# HEALING *the* SCHISM

*Karl Barth, Franz Rosenzweig, and the New Jewish-Christian Encounter*

STUDIES IN HISTORICAL & SYSTEMATIC THEOLOGY

# HEALING *the* SCHISM

*Karl Barth, Franz Rosenzweig, and the New Jewish-Christian Encounter*

## JENNIFER M. ROSNER

STUDIES IN HISTORICAL AND SYSTEMATIC THEOLOGY

LEXHAM ACADEMIC

*Healing the Schism: Karl Barth, Franz Rosenzweig, and the New Jewish-Christian Encounter*
Studies in Historical and Systematic Theology

Copyright 2021 Jennifer M. Rosner

Lexham Academic, an imprint of Lexham Press
1313 Commercial St., Bellingham, WA 98225
LexhamPress.com

First edition published by Fortress Press, Minneapolis (2015).

Print ISBN 9781683594932
Digital ISBN 9781-683594949          .
Library of Congress Control Number 2021933221

Lexham Editorial: Todd Hains, Allisyn Ma, Mandi Newell
Cover Design: Bryan Hintz
Typesetting: Abigail Stocker

*To Howard Loewen and Mark Kinzer, who served as faithful guides through the intellectual and personal journey of writing this book.*
*Without your wisdom and encouragement, I likely would not have embarked upon this project in the first place, and I certainly could not have finished it.*

# CONTENTS

# INTRODUCTION

—

# THE ELECTION OF ISRAEL AND CHRISTIAN THEOLOGY

In an article entitled "Salvation Is from the Jews," the late Richard John Neuhaus wrote the following with regard to Jewish-Christian dialogue: "I suggest that we would not be wrong to believe that this dialogue, so closely linked to the American experience, is an essential part of the unfolding of the story of the world."[1] The rivalrous and troubled tale of these two religious communities has been a constant thread in the history of the West, and the tumultuous events of the twentieth century have yielded a new chapter in the relationship between Christians and Jews. The burgeoning of this new relationship holds great promise for healing, reconciliation and redemptive partnership, and its full impact is still being played out. While we cannot be sure where this new trajectory will lead, we can point to the key events that provoked it and explore the ways in which Christians and Jews are responding to and engaging in it.

Scott Bader-Saye points to two "seismic events" in the twentieth century that shattered old models and paved the way for new ones. First, he describes the "demise of the Christendom paradigm, in which the church was positioned as the spiritual sponsor of Western civilization." Amidst an increasingly globalized society, Christianity has become merely one world religion among many. Second, Bader-Saye points to the Holocaust, "the systematic attempt by a 'Christian nation' to eradicate the Jews."[2] In 1980, it was estimated that by the end of the twentieth century, more would

---

1. Richard John Neuhaus, "Salvation Is from the Jews" in *Jews and Christians: People of God*, ed. Carl E. Braaten and Robert W. Jenson (Grand Rapids: Eerdmans, 2003), 65–77. Originally published in *First Things* 117 (November 2001): 17–22.

2. Scott Bader-Saye, *Church and Israel After Christendom: The Politics of Election* (Eugene: Wipf & Stock, 1999), 1.

have been written about the Holocaust than about any other subject in human history.[3] The Holocaust brought the plight of the Jewish people onto the center stage of world history, and Christians' eyes were opened to the dark streak of supersessionism and anti-Judaism that runs through Christian history.

To Bader-Saye's list of two seismic events, we must add two more. The creation of the modern state of Israel holds inestimable significance, and Jewish liturgy hails this event as the "first flowering of our redemption."[4] Questions about the theological significance of this political event abound, and Christians have found it "difficult, if not impossible, to see Israel as just another nation."[5] Finally, the latter half of the twentieth century saw the emergence of the Messianic Jewish movement, a development that has posed a significant challenge to the regnant understanding of the relationship between Judaism and Christianity. Messianic Jews refuse to accept a mutually exclusive construal of these two religious traditions, and their communities tangibly embody this posture.

These four factors have contributed to a widespread reassessment of the relationship between Christianity and Judaism, and the effects of this shift continue to ripple outward. The post-Holocaust era has seen a number of significant official Christian statements that chart a new way of relating to Judaism and the Jewish people,[6] and prevailing trends in biblical scholarship mirror this development.[7] The Jewish world has recognized

---

3. George M. Kren and Leon Rappoport, *The Holocaust and the Crisis of Human Behavior* (Teaneck, NJ: Holmes & Meier, 1994), 1.

4. *The Koren Siddur*, trans. Jonathan Sacks (Jerusalem: Koren, 2009), 522.

5. Gary Burge, *Whose Land? Whose Promise?: What Christians Are Not Being Told About Israel and the Palestinians* (Cleveland: Pilgrim Press, 2004), 12.

6. Among the most significant of these documents are the Catholic Vatican II statements *Nostra Aetate* and *Lumen Gentium*. For analysis of these and related Christian statements, see Michael B. McGarry, *Christology After Auschwitz* (Mahwah, NJ: Paulist Press, 1977) and Geoffrey Wigoder, *Jewish-Christian Relations Since the Second World War* (Manchester: Manchester University Press, 1988).

7. With regard to biblical scholarship, see, for example Paula Fredriksen, *Jesus of Nazareth, King of the Jews* (New York: Vintage, 2000); Pamela Eisenbaum, *Paul Was Not a Christian: The Original Message of a Misunderstood Apostle* (New York: HarperCollins, 2010); Amy-Jill Levine, *The Misunderstood Jew: The Church and the Scandal of the Jewish Jesus* (New York: HarperOne, 2007); and the work of Mark Nanos (much of which is available at www.marknanos.com). With regard to Pauline scholarship, Magnus Zetterholm has coined the term "radical new perspective" to designate a group of scholars for whom "the traditional dichotomy between

that the Christian reassessment of Judaism requires a response, and this response has likewise come in a variety of forms.[8] These developments represent a new kind of Jewish-Christian encounter, made possible by Christians increasingly recognizing and renouncing the supersessionism that has plagued Christian history, and Jews increasingly acknowledging that Christian theology is not inherently anti-Jewish.

While these various trends are far too diverse and multifaceted to adequately treat in one study, our purpose in the pages that follow is to explore and assess one individual thread in the fabric of this twentieth-century reappraisal between Christians and Jews. In particular, this study approaches these developments from a theological and doctrinal perspective, focusing specifically upon the Christological and ecclesiological revisions that have accompanied and provoked this widespread reassessment. We will begin by explicating a key doctrinal question posed by Catholic theologian Bruce Marshall, whose lucid and theologically rigorous approach will frame the entirety of this study. Through the lens of Marshall's question, each chapter will assess a key twentieth- or twenty-first century theologian (and, in the case of chapter 3, a group of theologians) who has significantly contributed to the theological reenvisioning of the relationship between Judaism and Christianity. Our goal will be, in essence, to retrace some of the key moments in the recasting of Christology and ecclesiology in light of Israel and point the way forward toward potential future directions in this unfolding intellectual trajectory.

The purpose of the present chapter is to lay the framework that will guide our study. After reviewing Marshall's perspective and setting up the key question that will govern our approach, we will further establish one of the theological mainstays of Marshall's criteria, namely the ongoing connection between the Jewish people and Jewish practice. We will then delineate the scope of this study by defining the "new Jewish-Christian encounter" and provide an overview of what is to follow.

---

Judaism and Christianity is not the fundamental assumption" (*Approaches to Paul: A Student's Guide to Recent Scholarship* [Minneapolis: Fortress, 2009], 161).

    8. For one significant expression of this Jewish response, see Tikva Frymer-Kensky et al., eds., *Christianity in Jewish Terms* (Boulder, CO: Westview Press, 2000).

## MARSHALL'S CHALLENGE

While Bruce Marshall has not (yet) written a complete work on the question of Israel and the church, he has treated this topic in a number of articles and chapters in books.[9] As we will see, his cogent approach prioritizes both a restructuring of traditional theological loci as well as an adherence to orthodox Christian doctrine. Marshall's desire to see the tradition reworked within the bounds of orthodoxy provides the framework for this study.

### A CHRISTIAN AFFIRMATION OF THE ELECTION OF ISRAEL

According to Marshall, the widespread reconception of the relationship between Judaism and Christianity has, from the Christian side, hinged upon one particularly significant fulcrum. In his words, "The theological point of departure for our century's critical reassessment of the church's relation to the Jewish people is the proposal, now commonly made, that Christians ought to share a wider range of beliefs with Jews than they have in the past, and one belief in particular: that the biological descendants of Abraham, Isaac and Jacob are permanently and irrevocably the elect people of God."[10] Part and parcel of this affirmation is a repudiation of the long-held Christian belief that the church has replaced Israel as God's elect. This, for Marshall, is the very definition of supersessionism. In order to renounce the supersessionist claims that have so perniciously clung to Christian theology, the church must come to share in the belief of Israel's permanent election. According to Marshall, such an affirmation entails upholding "at least" the following elements:[11]

---

9. See Bruce D. Marshall, *Trinity and Truth* (Cambridge: Cambridge University Press, 2000), esp. 169–79; Marshall, "Christ and the Cultures: The Jewish People and Christian Theology," in *The Cambridge Companion to Christian Doctrine*, ed. Colin E. Gunton (Cambridge: Cambridge University Press, 1997), 81–100; Marshall, "Elder Brothers: John Paul II's Teaching on the Jewish People as a Question to the Church," in *John Paul II and the Jewish People: A Jewish-Christian Dialogue*, ed. David G. Dalin and Matthew Levering (Lanham, MD: Rowman & Littlefield, 2008), 113–29; Marshall, "Christ and Israel: An Unsolved Problem in Catholic Theology" (The 20th Annual Aquinas Lecture presented at the Dominican School of Philosophy & Theology, Berkeley, CA, March 3, 2010). Also of interest is Marshall, "Truth Claims and the Possibility of Jewish-Christian Dialogue," *Modern Theology* 8:3 (July 1992): 221–40.

10. Marshall, "Christ and the Cultures," 81.

11. This list can be found in ibid. 82–83.

1.  The elect people of Israel are the biological ("according to the flesh," as Rom 9:3 states) descendants of Abraham, Isaac and Jacob.

2.  As such, a distinction between this biological family and all other peoples of the earth is presupposed.[12]

3.  This biological family receives God's favor as his "treasured possession" (Deut 10:14), not because of anything they have done but because of God's choice.

4.  To this people belong both the promise that they themselves will be blessed by God and that through them God's blessing will come to all peoples on earth.

5.  This elect people has special responsibilities toward God, namely to observe Torah, which is incumbent upon them alone.

As Marshall explains, the first two principles describe who the elect people are and the following three describe the content and consequences of their election.[13] In these five principles, Marshall is driving toward a larger point that is seldom recognized by Christians, namely the connection between the election of the Jewish people and the practice of Judaism. According to Marshall, theologians who seek to avoid supersessionism must affirm God's ongoing election of Israel and Israel's unique covenantal obligations.

Before addressing this point directly, it is important that we expand further on the second affirmation in Marshall's list, namely that a distinction between the Jewish people and all other peoples on earth is "presupposed."[14] That the Jewish people be identifiable as a unique people is an essential element of their election. In Marshall's words, "visible distinction

---

12. Marshall draws on the thought of Michael Wyschogrod, who emphasizes the "carnal" nature of Israel's election (see *The Body of Faith: God in the People Israel* [Northvale, NJ: Jason Aronson, 1996], 175–77.)

13. Marshall, "Christ and the Cultures," 82–83.

14. As we will see in chapter 3, this contention is a central tenet in the thought of R. Kendall Soulen.

from the nations is ... necessary for the election of Israel; it is among the constituent or integral parts of the existence of the Jewish people as God's chosen."[15] According to Marshall, Israel's election "would be void if the biological descendants of Abraham indeed received God's promised blessing, but had ceased to be identifiable as Abraham's descendants, that is, as Jews. The permanence of Israel's election thus entails the permanence of the distinction between Jew and Gentile."[16]

Marshall contends that the incarnation is the final safeguard that this distinction will always remain. Jesus' Jewishness and membership in the people of Israel is irreducibly constitutive of his identity. By virtue of God taking on Jewish flesh in the person of Jesus, "God's ownership of this Jewish flesh is permanent. In the end, when all flesh shall see the glory of the Lord, the vision of God will, so the traditional Christian teaching goes, be bound up ineluctably with the vision of this Jew seated at God's right hand."[17] Because Jesus' Jewish identity is only meaningful within the context of the Jewish people as a whole, "in owning with unsurpassable intimacy the particular Jewish flesh of Jesus, God also owns the Jewish people as a whole, precisely in their distinction from ... Gentiles; he cannot own one without also owning the other."[18] The incarnation of God in Jesus is the concentration and intensification of the indwelling of God in the Jewish people collectively.[19] God's singling out of this particular people (and this particular man) as his dwelling place in the world makes explicit the distinction of the Jewish people from the rest of the nations.[20]

"How then," Marshall asks, "is the distinct identity of the Jews, and so Israel's election, to be maintained?"[21] In his words, "the obvious answer is by Jewish observance of the full range of traditional Jewish law (*halachah*, which embraces both the written and oral Torah, that is, both biblical and rabbinic law—see Marshall's point 5, above). This observance, in which the

---

15. Marshall, "Christ and Israel," 10.

16. Marshall, "Christ and the Cultures," 91.

17. Marshall, *Trinity and Truth*, 178.

18. Ibid.

19. We will further explore the connection between God's incarnation in Christ and God's incarnation in the Jewish people in chapter 3.

20. While the "content" of election comes to be shared with the gentiles through Christ, the distinction between Jew and gentile remains. See Marshall, "Christ and the Cultures," 91.

21. Ibid.

Gentiles will surely have no interest and to which God's electing will does not obligate them, will be the chief means by which Abraham's descendants can be identified."[22] This leads us back to Marshall's key observation that affirming Israel's permanent election is inseparable from affirming the ongoing practice of Judaism.

Marshall makes this connection explicit in his assessment of Pope John Paul II's contribution to the conversation. While it is possible to affirm the election of the Jewish people without affirming the ongoing practice of Judaism—and vice versa—John Paul II is notable for maintaining a high regard for both. Speaking at the Chief Synagogue in Rome in 1986, the pope invoked the words of *Nostra Aetate*: "The Church of Christ discovers her 'bond' with Judaism by 'searching into her own mystery.' " According to the pope's interpretation, this statement implies that "the Jewish religion is not 'extrinsic' to us, but in a certain way is 'intrinsic' to our own religion. With Judaism, therefore, we have a relationship which we do not have with any other religion." Thus the pope declared to the Jews in Rome, "You are our dearly beloved brothers and, in a certain way, it could be said that you are our elder brothers."[23]

In light of the special bond that exists between Jews and Christians, John Paul II contends that Christian self-understanding must take into account not only the Jewish people, but the Jewish religion as well. In Marshall's words, "If another religion is intrinsic to our own identity, then we can only understand the import of our own beliefs—we can only grasp whom we ourselves are—by coming to know and appreciate the beliefs, the religion, of another community. When we say this about the relationship of the Church to Judaism, we are pinning down our own identity, in some irreducible way, on a community which is, as the pope goes on to say, clearly distinct from our own, and one whose beliefs are in some very important ways opposed to our own."[24]

---

22. Ibid. According to Michael Wyschogrod, a Christian reassessment of Torah lies at the heart of improved Jewish-Christian relations. In his words, "If the Christian view of the law as a law of death remains in force, then the estrangement between Christianity and Judaism will prevail" ("A Jewish View of Christianity," in *Abraham's Promise: Judaism and Jewish-Christian Relations*, ed. R. Kendall Soulen [Grand Rapids: Eerdmans, 2004], 162).

23. Quoted in Marshall, "Elder Brothers," 115.

24. Ibid., 116.

Significantly, that the pope's words were addressed to the Jews in Rome affirms that their physical descent from Abraham, Isaac, and Jacob makes them the referents of God's enduring covenant with Israel: "Not only is faithful Israel before Christ the root from which the gentiles live in Christ, but faithful Israel now, the Jews gathered with their chief rabbi in the Great Synagogue of Rome, are the root from which the gentile Church now lives in Christ."[25] The coming of Christ reinforces rather than diminishes the Jewish people's unique covenant with God, a covenant that necessarily undergirds and informs the church's identity.

While the pope's words make a strong claim with regard to Christianity's self-understanding, they also make an important point about Jewish existence. The pope recognizes the integral connection between Jewish identity and the practice of Judaism, namely that the former ultimately depends on the latter. As Marshall rightly explains, "The Jewish people cannot continue to exist in the long run without Judaism. ... The irrevocable election of the Jewish people evidently requires the permanence of their religion ... Without Judaism, the Jewish people would surely, if slowly, disappear from the earth, as other ancient people have done. They would cease to be a distinct people, and vanish into *gentilitas*, as medieval Christian theologians called the mass of us not descended from Abraham, Isaac, and Jacob."[26]

Marshall brings to the fore the reality that the election of the Jewish people cannot be affirmed and upheld without also affirming the ongoing practice of Judaism: "In permanently electing Israel, it seems that God has also permanently willed the practice of Judaism."[27] Judaism is the means by which the Jewish people uphold their covenant fidelity to God and remain distinct from all other peoples—tenets which Marshall identifies as being central to the doctrine of Israel's election.

Having established what a Christian affirmation of Israel's election entails, and what is at stake in maintaining such an affirmation, Marshall explains the difficult theological task that now confronts the church. Affirming Judaism as part and parcel of Jewish election requires that the church rethink its stance toward a religious tradition that has been

---

25. Ibid., 118.
26. Ibid., 122.
27. Ibid.

developed in distinction from—and often in tension with—the Christian tradition. In Marshall's words, "The discovery that Christians ought to share with Jews a belief in the permanent election of Abraham's children poses a challenge for Christian theology, one which in some respects has not been faced seriously since the second century."[28] The heart of the challenge focuses on how Christians can simultaneously affirm the irrevocable election of the Jewish people and "the universal, ecclesially mediated saving mission of Christ."[29]

While Marshall's Catholic ecclesiology equates "God's call to salvation in Christ" with "a call to enter and remain within the Catholic Church,"[30] his question retains its force outside a Catholic context. The question is equally relevant for Christians more generally who understand salvation to be mediated through Christ and his church and who affirm the universality of Christ's call to discipleship. How can these claims, which constitute mainstays of Christian orthodoxy, be upheld alongside the affirmation that "the existence of faithful Jews is not simply an empirical likelihood or a devout hope, let alone an evil God puts up with, but belongs to God's own good and unalterable purposes"?[31]

It is this question that will frame our study. As we survey a number of Jewish and Christian theologians, our assessment of their thought will be based upon the dual doctrinal affirmations sought by Marshall. We will pose the following question to each theologian: To what extent does their thought affirm (or contribute to the affirmation of) both the universal, ecclesially mediated saving mission of Christ and the irrevocable election of the Jewish people, which necessarily includes the ongoing practice of Judaism?

## A SURVEY OF EXISTING APPROACHES

While Marshall does not himself offer a definitive answer to how these doctrinal tenets may be affirmed, he identifies three ways in which theologians have generally approached this issue, noting difficulties with each of them.

---

28. Marshall, "Christ and the Cultures," 91.
29. Marshall, "Christ and Israel," 3.
30. Marshall, "Elder Brothers," 121.
31. Ibid., 122.

He also tentatively pioneers a fourth possibility, though he raises questions about the adequacy of this option as well.[32] Let us review each of these in turn. First, one may assert that "the Jews, or at least some of them, are not really called to life in the Church, or at least not in the same way, or to the same life, that the gentiles are." In its strongest form, this stance affirms two separate "saving arrangements in the world, one through carnal election and Torah for Jews, the other through faith in Jesus Christ for gentiles."[33] Classically termed the "two covenant" approach, this stance upholds the ongoing election of the Jewish people and the ongoing practice of Judaism, but denies the universal scope of Christ's salvific mission, at least to the extent that that mission involves universal participation and involvement in the Christian church.[34]

According to Marshall, for Christians to take this stance is tantamount to giving up their "most central, identity-forming convictions" and thus acting in "infidelity to … God."[35] From a Christian perspective, "the 'two covenants' view does not so much understand the faith as undercut it."[36] In its weaker form, this position may assert that God wills that the Jewish people enter a saving relationship with Christ, but that "Christ's saving purpose for the Jews is dormant, as it were, until the eschaton."[37] This weaker form is theologically tenuous, for it is difficult to make the case biblically that Christ's purposes presently do not apply to the express people to whom and for whom he came.

The second option is to assert that God's saving purposes are offered "figuratively" through the "old law" and then enacted "with temporally unsurpassable clarity by the incarnation of the Word" whose life, death and resurrection inaugurates a new law.[38] This position has been upheld in

---

32. Marshall expounds the first three options in "Elder Brothers" and the fourth in "Christ and Israel."

33. Marshall, "Elder Brothers," 123.

34. Again, while Marshall approaches these questions from a Catholic perspective, they are equally relevant for the Christian church more broadly speaking. Since, for the past 1700 years at least, Judaism and Christianity have essentially been two entirely separate religions, for a Jew to enter the Christian church has been (with very few exceptions) incompatible with living as a Torah-observant Jew.

35. Marshall, *Trinity and Truth*, 177.

36. Marshall, "Elder Brothers," 123.

37. Ibid., 124.

38. Ibid.

a variety of ways throughout Christian history, and its adherents are often deeply committed to "God's love for Abraham's fleshly descendants as an irrevocable element of his saving design in Christ." However, according to this proposed solution, it is "difficult to find room for the thought that God wills the permanent practice of Judaism." Judaism as a religious system may be tolerated, but it is no longer seen as God's appointed route to covenant faithfulness for the Jewish people. In Marshall's estimation, "to the extent that Jewish election depends on the practice of Judaism, this second approach seems incompatible with the permanent election of Israel."[39] That God's history with the Jewish people reaches its climax in Christ is a touchstone of Christian doctrine, but this does not solve the problem that Marshall raises. In his words, "the notion that the law of Moses finds its complete fulfillment in Christ and the Church is ... indispensable for Christianity. But this ancient idea is not the solution to the problem of supersessionism. It is the problem."[40]

Marshall describes a third option that has recently emerged and is embodied by a certain strand of Messianic Judaism. According to this model, "the Jews are called to faith in Christ and to Christian communal life, but in such a way that they retain enough Judaism to be recognizable as Jews, including, among other things, their own worship and the continued observance of Jewish dietary laws."[41] Marshall points to Messianic Jewish theologian Mark Kinzer as a representative of this position, noting that Michael Wyschogrod (an Orthodox Jew) endorses Kinzer's conclusions in principle without himself ascribing to the core tenets of Messianic Judaism. While Marshall acknowledges that this model upholds "both the necessity of distinctively Jewish practice and identity for Jewish election, and the universality of Christ's saving mission,"[42] he questions whether this option represents an undesirable form of syncretism. Does it offer the best of both worlds, or does it fail to be faithful to either? Would either the Jewish or the Christian community recognize Messianic Judaism as a

---

39. Ibid.

40. Bruce D. Marshall, "Quasi in Figura: A Brief Reflection on Jewish Election, after Thomas Aquinas," *Nova et Vetera* 7, no. 2 (2009): 481.

41. Marshall, "Elder Brothers," 124–125.

42. Ibid., 125.

genuine manifestation of its core beliefs and traditions? From a Christian perspective, Marshall wonders how this option manifests the reality that "by his Cross, Christ has united Jews and gentiles in one body (cf. Eph 2:11–22)." According to this third option, "it sometimes seems as though Christ has two bodies—two churches—neither of which has a universal saving mission. With that, the sense in which Christ himself has a single saving purpose for all ceases to be apparent."[43]

In "Christ and Israel: An Unsolved Problem in Catholic Theology," Marshall puts forward a fourth option that does not fall prey to the weaknesses of the three positions just outlined. He begins his proposal by admitting that, with regard to the universal saving mission of Christ and the ongoing election of the Jewish people, "I do not quite know how these two important teachings fit together. No traditional or contemporary way of handling this question really seems to be successful. The main approaches to the problem, so far as I am aware of them, end up playing one of the teachings off against the other, though they do not usually do this by design … I will suggest an alternative approach, but only tentatively, since the idea I want to propose itself seems less than fully satisfactory."[44] In what follows, Marshall expands upon a phrase in the *Catechism of the Catholic Church* which reads: "When one considers the future, God's People of the Old Covenant and the new People of God tend towards similar goals: expectation of the coming (or the return) of the Messiah. But one awaits the return of the Messiah who died and rose from the dead and is recognized as Lord and Son of God; the other awaits the coming of a Messiah, whose features remain hidden till the end of time; and the latter waiting is accompanied by the drama of not knowing or of misunderstanding Christ Jesus (§840)."

As Marshall interprets this passage, Jews (via "communal *halakhic* life"[45]) and Christians (via "communal Eucharistic life") await one and the same coming Messiah.[46] Accordingly, "Christians must see Jewish

---

43. Ibid.

44. Marshall, "Christ and Israel," 2–3.

45. *Halakhah* (which derives from the Hebrew verb "to go" or "to walk") refers to the communally authoritative applications of the Torah to the changing circumstances of daily life. *Halakhah* "embraces personal, social, national, and international relationships, and all the other practices and observances of Judaism" (*Encyclopedia Judaica*, 2nd ed. (2006), s.v. "Halakhah").

46. Marshall, "Christ and Israel," 16.

anticipation of the one to whom the law and the prophets bear witness as aimed, in reality, at no one other than Christ Jesus. As such the messianic expectation of the Jewish people mysteriously joins them to Jesus Christ, in his full revealing yet to come." Thus, faithful Jewish observance turns out to be the means by which Jews are joined to Christ and wait with the church for his coming: "Because it joins to Christ, a Torah-observant life, given by God to set his elect people forever apart from the nations, cannot be opposed to a certain kind of membership in the new people of God. It must be Israel's divinely willed way of belonging, however unexpectedly, to the new people of God."[47]

For Marshall, this recognition allows the church to affirm Jewish observance without concluding that it somehow contradicts Christ's universal mission. Marshall admits that this position too poses a number of difficulties, and he wonders whether it is "a genuine solution to the problem with which we have been concerned, or merely another way of redescribing it."[48] One possible objection to this proposal is that it "reconciles the election of Israel with the call of every human being to life in Christ by severing, at least for some human beings, the connection between union with Christ and the sacraments of the Church."[49] If this is the case, it is indeed an "unhappy conclusion," for according to Catholic ecclesiology "the sacraments of the Church [are] ... integral to the paschal mystery in which every human being is called to share."[50] While Marshall is not confident that this fourth option adequately resolves the tension, he is hopeful that his investigation provides a better explication of the question and its complexity, which he deems a worthwhile endeavor in its own right. As Marshall admits, a satisfactory resolution to this issue has repeatedly proven elusive.

Marshall's challenge merits sustained consideration, if only to more thoroughly trace the contours of the tension and better understand the reasons why it has not been adequately resolved. The present study is an attempt to further probe the question Marshall raises, and at the end of our

---

47. Ibid. Marshall is drawing the phrase "new people of God" from *Nostra Aetate* 4 and *Lumen Gentium* 9, 13.

48. Marshall, "Christ and Israel," 14.

49. Ibid.

50. Ibid., 15.

study, we will return to Marshall's four options in light of the theological trajectory we are exploring.

## GOD, ISRAEL, AND TORAH

As we saw above, Marshall assumes a tight connection between the Jewish people and Jewish practice, which leads him to insist that affirming Israel's irrevocable election must entail an endorsement of the ongoing practice of Judaism. Marshall's clear and resolute assertion of this connection is among the factors that make his framing of the issue so pertinent to our study. Christians seldom recognize the connection between Israel and Torah, and it has become one of the most ardently debated topics in modern Judaism. If we are going to follow Marshall's framework in this regard, we must briefly demonstrate why Marshall's perspective is defensible and distinguish it from the well-established positions with which Marshall tacitly disagrees.

Traditionally, the identity of the Jewish people has hung on three fundamental realities: God, Israel and Torah.[51] The tight theological interweaving of these doctrinal pillars undergirds Jewish history and self-understanding, as can be seen throughout the liturgy that shapes Jewish communal life. The traditional blessing that is recited before daily Torah study or a public reading of the Torah reads as follows: "Blessed are You, Lord our God, King of the Universe, who has chosen us from all peoples and who has given us His Torah."[52] This blessing is but one window into the centrality of God, Israel and Torah as the three cornerstones of Judaism. David Novak makes explicit the following basic relations underlying this blessing: "(1) Israel is related to God because of God's election of her; (2) Israel is related to God because of God's revelation of the Torah to her; (3) Israel is disjunct from the nations of the world because of God's election of her."[53]

---

51. Some Jewish thinkers add the land of Israel as a fourth "cornerstone" of Judaism. See, for example, Hayim Halevy Donin, *To Be a Jew: A Guide to Jewish Observance in Contemporary Life* (New York: Basic Books, 1972), 12–18.

52. *The Koren Siddur*, 506.

53. David Novak, *The Election of Israel: The Idea of the Chosen People* (Cambridge: Cambridge University Press, 1995), 10.

Until the modern era, these basic relations informed the very lifeblood of Jewish identity, and it is these relations that undergird the election of Israel in Marshall's thought and in the present study. However, modern Judaism comprises a vast spectrum of thought and practice along which the relationship between God, Israel and Torah is variously and diversely construed. While the range of Jewish thought on this issue is far too vast and complex to rehearse here, a few preliminary remarks must be made. In the pages that follow, we will briefly explore the longstanding theological and historical markers of Jewish identity as well as the serious challenge that modernity dealt to Judaism and traditional Jewish self-understanding.

### THE JEWISH PEOPLE AND JEWISH PRACTICE

The exodus from Egypt marks the foundational moment in God's election and calling of the people of Israel, and the giving of the Ten Commandments on Mount Sinai casts the shape and structure of this covenantal partnership. The deliverance from Egypt and the giving of the Torah are not properly two separate events, but two sides of one single event.[54] God's self-revelation to the Israelites was not an end in itself; it had as its goal Israel's commitment to following and obeying God. In the words of Jon Levenson, "The community comes into the fuller knowledge of God through a life of observance to the *mitsvot*. History is the foreground of observance, but observance is the teleological end of history."[55] In other words, God's self-revelation to the people of Israel was the beginning of an enduring covenantal relationship between Israel and God. Israel's covenantal life has as its goal knowing and honoring God, and the Torah is the revealed means by which Israel is instructed to do so. The historical account of God's revelation is the necessary prologue to this covenantal relationship: "What endures is the mutual relationship between unequals

---

54. In the words of Jonathan Sacks, "The Exodus was only the prelude to Israel's birth as a nation. The decisive event took place not in Egypt nor even when they left, but seven weeks later as they stood at the foot of Mount Sinai. It was there that they heard the voice of God and received the Ten Commandments, the most famous of all moral codes. For Judaism, this was the supreme moment of revelation" (Jonathan Sacks, *A Letter in the Scroll: Understanding Our Jewish Identity and Exploring the Legacy of the World's Oldest Religion* [New York: Free Press, 2000], 117).

55. Jon D. Levenson, *Sinai and Zion: An Entry into the Jewish Bible* (New York: HarperOne, 1985), 44. A *mitzvah* (pl. *mitzvot*) is a commandment or the fulfillment of a commandment of Jewish law.

which is the substance of covenant. That relationship does not lack concreteness; on the contrary, it is healthy only to the extent that the will to fulfill specific *mitsvot* is present."[56]

God's call of Abraham in Genesis 12, the incipient genesis of the people of Israel, finds its fullest form in the Sinaitic covenant in the book of Exodus. According to Levenson, "The covenant without stipulations, the Abrahamic covenant of Genesis 15 and 17, is only a preparation for the Sinaitic covenant, into which it is absorbed. Thus, the observance of the Mosaic Torah is the opposite of an obstacle to a loving and intimate relationship with God. It is the vehicle and the sign of just that relationship."[57] The book of Deuteronomy gives passionate expression to the covenantal relationship between God and Israel. For example, Deuteronomy 10:12-15 reads:

> And now, Israel, what does the LORD your God ask of you but to fear the LORD your God, to walk in obedience to him, to love him, to serve the LORD your God with all your heart and with all your soul, and to observe the LORD's commands and decrees that I am giving you today for your own good? To the LORD your God belong the heavens, even the highest heavens, the earth and everything in it. Yet the LORD set his affection on your ancestors and loved them, and he chose you, their descendants, above all the nations—as it is today.

These verses offer a snapshot of God's sovereign transcendence, God's election of Israel as a unique people with whom he intimately covenants, and obedience to the *mitzvot* as Israel's reciprocal covenantal obligation. As Levenson explains:

> Covenant-love is mutual; it distinguishes a relationship of reciprocity. On God's side lies an obligation to fulfill the oath he swore to the Patriarchs, to grant their descendants the promised land, to be their God. Israel, for her part, is to realize her love in the form of observance of her master's stipulations, the *mitsvot*, for they are the words of the language of love, the fit medium in which to respond to the passionate advances of the divine suzerain. It is not a question of law or love, but law conceived in love, love expressed in law.

---

56. Ibid., 45.
57. Ibid.

The two are a unity. To speak of one apart from the other is to produce a parody of the religion of Israel. The love of God moves Israel to embrace the norms of Sinai.[58]

Thus, observance of Torah as Israel's response to God's electing love is part and parcel of Israel's election. According to Novak, "Jewish adherence to the commandments is not law in place of grace, but, rather, a faithful Jewish response to God's most gracious commandments."[59] In other words, for Judaism, faithful living is embodied through the concrete practices prescribed by Torah. It is through such practices that Jewish theology is made manifest. The uniqueness of Judaism thus includes both theology and praxis, which cannot be separated from one another. According to Michael Fishbane, "The self-understanding of the Jewish people was and is that of a distinct people, a people whose uniqueness is constituted by its spiritual link with God and expressed through the ritual and ethical requirements of the covenant (the Torah and its traditional elaborations). God is therefore central to Judaism, but not in any abstract or impersonal sense. Rather, God is always the One who establishes a covenant, who reveals the Torah, who requires obedience and sanctity, who guides the people's destiny and so on."[60]

As we saw in Deuteronomy 10, God is made known through God's acts as both the creator of the universe and the one who elects Israel. Israel is in turn called to make God known through concrete practices; Torah obedience effectually discloses God to the world. As the climactic moment in Jewish worship, the liturgy of the Shema illustrates this covenantal reciprocity. Judaism's central declaration of God's oneness and lordship ("Hear, O Israel, the LORD is our God, the LORD is One" [Deut. 6:4]) is immediately followed by an exhortation to obedience ("You shall love the LORD your God with all your heart, with all your soul, and with all your strength; and let these words which I command

---

58. Ibid., 77.

59. David Novak, "From Supersessionism to Parallelism in Jewish-Christian Dialogue," in *Jews and Christians*, 107.

60. Michael Fishbane, *Judaism: Revelation and Traditions* (New York: HarperOne, 1987), 21.

you this day be upon your heart ..." [Deut. 6:5]).[61] In Judaism, "there is no simple love of God that is not concretized through some customary form of behavior and no strict observance of these behaviors that is not also to be regarded as an expression of the love of God."[62]

In Devarim Rabbah, a midrashic commentary on the book of Deuteronomy, we find the following anecdote that aptly illustrates this concept: "A king's son said to him, 'Make me visibly identifiable in the midst of the country that I am your son.' His father said to him, 'If your request is that all should know that you are my son, then wear my royal purple garment and place my crown upon your head; then all will know that you are my son.' So did the Holy-One-blessed-be-He say to Israel, 'If you desire that you should be identified as my children, engage in the Torah and its commandments and all will see that you are My sons.' "[63] Throughout the history of the people of Israel, obedience to Torah has been a basic presupposition and fundamental constitutive element of Jewish self-understanding. As Marshall observes, it is that which has kept the Jewish people distinct from other nations and recognizable as God's covenant people. As Hayim Halevy Donin explains, "Torah is the embodiment of the Jewish faith. It contains the terms of ... covenant with God. It is what makes a Jew a Jew."[64] However, as we will explore in the following section, the forces of modernity assailed the fundamental connection between God, Israel, and Torah, and modern Judaism reflects the varied Jewish responses to this comprehensive challenge.

## THE EMERGENCE OF MODERN JUDAISM

The intimate connection between God, Israel, and Torah was not seriously challenged until the seventeenth century, during which a changing environment both internal and external to the Jewish people ushered

---

61. In the Jewish liturgy, the Shema is immediately preceded by the Ahavah Rabbah, a passionate declaration of God's love for Israel. Israel's recitation of the Shema is founded upon God's love for Israel and calls for Israel's reciprocal love for God. See *The Koren Siddur*, 96–100.

62. Fishbane, *Judaism: Revelation and Traditions*, 18.

63. Devarim Rabbah 7.10, quoted in David Novak, *Halakhah in a Theological Dimension* (Chico, CA: Scholars Press, 1985), 120.

64. Donin, *To Be a Jew*, 27.

Judaism into a period of fundamental redefinition.[65] According to Norbert Samuelson, these changes forced the Jewish people to "rethink and even reconstruct the very idea of what they thought it meant to be a Jew."[66] In the wake of modernity, for the first time in history, a vision of Israel without Torah (and in some cases without God) would emerge. In light of this history, the connection between Israel and Torah upheld by Marshall and the Jewish theologians engaged in this study is thrown into sharp relief.

Perhaps the most fundamental historical factor undergirding the emergence of modern Judaism was the rise of the secular nation-state. As it gradually deposed the Holy Roman Empire, this new system of economic and political entities introduced a distinction between "secular" and "religious" life, whereby, for the most part, the state was issued dominion over secular affairs (primarily defined as matters affecting relations between people) and religion maintained dominion over religious affairs (those matters affecting relations between people and God). To the extent that a state "modernized," it separated religious affiliation from national citizenship and, in principle, granted freedom of religion.[67]

This sweeping political development led to widespread Jewish emancipation, whereby discriminatory laws were abolished and Jews were enabled to attain full citizenship along with its attendant rights and privileges. Jews were first emancipated in the United States, whose constitution extended equal rights to all Americans. The French Revolution ushered in the emancipation of French Jewry, and other Western European nations soon followed suit. As Jacob Neusner explains, "The process was not smooth or easy, and the Jews were never really fully integrated into the political life of Western European countries. But [emancipation] marked an immense change in Jews' status and condition."[68]

---

65. See Alan T. Levenson, *An Introduction to Modern Jewish Thinkers: From Spinoza to Soloveitchik*, 2nd ed. (Lanham, MD: Rowman & Littlefield, 2006), 1–4.

66. Norbert Samuelson, *An Introduction to Modern Jewish Philosophy* (Albany, NY: State University of New York Press, 1989), 21.

67. Ibid. See also Leora Batnitzky, *How Judaism Became a Religion: An Introduction to Modern Jewish Thought* (Princeton: Princeton University Press, 2011).

68. Jacob Neusner, *The Way of Torah: An Introduction to Judaism* (Belmont, CA: Wadsworth, 1993), 148.

In order to grasp the significance of Jewish emancipation, it is important to understand the nature and structure of pre-emancipation Jewish
life. Before the modern period, "Jewish society was corporate, segregated,
and collective in emphasis."[69] Accordingly, Jews in Europe spoke a common
language (Yiddish), and regarded themselves as a separate nation living
within other nations, and awaiting their ultimate return to their own land.
The central social ideal was study of Torah, which would result in heavenly
reward. The obligation to study the Torah, leading to an intense appreciation for intellectualism, prevented the sanctification of economic activity
as an ultimate goal and ensured tradition's effective control over the people's value structure. Indeed, the study of tradition was the chief purpose
of living. The community itself was governed by its own classical legal
tradition, with the rabbi as judge and community official.[70]

This model of Jewish communal existence, which encompassed all
aspects of life (economic, political, familial, legal, cultural, educational,
etc.), characterized Judaism for over a thousand years, "from the far west
of Morocco to Iran and India and from Egypt to England."[71] It is this all-
encompassing collective reality that would be eroded by modernity.

Political emancipation coincided with and was fueled by the *Haskalah*,
or Jewish Enlightenment, during which the Enlightenment emphasis on
reason and intellect found its way into distinctively Jewish endeavors.
Jews were encouraged to study secular subjects, to learn both Hebrew and
European languages, and to enter fields such as agriculture, crafts, the
arts, and science. Jews deeply influenced by the *Haskalah* worked hard
to assimilate into European society in dress, language, manners and loyalty to the ruling power.[72] As pre-emancipation Judaism gave way to the
Enlightenment ideals of the secular nation-state, active participation in
civil society quickly became a central goal of European Jewry.

Amidst this rapidly changing environment, Jews were forced to reassess
their self-understanding (and the very meaning of Judaism) in previously

---

69. Ibid., 151.

70. Ibid., 151–152.

71. Ibid., 11. Neusner divides Jewish history into four main eras: The First Age of Diversity
(c. 500 BCE–70 CE), The Age of Definition (c. 70 CE–640), The Age of Cogency (c. 640–1800),
and The Second Age of Diversity (1800 to the present). See ibid., esp. ch. 4.

72. See *Encyclopedia Judaica*, 2nd ed. (2006), s.v. "Haskalah."

alien categories. The separation of religious and national identity so fundamental to the nation-states in which Jews sought full participation was completely foreign to Judaism. According to Samuelson, "Classical rabbinic Judaism, like all other pre-Reformation religions in the western and mediterranean worlds, was in its very conception antithetical to such a separation. The Jewish people, insofar as they were a people governed by a law, were a nation; but they were not simply a state. They were a nation called into existence and given a law by God ... There was no way to distinguish what, in the communal and private lives of the Jewish people, was religious and what was national."[73]

Correlatively, Neusner explains that in premodern Judaism "the conception of an individual who framed identity separately from the community found no resonance in the Judaic system. Consequently, the advent of the nation-state, which recognized not communities ... but only individuals, produced a category that the received religion did not comprehend: the individual Jew."[74] Modernity's emphasis on the individual as the fundamental category of identity and the nation-state's reification of a division between religious and secular spheres posed an unprecedented challenge to Jewish self-understanding: "The received Judaism did not (and did not have to) deal with the possibility that Jews could ever be individual, let alone secular, that is to say, anything other than holy Israel, all together, all at once. It made no provision for Jews to be something else, unless they ceased, of course, to be Jews at all. The Judaism of the Torah surely could not imagine the Jews ever to be something in addition, over and above Israel."[75]

The secularization, individualization and fragmentation of modern society significantly eroded the all-encompassing and communal nature of Jewish identity. As Jews came to share in the aspirations and values of the nations in which they were citizens, a host of questions emerged. For example, "Would one work on the Sabbath in order to afford the same clothing and housing and transportation as one's neighbors? Would one eat only kosher food and absent oneself from the voluntary societies that

---

73. Samuelson, *Modern Jewish Philosophy*, 23.

74. Jacob Neusner, *Judaism in Modern Times: An Introduction and Reader* (Cambridge: Blackwell, 1995), 3.

75. Ibid.

played such a large role in European culture? Would one send one's child to *heder* [Jewish day school], or to the best high school in the area? Would one encourage one's son to go to Tuebingen University to get a law degree, even if it meant the temptations of baptism for career advancement or intermarriage?"[76]

The spectrum of Jewish response to these questions ranged from an attempt to maintain enclaves of distinct Jewish life untouched by society's rapid modernization, to selective accommodation of traditional models of Jewish existence to the exigencies of secular society, to wholesale abandonment of Jewish particularity and full acculturation to the surrounding environment. The question and extent of accommodation and acculturation increasingly came to define modern Judaism. Secularized society had made distinctively Jewish ways of life optional for the Jewish people, and certain social incentives accompanied the shedding of Jewish observance. As Levenson explains, "In the medieval world one could be a sinful Jew, or even an apostate, but one could not maintain a detached posture regarding the norms of Jewish life. In our secularized atmosphere, however ... one may be a Jew in name and little else. To state this reality more optimistically, we are all 'Jews by choice.'"[77]

Neusner lists six "Judaisms" that emerged in the modern era—three from the nineteenth century (Reform, Orthodox and Conservative) and three from the twentieth century (Zionism, Jewish Socialism and Yiddishism, and American Judaism of Holocaust and Redemption). According to Neusner, the primary challenge facing nineteenth-century Judaism was integration versus segregation, and each emergent stream of Judaism represented a different response to this tension. Each of the three nineteenth-century Judaisms viewed Judaism fundamentally as a religion (thus perpetuating the divide between religious identity and national identity), and despite the innovations they employed, each maintained a significant amount of continuity with the received tradition. Moreover, despite their differences, each of these Judaisms identified this sense of continuity as paramount in modern Jewish existence. In Neusner's words, "The nineteenth-century Judaisms outlined the grounds for establishing a single and continuous

---

76. Levenson, *Modern Jewish Thinkers*, 3.
77. Ibid., 30.

relationship with 'the past,'" as each "composed a statement of a self-conscious explanation of who it was in relationship to the received system."[78]

The nineteenth-century concern with continuity all but disappeared in the Judaisms of the twentieth century, which depart much more radically (and intentionally) from the received tradition. Neusner dubs the twentieth century the "post-Christian" century, emphasizing the massive anti-Christian forces that dominated this century of "perpetual war ... alongside the celebration of the all-powerful state."[79] Nazism, Communism, and secularism launched a powerful attack against both Christian and Judaic ideals, such that "we cannot find it surprising ... that the first 'post-Christian' century also marked the last century of Judaism in most of Europe."[80]

In attempting to cope with the Holocaust and respond to fundamental questions of survival, the Judaisms of the twentieth century "took up political, social, economic, but not theological questions."[81] These Judaisms did not address issues that were unique to the Jewish people, but rather confronted in Jewish terms the sweeping crisis that faced the Western world as a whole. In other words, twentieth-century Judaisms depart from the core issues that have defined Jewish identity throughout the ages and focus instead on practical means of survival amid the threat posed by the immediate situation and surroundings. Unlike the Judaisms of the nineteenth century, these Judaisms did not make use of the intellectual resources of the received tradition, which they treated with utter disinterest.[82]

As Neusner explains, "The urgent issues of the nineteenth century demanded attention to doctrine and individual deed: what should I think? what should I do? The critical concerns of the century beyond focused upon public policy: how shall we survive? where should we go?"[83] While intellectuals and philosophers served as the pioneers of nineteenth-century Judaisms, twentieth-century Judaisms were dominated by organizers and mobilizers. Furthermore, Judaism in the twentieth century was increasingly conceived along ethnic lines rather than religious lines.

---

78. Neusner, *Judaism in Modern Times*, 34.
79. Ibid., 125.
80. Ibid., 125–126.
81. Ibid., 128.
82. Ibid., 129–130.
83. Ibid., 135–136.

Whereas nineteenth-century Judaisms focused on Judaism as a religion, the twentieth century emphasis fell on the peoplehood of the Jews.

While much more could be said about the emergence of modern Judaism(s), the main point of relevance for our study is to set in context the understanding of Judaism with which we are concerned. While no extant Judaism or Jewish community is immune to or unaffected by the developments of the modern era, the diversity among the Judaisms described by Neusner provides the backdrop for the common thread that runs between the Jewish thinkers we will be engaging. Unlike the twentieth century Judaisms Neusner describes, the Judaism of interest in this study is, in continuity with the received tradition, thoroughgoingly theological. The Jewish thinkers with whom we will interact view the indelible connection between Israel and Torah as paramount in defining Judaism and Jewish self-understanding. While the Jewish thinkers represented in this study are far from theologically monolithic, they share a common emphasis on this central theological connection. Collectively, they reflect a commitment to a Judaism built upon the biblical relationship between God, Israel, and Torah that self-consciously stands in theological and historical continuity with the received tradition.

It is this stream of modern Judaism that underlies Marshall's understanding of the election of Israel, making his thought stand out among Christian perspectives on Judaism and the Jewish people. While motivated by different historical, theological, and exegetical concerns, Christianity in general tends to conceive of the Jewish people without regard to Jewish practice. Marshall exposes the incoherence of such a position, insisting that the church rethink not only its posture toward the Jewish people, but perhaps more significantly its stance toward Judaism as a religious tradition. Marshall's formulation of this issue and understanding of this connection will thus provide the overarching framework of this study.

Particularly of interest in this study is the interaction between a group of theologically engaged modern Jews and their confessionally committed Christian interlocutors. The Jewish thinkers we will engage uphold the ideals of traditional Judaism yet press toward an understanding of Judaism that takes into account the deep connection between Judaism and Christianity. While their traditionalist perspective on God, Israel, and Torah sets them apart from the twentieth-century Judaisms described by Neusner, their willingness to theologically engage Christianity sets them apart from the vast majority of traditional Jews. In other words, what makes the Jewish thinkers in this study unique is both their commitment to upholding traditional Judaism and their insistence that traditional Judaism cannot be conceived without regard to Christianity.

The theological interchange between this group of Jewish thinkers and their orthodox Christian counterparts forms the very heart of the new Jewish-Christian encounter, whose contours we will explore below. As we will see, this encounter stands apart from other forms of twentieth-century Jewish-Christian dialogue[84] and comprises an emergent intellectual tradition that is deeply shaping the self-identities of its participants.

---

84. While the spectrum of Jewish-Christian engagement in the twentieth century is far too diverse to be easily characterized, perhaps a brief look at the stance of four representative theologians will help identify what sets the new Jewish-Christian encounter apart from the rest of twentieth-century Jewish-Christian dialogue. From the Christian side, the works of Hans Küng and Paul van Buren are sufficiently illustrative of Christian approaches that, in Marshall's terms, do not affirm the "universal, ecclesially mediated saving mission of Christ." While both Küng and van Buren have made a deep impact upon twentieth-century Jewish-Christian dialogue, each makes substantial theological sacrifices in their interfaith engagement. Küng advocates a "wider ecumenism" within which a Christian stance toward other religions displays "neither arrogant absolutism, not accepting any other claim, nor a weak eclecticism accepting a little of everything, but an inclusive Christian universalism claiming for Christianity not exclusiveness, but certainly uniqueness" (Hans Küng, On Being a Christian [trans. Edward Quinn, New York: Image Books, 1984], 112; see also Hans Küng et al., Christianity and the World Religions: Paths to Dialogue with Islam, Hinduism, and Buddhism [trans. Peter Heinegg, New York: Doubleday, 1986]). Van Buren posits that Christ's mission vis-à-vis the Jewish people is significantly different from his mission vis-à-vis gentiles. With regard to Israel, Christ came to issue a call to renewed Torah-faithfulness, to "be Israel, better than you are being it in practice." Jesus was in the line of prophets, priests, Pharisees, and rabbis who were calling Israel back to obedience, beginning with Jeremiah and continuing up through the rabbis at Javneh and rabbinical Judaism today. "Jesus' call to his people in his lifetime and to this day is rather that they be Jews as he was a Jew, that they be God's Jews" (Paul van Buren, A Theology of the Jewish-Christian Reality, Part Two: A Christian Theology of the People Israel [Lanham, MD: University Press of America, 1995], 258). From the Jewish side, the thoughts of Martin Buber and Joseph Soloveitchik, both significant twentieth-century figures with regard to Jewish-Christian engagement, again illustrate what sets the new Jewish-Christian encounter apart. While Buber engaged in deep and ongoing dialogue with Christians, and found in the Jewish Jesus a "great brother," he sacrifices the central connection between Israel and Torah that characterizes traditional Judaism (see Martin Buber, Two Types of Faith, trans. Norman P. Goldhawk [Syracuse: Syracuse University Press, 2003], 12). Soloveitchik believed that it was important for Jews and Christians to partner "in all fields of constructive human endeavor" (by which he means combating disease, alleviating human suffering, protecting human rights, helping the needy, etc.), but denied that any true theological engagement was possible between adherents of two different faiths. In his words, "It is important that the religious or theological logos should not be employed as the medium of communication between two faith communities whose modes of expression are as unique

## THE NEW JEWISH-CHRISTIAN ENCOUNTER

The widespread positive engagement between Jews and Christians in the post-Holocaust era is perceptible from many angles and has taken a variety of forms. Our interest in this study is limited to one particular strand of this improved relationship, the aims and means of which have yielded a nascent intellectual tradition. The new Jewish-Christian encounter is not merely a sharing across mutually agreed upon communal and doctrinal boundaries; in many ways, it is a fundamental redrawing of those historically entrenched boundaries.

As Christian theologians Carl Braaten and Robert Jenson note, "Theologians and scholars of both Judaism and Christianity are today radically rethinking the relation between their two covenant communities."[85] From the Jewish side, the recognition that Christianity's posture toward Judaism is shifting has elicited a reciprocal openness to dialogue and engagement. In the words of Fritz Rothschild, "Jews can no longer afford to treat Christianity with the benign neglect of past generations. Apart from such historical facts as the Holocaust and the crisis of religious faith in the postmodern world, we now face a situation where Christians are, perhaps for the first time, ready to listen to what Jews have to say, and are ready for a fruitful dialogue instead of turning such encounters into occasions for missionary propaganda or mere apologetics."[86]

While literature on twentieth-century Jewish-Christian dialogue abounds, two publications in particular reflect the promising direction of the new encounter with which we are concerned. In 2003, Carl Braaten and Robert Jenson edited a collection of essays entitled *Jews and Christians: People of God*.[87] Most of the essays in the book originated as papers that were presented at a gathering in 2001 hosted by Augsburg College and

---

as their apocalyptic experiences" (Joseph B. Soloveitchik, "Confrontation," *Tradition* 6, no. 2 [Spring-Summer 1964]: 26, 24).

85.  Carl E. Braaten and Robert W. Jenson, "Introduction," in *Jews and Christians*, vii.

86.  Fritz A. Rothschild, "General Introduction," in *Jewish Perspectives on Christianity*, ed. Fritz A. Rothschild (New York: Crossroad, 1990), 2.

87.  The contributors whose works are most relevant to our study are Robert Jenson, Jon Levenson, George Lindbeck, Richard John Neuhaus, David Novak, Peter Ochs, Wolfhart Pannenberg, and R. Kendall Soulen.

sponsored by the Center for Catholic and Evangelical Theology. According to the editors, "The Christian scholars represented in this volume all repudiate supersessionist theory, which holds that in the providence of God the church is a 'new Israel' in such a fashion that there can be no other, thus removing Judaism from God's saving plan."[88] The book includes essays by leading Jewish scholars who are responding to "new Christian theology of Judaism with new Jewish understanding of Christianity."[89]

The conference that gave rise to the Braaten and Jenson volume built upon a development that had occurred the previous year. In 2000, an interdenominational group of Jewish scholars drafted the document *Dabru Emet: A Jewish Statement on Christians and Christianity* as a Jewish response to the widespread Christian reassessment of Judaism. The statement was accompanied by the publication of a collection of essays entitled *Christianity in Jewish Terms*, in which leading Jewish and Christian scholars address side by side the central theological issues that both unite and divide Judaism and Christianity. The preface to this volume begins as follows: "Over the past few decades there has been a dramatic and unprecedented shift in Jewish and Christian relations. Throughout the nearly two millennia of Jewish exile, Christian theologians and clerics have tended to characterize Judaism as a failed religion or, at best, a religion that prepared the way for Christianity and that is completed in and replaced by Christianity. In the four decades since the Holocaust, however, Christianity has changed dramatically."[90]

The five editors[91] of *Christianity in Jewish Terms* point specifically to the public remorse expressed by Christian theologians and church bodies about the mistreatment of Jews over the last two millennia, as well as the growing Christian acknowledgment that "Christian theologies, liturgies,

---

88. Braaten and Jenson, "Introduction," viii. We will be interacting much more closely with the history and repudiation of supersessionism in chapter 3. For a theological perspective on the church's self-designation as the "new people of God," see Mark Kinzer, *"Lumen Gentium*, through Messianic Jewish Eyes," in *Israel's Messiah and the People of God: A Vision for Messianic Jewish Covenant Fidelity*, ed. Jennifer M. Rosner (Eugene, OR: Cascade, 2011), 156–174.

89. Braaten and Jenson, "Introduction," viii.

90. Tikva Frymer-Kensky et al., "Preface," in *Christianity in Jewish Terms*, ed. Tikva Frymer-Kensky et al. (Boulder, CO: Westview, 2000), ix.

91. These editors are Tikva Frymer-Kensky, David Novak, Peter Ochs, David Fox Sandmel, and Michael Signer.

and Bible teachings can and must be reformed so that they acknowledge God's enduring covenant with the Jewish people and celebrate the contribution of Judaism to world civilization and to Christian faith itself."[92]

The editors of and contributors to these two volumes are among those who are leading the new Jewish-Christian encounter, and the theological disposition of their work makes this encounter unique.[93] As we seek to illustrate and interpret this emerging intellectual tradition, four interrelated descriptors emerge. These dialogical distinctives build upon one another, and the sum turns out to be far greater than the parts. First, the Jewish-Christian engagement represented in this stream of dialogue reflects a commitment to theological and doctrinal rigor. The theologians of the new Jewish-Christian encounter are unabashedly committed to their respective traditions, and they view their religious particularity as an asset rather than a liability in their interfaith work. Second, these scholars are attempting to understand the religious tradition of the other in the terms and categories of their own religion. This approach enables rich theological exchange, for the religious particularity of the other is engaged in relation to (rather than in isolation from) one's own deeply held convictions. Third, the theologians representing the new Jewish-Christian encounter perceive a deep underlying commonality between Judaism and Christianity. While they do not minimize or ignore the significant theological and historical differences between these two religious communities, they recognize that the bond between these two entities is non-analogous to any other pair of religious traditions. Finally, and perhaps most significantly, these theologians are beginning to reconceive their own religious identity and self-understanding in light of their encounter with one other. If Judaism and Christianity are mysteriously and indelibly bound together, then it follows that they can only properly be defined with reference to one another. In the pages that follow, we will further describe and explain each of these

---

92. Frymer-Kensky et al., "Preface," ix.

93. Peter Ochs recognizes the contribution of postliberal Christianity to the new Jewish-Christian encounter, and he coins the term "aftermodern Jewish philosophers" to refer to the Jewish counterparts of postliberal Christian theologians. See Peter Ochs, "A Rabbinic Pragmatism," in *Theology and Dialogue: Essays in Conversation with George Lindbeck*, ed. Bruce D. Marshall (Notre Dame: University of Notre Dame Press, 1990), 213–248. Also of relevance is Ochs' book *Another Reformation: Postliberal Christianity and the Jews* (Grand Rapids: Baker, 2011).

four key markers of the new Jewish-Christian encounter. We will also say a word about boundary redefinition and the threat of syncretism before moving on to an overview of the present study.

## DISTINCTIVE #1: COMMITMENT TO
## THEOLOGICAL AND DOCTRINAL RIGOR

Authentic engagement between Jews and Christians cannot ignore the differences between these two religious communities. These differences are not merely superficial and cosmetic; rather, they lie at the heart of each community's self-understanding and have fueled the tense relationship between Jews and Christians. In an atmosphere of healing and reconciliation, proponents of Jewish-Christian dialogue may be tempted to bury these differences in an effort to highlight the multiple grounds for improved relations. In fact, much of the dialogue thrives upon avoiding doctrinal discussions and disagreements. According to Bruce Marshall, the divergent truth claims of Judaism and Christianity make it tempting to "account for the possibility of dialogue between Jews and Christians by doing away with particularism about truth altogether, or, less drastically, by ignoring it for the purposes of dialogue. Different versions of this strategy enjoy wide currency in Christian theology of religions and of inter-religious dialogue."[94]

According to the ethos of the new Jewish-Christian encounter, to deny the very real theological differences between Christians and Jews is to preclude the possibility of genuine engagement. Doctrinal particularity cannot be permitted to bow at the altar of interfaith amity. As David Novak asserts in *Christianity in Jewish Terms*, "One cannot use understanding of the other as any kind of escape from full commitment to the authority of Judaism for Jews or of Christianity for Christians."[95] Braaten and Jenson likewise affirm this commitment to doctrinal particularity, and the contributors to their co-edited volume "have avoided the pitfalls so common in 'dialogue,' of watering down distinctive beliefs to accommodate their partners." For example, the Jewish theologians represented in

---

94. Marshall, "Truth Claims," 230.
95. David Novak, "What to Seek and What to Avoid in Jewish-Christian Dialogue," in *Christianity in Jewish Terms*, 2.

Jews and Christians "are not asking Christian theologians to compromise their trinitarian interpretation of God or their incarnational belief in Jesus' Messiahship."[96]

Along these lines, Novak delineates two poles that must be avoided if true dialogue is to take place. On the one hand, neither religious community can posture itself triumphantly, as if "the final truth has already been given to my community alone."[97] A triumphalist stance assumes that "there is no commonality to discover between the two religions, and that therefore there is nothing to learn from the dialogue."[98] However, the opposite extreme must also be avoided. "When triumphalism is abandoned too hastily as a historical embarrassment in a pluralistic world, the authority of the tradition is usually compromised in such a way that both the other community and one's own community lose their phenomenological integrity. The precipitous abandonment of triumphalism usually leads to the worse stance of relativism."[99] According to Novak, "Relativism on the part of either Jews or Christians is as inauthentic about its own faith as it is about the faith of the other."[100]

Novak points to both the allure and the danger of secularity, cautioning that dialogue on the basis of some form of "secular agreement," in which "Jews and Christians bracket the historical character of their respective faiths for the sake of some broader international consensus" in effect replaces faith by something antithetical to it.[101] In the words of Randi Rashkover, "The Christian is always a Christian and the Jew always a Jew, regardless of their conversation partners. A Jewish-Christian dialogue relegated to the secular realm is a contradiction in terms."[102] In other words, the respective truth claims of Judaism and Christianity must be brought to the table if true Jewish-Christian dialogue is to take place.

---

96. Braaten and Jenson, "Introduction," viii–ix.

97. Novak, "What to Seek and What to Avoid in Jewish-Christian Dialogue," 5.

98. Ibid., 6.

99. David Novak, *Jewish-Christian Dialogue: A Jewish Justification* (New York: Oxford University Press, 1989), 17.

100. Ibid., 18.

101. Ibid., 11.

102. Randi Rashkover, "Jewish Responses to Jewish-Christian Dialogue: A Look Ahead to the Twenty-First Century," *Cross Currents* 50, no.1-2 (Spring-Summer 2000): 215.

This commitment to one's tradition is a hallmark of the new Jewish-Christian encounter. Recognizing the peril of diluting doctrine for the sake of religious agreement, the theologians of interest in this study refuse to ignore or disregard the theological particularities of Judaism and Christianity.

DISTINCTIVE #2: ASSESSMENT OF THE
OTHER'S TRADITION IN LIGHT OF ONE'S OWN

While not sweeping aside the differences between Jews and Christians, the theologians of the new Jewish-Christian encounter seek to thoroughly understand the religious claims of the other. Furthermore, the desired understanding is not based upon detached observation but rather upon mutual engagement and reciprocal openness. Hence, the editors of *Christianity in Jewish Terms* write: "We believe it is time for Jews to learn about Christianity in Jewish terms: to rediscover the basic categories of rabbinic Judaism and to hear what the basic categories of Christian belief sound like when they are taught in terms of this rabbinic Judaism."[103]

This constructive approach to dialogue requires a certain vulnerability and precludes a theologically aloof posture toward the tradition of the other. It is in effect to allow the other's tradition to interface with one's own sense of religious consciousness. To do so evades a destructive and alienating process of "othering" that distorts the relative proximity of these two religious communities. This approach to dialogue is visible through the various chapters of *Christianity in Jewish Terms*, which treat a number of theological loci that are common to both traditions—God, Scripture, commandment, suffering, embodiment, redemption, etc. To assess Judaism and Christianity in terms that are common to both is to uncover vast territories of theological overlap amid the clear areas of difference.

As we proceed through this study, we will track the progression of this dialogical posture, noting the ways in which the acknowledged areas of resonance broaden and deepen as the new Jewish-Christian encounter takes root and gains momentum. As we will see, Karl Barth and Franz Rosenzweig served as key forerunners of the new Jewish-Christian encounter, as their thoughts reflect a conscious awareness of the deep

---

103. Frymer-Kensky et al., "Preface," x.

theological resonance between Judaism and Christianity. While these two theologians assess the religious tradition of the other in the terms of their own religious self-understanding, they both ultimately construe Judaism and Christianity as being mutually exclusive. This disposition does not disappear in the post-Holocaust era, though the theologians we will assess who build on the work of Barth and Rosenzweig begin to discern a greater degree of theological and doctrinal common ground between Judaism and Christianity. Finally, as we will see in the last chapter of this study, Messianic Judaism refuses a mutually exclusive paradigm and provides the theological scaffolding for a model of understanding in which maximal continuity between these two traditions prevails. Standing somewhere in the boundary space between Judaism and Christianity, Messianic Judaism is both an insider and an outsider to both traditions and has the unique ability to evaluate each tradition in light of the other.

### DISTINCTIVE #3: RECOGNITION OF UNDERLYING THEOLOGICAL COMMONALITY BETWEEN JUDAISM AND CHRISTIANITY

As we stated above, the engagement between Christians and Jews is non-analogous to any other interfaith endeavor. The new chapter that has commenced in the relationship between Judaism and Christianity has highlighted the shared canon, heritage, and history of these two religious traditions.

The inherent connection between Judaism and Christianity is perhaps more apparent to Christians than it is to Jews. Indeed, the very fabric of Christianity emerges out of the covenantal history between God and Israel. John Howard Yoder has dubbed Judaism a "non-non-Christian religion,"[104] pointing to Judaism's singular status from the perspective of Christianity. In accordance with this understanding, Robert Jenson is dubious that "the sorts of conversation usually called 'interreligious dialogue' are at all appropriate between Judaism and Christianity. ... For Christianity, Judaism cannot be an 'other religion,' and this is true whether or not Judaism can

---

104. John Howard Yoder, *The Jewish-Christian Schism Revisited*, ed. Michael G. Cartwright and Peter Ochs (Grand Rapids: Eerdmans, 2003), 147–59.

say anything reciprocal about Christianity."[105] As we saw above, Pope John Paul II understood Judaism to be mysteriously intrinsic to Christianity. This acknowledgment of fundamental commonality deeply informs the new Jewish-Christian encounter. According to Braaten and Jenson, the new theological exchange "goes to the roots of that 'olive tree' of which both Judaism and Christianity are somehow branches (Rom. 11:17)."[106]

While the bond between Christianity and Judaism may not be as immediately apparent from the side of rabbinic Judaism, Jewish theologians are likewise recasting the relationship between these two religious communities. As Jewish theologian Michael Wyschogrod explains:

> In the Church, the vocabulary of Israel is used—covenant, election, suffering servant, and redemption—and the book that Israel hears as the word of God is for the first time heard by a people that is not the seed of Abraham. Can anything but joy fill the heart of Israel as it observes the mysterious way in which the God of Israel begins to be heard by the nations? Is it not the faith of Israel that, in the fullness of time, the God of the patriarchs will become the God of all peoples and, if this is not just an idle dream, must Israel not be ready to perceive signs of this even in the travail of history?[107]

As Wyschogrod's perspective makes clear, to evaluate Christianity in Jewish terms is to discern the mysterious way in which Christianity and Judaism hasten toward a common *telos*. As we will see throughout our study, renewed emphasis on two key theological doctrines have been central catalysts for discovering anew the deep bond between Judaism and Christianity: the Jewishness of Jesus and the election of Israel. Both of these doctrines figure prominently in the theology of Karl Barth, and Franz Rosenzweig reflects extensively on the unique vocation of the Jewish people while hinting at Jesus' role as a bridge between Judaism and Christianity. The significance of these two theological foci only increases among post-Holocaust

---

105. Robert W. Jenson, "Toward a Christian Theology of Judaism," in *Jews and Christians*, 2.
106. Braaten and Jenson, "Introduction," ix.
107. Michael Wyschogrod, "Israel, the Church, and Election," in *Abraham's Promise*, 183.

scholars, and these doctrines are effectually fused in the thought of Mark Kinzer.

## DISTINCTIVE #4: REASSESSMENT OF ONE'S OWN TRADITION IN LIGHT OF THE OTHER'S

The most significant aspect of the new Jewish-Christian encounter is the way in which its pioneers and participants are rethinking their own religious self-understanding as a result of theological engagement with the other. The three distinctives we have just traced culminate in this final marker, which opens significant new avenues for the future of the dialogue. This phenomenon represents something far beyond constructing a Christian theology of Judaism or a Jewish theology of Christianity; it essentially presses toward redefining the essence of and relation between these two communities. Once again, this revised sense of religious self-identity is apparent on both the Jewish and the Christian sides of the dialogue, though there is perhaps more at stake (and potentially more theological yield) from the Christian side.

In "Truth Claims and the Possibility of Jewish-Christian Dialogue," Bruce Marshall attempts to outline the parameters of a dialogue that opens up "the possibility of Christians learning things from Jews about how to be Christians." The very posture of this goal reflects this fourth distinctive of the new Jewish-Christian encounter. As Marshall expands upon what such a goal actually entails, he explains that "to say that Christians should expect to learn from Jews is to say that they should expect to accept Jewish truth claims; that is, they should expect to hold true sentences that Jews hold true, interpreted as Jews interpret them."[108] Marshall's model for dialogue does not merely envision a Christian affirmation of the validity of Jewish truth claims for Jews; rather, he is concerned that Christians uphold these truth claims as valid for Christianity as well. Such a concern reveals the sheer novelty of the new Jewish-Christian encounter as well as its most theologically daring characteristic.

What Marshall seeks on a doctrinal level, Richard John Neuhaus presses from an ecclesiological angle. In his words, "The salvation that is from the

---

108. Marshall, "Truth Claims," 232.

Jews cannot be proclaimed or lived apart from the Jews. ... The Christian story and the Jewish story are of theological interest only as they participate in the story of the one God of Israel. Along the way there are many stories, but ultimately the story of salvation, like the phrase 'people of God,' has no plural."[109] Neuhaus contends that theological commonality between Jews and Christians must produce communal unity. To emphasize the oneness of God's people is to claim that even amid their doctrinal differences, these two communities are enduringly bound together in the plan and purposes of God.

Ultimately, from a Christian perspective, if this permanent and thoroughgoing connection between Jews and Christians is real, it must work its way through every doctrine of Christian theology. If Judaism is somehow intrinsic to Christianity, then Christianity's self-understanding is necessarily distorted to the extent that it excludes consideration of Judaism and the Jewish people. Christianity is increasingly awakening to this reality, and Christian theology is just beginning to fully acknowledge and integrate this realization into its own identity.

From the Jewish side, theologians are likewise discovering that understanding Christianity can in turn inform their self-understanding as Jews. In his book *Intersecting Pathways: Modern Jewish Theologians in Conversation with Christianity*, Marc Krell examines a handful of Jewish thinkers whose theologies of Judaism develop out of a cultural and theological interchange with Christianity. Krell explains that, "in their efforts to better conceptualize Jewish identity in relation to Christianity, these Jewish thinkers ... not only reflect upon the relationship between Judaism and Christianity, but their engagement with Christian thought and culture leads to a reconstruction of Jewish theology."[110] Not surprisingly, Franz Rosenzweig appears at the top of Krell's list of Jewish thinkers who represent this trend.[111]

While Wyschogrod is not among those assessed in Krell's book, his thought deeply embodies the quality we are describing. In an essay entitled

---

109. Neuhaus, "Salvation Is from the Jews," 70.

110. Marc A. Krell, *Intersecting Pathways: Modern Jewish Theologians in Conversation with Christianity* (Oxford: Oxford University Press, 2003), 6.

111. Krell also examines the thought of Irving Greenberg, which we will engage in chapter 3.

"The Impact of Dialogue with Christianity on My Self-Understanding as a Jew," Wyschogrod explains the way in which Christianity has "sharpened my theological appetite."[112] He asserts that contact with Christianity has "enriched rather than impoverished my Judaism," for the sharpening he has experienced through his interaction with Christians is ultimately in the service of inner-Jewish concerns. He concludes the essay by encouraging readers that "there is a form of Christianity that does not intend to replace Israel as the people of God but join it as adopted sons and daughters in the household of God. The existence of this Christianity has helped me shape a Jewish identity that can live in deep appreciation of this new Christianity."[113]

The four markers just outlined comprise the uniqueness of the new Jewish-Christian encounter. We will see the way in which these distinctives characterize the perspectives held by the thinkers engaged in this study, and we will ultimately attempt to point toward future possibilities that have opened up in light of this particular approach to Jewish-Christian dialogue. Before moving on to an overview of the contents of this study, it is important to address the tendency toward syncretism that some may perceive in the description of this dialogical approach.

### A WORD ON BOUNDARY REDEFINITION
### AND THE THREAT OF SYNCRETISM

As we have already noted, the theologians of the new Jewish-Christian encounter demonstrate a willingness to rethink the traditional boundaries and boundary markers between Judaism and Christianity. Their distinctiveness lies in both their commitment to their respective traditions and their shared desire to overcome the historical divide between those traditions. The erosion of a mutually exclusive understanding of these two religious traditions has caused some to fear that the ultimate result will be a syncretistic hybrid that neither community will be able to claim or recognize as authentic.

This concern has been explicitly stated by David Novak, who specifically names syncretism as something to be avoided in Jewish-Christian

---

112. Michael Wyschogrod, "The Impact of Dialogue with Christianity on My Self-Understanding as a Jew," in *Abraham's Promise*, 229.

113. Wyschogrod, "The Impact of Dialogue," 236.

dialogue. He describes syncretism as idolatry (i.e., worship of a "strange god") and steadfastly asserts "this dialogue cannot stand syncretism in any form."[114] It is clear that Messianic Judaism is among the targets Novak has in his sights, for he claims "one cannot live as a Jew and a Christian simultaneously."[115] As we saw above, Novak is insistent that the dialogue acknowledge the differences between Judaism and Christianity, and from his perspective, Messianic Judaism fails to respect the irreducibly divergent truth claims upon which authentic Jewish-Christian dialogue is built. Novak is not alone in expressing this concern. According to Edward Kessler, "Many involved in Jewish-Christian dialogue view Messianic Judaism as undermining the mutual respect that has been built up in recent years."[116]

We will recall that Marshall has also raised the question of whether Messianic Judaism represents an undesirable form of syncretism, though his concern is phrased much more tentatively than Novak's. In his presentation of Mark Kinzer's thought as a possible avenue for affirming both the irrevocable election of Israel and the universal saving mission of Christ, Marshall quotes John Paul II: "Each of our religions, in the full awareness of the many bonds which unite them to each other ... wishes to be recognized and respected in its own identity, beyond any syncretism and any ambiguous appropriation."[117] Marshall then raises a few specific questions with regard to Messianic Jewish theology, though it is not clear how the particular concerns he raises connect to John Paul II's caution against syncretism. Despite these concerns, Marshall claims that Kinzer's approach "deserves more attention than it has yet received."[118]

While the apprehension about syncretism must be duly noted, this study seeks to explore whether Messianic Judaism may represent a fundamental step forward in this new dialogical trajectory rather than a threat to it. The features of the Messianic Judaism we will be assessing uphold the fundamental tenets of the new Jewish-Christian encounter and depart

---

114. Novak, "What to Seek and What to Avoid in Jewish-Christian Dialogue," 4.

115. Ibid., 5.

116. Edward Kessler and Neil Wenborn, eds., *A Dictionary of Jewish-Christian Relations* (Cambridge: Cambridge University Press, 2008), 292.

117. John Paul II, *Spiritual Pilgrimage: Texts on Jews and Judaism 1979–1995* (New York: Crossroad, 1996), 64 (no. 5 of the "Address"); quoted in Marshall, "Elder Brothers," 125.

118. Marshall, "Elder Brothers," 125.

significantly from the Messianic Judaism Novak indicts.[119] This emergent
Messianic Judaism is slowly making inroads into Jewish-Christian dialogue,
and a number of scholars—including Marshall, as we saw above—are calling for a more serious assessment of its potential role in and contribution
to the dialogue.[120] At this point, we cannot discern the future development
of this strand of Messianic Judaism nor its prospective involvement or
acceptance in the wider Jewish-Christian dialogue. Within the purview of
this study, our goal is to demonstrate the way in which Kinzer's Messianic
Jewish theology reflects the essential features of the new Jewish-Christian
encounter and fits within its distinct trajectory.

Before providing an overview of the present study, let us review what
we have covered so far. We began by explicating Marshall's incisive challenge to Christian theology, namely the affirmation of both the universal,
ecclesially mediated saving mission of Christ and the irrevocable election
of Israel, which includes the ongoing practice of Judaism. We noted the
way in which Marshall's understanding of Israel's irrevocable election
presupposes a tight connection between Israel and Torah, a connection
that is upheld by the Jewish thinkers treated throughout this study. By
briefly reviewing the history of modern Judaism, we identified the way in
which the thoroughly theological approach to Judaism of interest in this
study departs from the prevailing trends in nineteenth-and twentieth-
century Judaism. Finally, we have reviewed four key characteristics of
the new Jewish-Christian encounter and addressed directly the question
of syncretism, particularly with regard to Messianic Judaism. Let us now

---

119. Novak claims that the acceptance of Messianic Jews subtly endorses "a new form of
proselytizing … designed specifically to lure us eventually, if not immediately, away from what
we believe is our own true covenantal identity" (David Novak, "When Jews Are Christians," in
*Talking with Christians: Musings of a Jewish Theologian* [Grand Rapids: Eerdmans, 2005], 220).
As we will see in chapter 4, one of Mark Kinzer's primary concerns is to uphold and advocate
for the covenantal obligations of all Jews, including Messianic Jews. Novak likewise asserts
that Messianic Jews "see the messiahhood of Jesus as the sole point of difference between
themselves and their fellow Jews," effectively choosing "to ignore the testimony of intervening history" (Novak, "When Jews Are Christians," 221). Kinzer, however, pays particular
attention to the contours of the "intervening history" and ultimately purports a theological
understanding of the schism that that history has brought about.

120. See, for example, Wolfhart Pannenberg's statements in "A Symposium on Dabru
Emet" in *Jews and Christians*, 185, and Christian Rutishauser's claim in " 'And after the fire a
soft murmuring sound … ' The Abiding Significance of Judaism for Christian Identity," *Studies
in Jewish-Christian Relations* 2, no. 2 (2007): 150.

chart the course of our study, which builds upon each of these preliminary points.

## OVERVIEW OF STUDY

### APPROACH AND METHODOLOGY

In an attempt to map out the new Jewish-Christian encounter from its nascent origins in the thought of key early twentieth-century pioneers to its current manifestation at the beginning of the twenty-first century, this study will take a historical approach to describing and assessing this emerging intellectual tradition. Our goal in this study will be threefold: first, to trace key influences in the theological genesis of this developing strand of Jewish-Christian dialogue (chapters 1 and 2); second, to outline dominant features of its present incarnation (chapters 3 and 4); and finally, to identify potential future directions for this trajectory (conclusion). Ultimately, our interest lies in the way in which the theologians we are engaging redefine the relationship between Judaism and Christianity while maintaining a commitment to their own respective communities and theological convictions. Therefore, while this study utilizes a historical lens to trace the emergence and contours of the new Jewish-Christian encounter, charting this trajectory is ultimately in service of elucidating the central doctrinal developments that concern us throughout.

Marshall's challenge will inform this sustained doctrinal focus, and each chapter will assess the contribution of a particular theologian (or group of theologians) with regard to Marshall's key question. Our concern will be to evaluate the ability of these theologians—and the new Jewish-Christian encounter more broadly—to affirm both the irrevocable election of Israel (which necessarily includes the ongoing practice of Judaism) and the universal, ecclesially mediated saving mission of Christ. Because these doctrinal concerns comprise the central focus of this study, this work ultimately fits much more readily in the field of systematic theology than historical theology.

OUTLINE OF CHAPTERS

Chapter 1 will explore the relevant facets of Karl Barth's theology, particularly his doctrine of election and its relationship to the command of God. Barth's theology prefigures the post-Holocaust reassessment of the relationship between Judaism and Christianity, and his christological configuration of both election and command raises a set of highly pertinent questions with regard to Jesus' Jewishness and the church's relationship to the people of Israel. We will identify the greatest assets and the greatest limitations of Barth's theology with regard to Marshall's criteria, keeping in mind the far-reaching impact his theology has made upon the next generation of Christian (and Jewish) theologians.

In chapter 2, we will outline Franz Rosenzweig's novel construal of the relationship between Judaism and Christianity, including the correlative vocations and mutual contingency he assigns to these two communities. The impact Rosenzweig's thought has had on twentieth-century Jewish theology is comparable to Barth's influence in the Christian sphere, as both thinkers pioneered models that must be reckoned with by subsequent generations of theologians.[121] We will offer an assessment of Rosenzweig's implicit Christology as well as his robust doctrine of the election of Israel, ultimately assessing what his thought contributes to Marshall's desired theological affirmations.

Chapter 3 delineates six key theological focal points that build upon the frameworks of Barth and Rosenzweig and have gained considerable attention in the work of post-Holocaust Jewish and Christian theologians.

---

121. The most notable study to date that pairs Barth and Rosenzweig is Randi Rashkover's 2005 book *Revelation and Theopolitics: Barth, Rosenzweig and the Politics of Praise* (London: T&T Clark). Rashkover offers a comparative reading of these two theologians and "uses this new reading as the basis for a philosophically justified theopolitics" (ibid., 3). Her work on Barth and Rosenzweig focuses on their common rejection of a liaison between religion and the state, which in both cases stems from their robust doctrines of election.

Another noteworthy publication that treats both Barth and Rosenzweig is Mark Lilla's 2007 book *The Stillborn God: Religion, Politics, and the Modern West* (New York: Random House). While the scope of this book goes far beyond the work and influence of these two thinkers, Lilla dedicates a chapter to explaining the parallel impact made by Barth and Rosenzweig on the political environment of twentieth-century Germany. According to Lilla, neither Barth nor Rosenzweig "recognized the connection between the rhetoric of their theological messianism and the apocalyptic rhetoric that was beginning to engulf German society." While Lilla claims no causal relationship between their work and the political developments in Germany, he asserts that their writings did "unwittingly help to shape a new and noxious form of political argument, which was the theological celebration of modern tyranny" (ibid., 278).

This chapter will assess both the theological concepts themselves as well as the key thinkers who are developing them. While the thought of Barth and Rosenzweig anticipates the new Jewish-Christian encounter, these theologians chisel out the precise contours of this dialogical trajectory and draw it forward. Their ability to remain committed to their respective religious communities while creatively recasting the traditional models of Judaism and Christianity marks them as key theological architects of this developing intellectual tradition.

Chapter 4 examines the work of Messianic Jewish theologian Mark Kinzer, whose unique theological project both builds upon and extends the trajectories of Barth, Rosenzweig, and the post-Holocaust theologians of chapter 3. If one of the hallmarks of the new Jewish-Christian encounter is rethinking the self-definitions of Judaism and Christianity in light of one another, Kinzer's thought embodies this endeavor par excellence. Our assessment of Kinzer's work will explore the implications of his thought as well as identify areas that require further clarification. Because Kinzer has not yet presented systematic reflections on the key theological doctrines that his work both builds upon and departs from, our appraisal of his thought must remain provisional.

Finally, we will offer some concluding remarks on the intellectual tradition represented by these theologians, particularly the degree to which their thought contributes to an affirmation of Marshall's theological criteria. In light of both the theological achievements and remaining limitations of the thinkers addressed in this study, we will point forward to potential future directions of this unique intellectual tradition.

# 1
—

# "SALVATION IS OF THE JEWS": KARL BARTH'S DOCTRINE OF ISRAEL AND THE CHURCH

## INTRODUCTION

Karl Barth has been described as a "theological Everest,"[1] and any attempt at Christian theological reflection in the twenty-first century must reckon with his impact and influence. From beginning to end, the content of Barth's theology is deeply informed by and connected to the historical circumstances in which he lived and wrote. In fact, Barth's theology is only properly understood when it is placed in its historical context. Though Barth's theology is organized systematically, what lies behind the system is the social and political context in which he lived.[2] For these reasons, Timothy Gorringe claims that "Barth must be read 'prophetically' rather than 'systematically,' as a theologian who is above all concerned with the way in which God's Word shapes history, rather than in setting out an account of the divine essence."[3]

Latent within Barth's theology and constant throughout his entire career is his intense and active interest in and engagement with politics and social ethics. Barth was continually assessing the situation of his time

---

1. Colin Brown, *Karl Barth and the Christian Message* (London: Tyndale, 1967), 9.

2. See Timothy Gorringe, *Karl Barth: Against Hegemony* (New York: Oxford University Press, 1999), 292–301. Gorringe includes an appendix entitled "Barth's Work in Context" in which he provides a helpful timeline that charts each year from the year Barth first published theology (1909) until his death (1968). He includes in the timeline major historical events of that year, cultural novelties of that year, significant events in Barth's life at that time, what Barth published during that year, and other significant publications of that year.

3. Gorringe, *Karl Barth: Against Hegemony*, 8.

and writing theology that was highly relevant to his social, political, and religious context, and these elements determined the form and structure of his theology. Barth's practice of exegeting his surroundings in order to express his theological ideas—constructing theology with the Bible in one hand and the newspaper in the other—buttresses both the logic and the delivery of his theological system. It is for this reason that Friedrich-Wilhelm Marquardt postulates that Barth's methodology is his theological biography.[4] His development as a theologian was deeply connected with the historical setting that encircled him, and for our purposes it is significant to note that Barth's writing is informed by three of the four major historical factors we noted at the beginning of the last chapter.[5]

With regard to our specific focus in this study, Barth is among the most significant Christian pioneers of the new Jewish-Christian encounter, and both the context and the content of Barth's writings open new theological avenues for conceiving of the relationship between Judaism and Christianity. Barth's theology sets the course for a Christian understanding of salvation history, election, and Christian mission in which Israel figures prominently. In the words of Mark Lindsay, "While it would be disingenuous to suggest that Barth was a deliberate pioneer of interfaith theological dialogue in the same sense as people like Paul van Buren and Hans Küng, it would be equally incorrect to suggest that Barth was entirely ambivalent about the state of Jewish-Christian relations, or that he did not work hard to eliminate the anti-Jewish elements that had for

---

4. Friedrich-Wilhelm Marquardt, *Theologie und Sozialismus: Das Beispiel Karl Barths*, 3rd ed. (Munich: Kaiser, 1985), 230. In reflecting on his own theological method, Barth explained that: "As far as I can recall there was no stage in my theological career when I had more than the very next step forward in mind and planned for it. On each occasion this step developed from the steps which I had already taken, and followed from my view of what was possible and necessary in each changing situation. ... I used what I thought that I had learned and understood so far to cope with this or that situation, with some complex of biblical or historical or doctrinal questions, often with some subject presented to me from outside, often in fact by a topical subject, e.g. a political issue. It was always something new that got hold of me, rather than the other way around. ... I hardly ever had anything like a programme to follow at all costs. My thinking, writing and speaking developed from reacting to people, events and circumstances with which I was involved, with their questions and their riddles" (cited in Eberhard Busch, *Karl Barth: His Life from Letters and Autobiographical Texts* [Grand Rapids: Eerdmans, 1994], 418–21).

5. These four major shifts are the demise of Christendom, the Holocaust, the creation of the modern state of Israel and the emergence of Messianic Judaism. See Introduction above.

so long contaminated the Church's teaching."[6] In a book entitled *Prospects for Post-Holocaust Theology*, Stephen Haynes claims that "It is not an exaggeration to say that Barth's understanding of Israel has had the kind of influence on Protestant theology that '*Nostra aetate*' has had on Catholic thinking about Israel."[7]

In our attempt to trace the theological origins of the new Jewish-Christian encounter, Barth's impact upon twentieth-century construals of Israel and the church positions his theology as our starting point. With Marshall's framing question in mind, our assessment of Barth will focus upon the extent to which he upholds both the universal, ecclesially mediated saving mission of Christ as well as the irrevocable election of Israel (which necessarily entails the ongoing practice of Judaism).[8]

My investigation of Barth's Christology, as well as his treatment of Israel as a people and Judaism as a religion, is undergirded by two specific loci of Barth's thought: election and ethics. For this reason, my explication of Barth's work will focus primarily on the *Church Dogmatics*, and volume II/2 in particular.[9] While my assessment of Barth will not be limited to his thoughts in this volume, it will serve as the foundation of the discussion as I seek to put Barth's theology in conversation with Marshall's question. In order to put this particular section of Barth's theology in context, I will briefly review the structure of the *Dogmatics*. In volume I, Barth lays the framework for his entire theological project by explicating the threefold form of the word of God and establishing the Trinitarian grid that informs his theological program. Volume II is dedicated to Barth's doctrine of God, and the second half of this volume expounds the two overarching concepts that anchor our particular study: the "Election of God" (§§32–§35) and the "Command of God" (§§36–§39). It is within these pages that Barth offers his most thorough reflections on "Israel and the Church" and "Gospel and

---

6. Mark Lindsay, *Barth, Israel, and Jesus: Karl Barth's Theology of Israel* (Burlington, VT: Ashgate, 2007), 5.

7. Stephen Haynes, *Prospects for Post-Holocaust Theology* (Atlanta: Scholars Press, 1991), 48.

8. For a fuller explanation of Marshall's criteria, see the introduction of this study (esp. Marshall's Challenge, pp. 4–14).

9. For a treatment of Barth's view of Israel from his earlier work, see Douglas Harink, "Barth's Apocalyptic Exegesis and the Question of Israel in *Römerbrief*, Chapters 9–11," *Toronto Journal of Theology* 25, no.1 (Spring 2009): 5–18.

Law." In volumes III, IV and what would have been V, Barth lays out the three primary movements of his theology: creation, reconciliation and redemption. Building upon the theological groundwork of volumes I and II, the later sections of the *Dogmatics* reflect Barth's thought in its most thorough and developed form.

With regard to our particular doctrinal focus, that Barth treats election and ethics in the same volume reveals one of the central thrusts of his entire theological system. As Barth lays out his doctrine of election, he characteristically begins with Jesus Christ, who is both the elect man and the electing God. For Barth, the election of the community of God (Israel and the church) and the election of the individual take place within the election of Christ. While, according to Barth, "the doctrine of election is the sum of the Gospel,"[10] one cannot speak of the gospel without in the same breath speaking about the law. In electing human beings, God calls them to obedience and responsibility. In Barth's words: "It is as He makes Himself responsible for man that God makes man, too, responsible. Ruling grace is commanding grace. ... The one Word of God is both Gospel and Law."[11] Just as God is made known in his acts, so too is humanity. Humans, therefore, cannot remain neutral in the face of God's election, which claims them in their entirety. According to Barth, "The love of God in Jesus Christ intends and seeks and wills us in our totality."[12]

Thus, for Barth, election and ethics are inseparable. God's election of Jesus Christ is God's primary self-disclosing act, and humanity's inclusion in that election necessarily implies its accountability. Humanity's election is actualized in its recognition of and obedience to the claim and command of God. As Barth puts it, "God actualises His covenant with man by giving him commands, and man experiences this actualisation by the acceptance of these commands."[13] Human beings—whether they recognize it or not—are elected in Jesus Christ to be covenant partners with God and

---

10. Karl Barth, *Church Dogmatics*, eds. T. F. Torrance and G. W. Bromiley, trans. G. W. Bromiley, 14 vols. (London: T&T Clark, 2004), II/2, 3.

11. Ibid., 511.

12. Ibid., 662.

13. Ibid., 679.

are therefore placed under the divine command.[14] As we will see, this tight connection between election and ethics significantly undergirds Barth's ecclesiological framework and thereby informs his contribution to providing an answer to Marshall's question. Throughout this chapter, as we gain an increasingly clear understanding of these facets of Barth's thought, our explication will gradually give way to assessment and critique.

## THE ELECTION OF GOD IN BARTH'S THEOLOGY

### THE ELECTION OF JESUS CHRIST

Barth posits that theology must begin with Jesus Christ,[15] and his discussion of election is therefore christologically grounded. God's movement toward humanity in Christ creates an irrevocable partnership that is constitutive of God's very being. God's election of Christ is "the decree of God behind and above which there can be no earlier or higher decree and beside which there can be no other, since all others serve only the fulfilment of this decree."[16] As Barth will discuss in volume III of the *Church Dogmatics*, all of creation provides the setting for the divine-human covenant relationship grounded in the election of Christ. In Barth's words, "The purpose and therefore the meaning of creation is to make possible the history of God's covenant with man which has its beginning, its centre and its culmination in Jesus Christ."[17]

The election of Christ makes manifest God's decision to be gracious toward humanity , and this grace of God forms the very heart of the gospel: "In the beginning, before time and space as we know them, before creation, before there was any reality distinct from God which could be the object of the love of God or the setting for His acts in freedom, God anticipated

---

14. Ibid., 656.

15. See ibid., 4.

16. Ibid., 94. For Bruce McCormack's account of the Trinitarian implications of Barth's doctrine of election, see "Grace and Being: The Role of God's Gracious Election in Karl Barth's Theological Ontology," in *The Cambridge Companion to Karl Barth*, ed. John Webster (Cambridge: Cambridge University Press, 2000), 92–110. For an alternate assessment, see George Hunsinger, "Election and the Trinity: Twenty-Five Theses on the Theology of Karl Barth," *Modern Theology* 24, no. 2 (April 2008): 179–98. McCormack offers a direct response to Hunsinger's theses in "Election and the Trinity: Theses in Response to George Hunsinger," *Scottish Journal of Theology* 63, no.2 (March 2010): 203–24.

17. Barth, *Church Dogmatics* III/1, 42.

and determined within Himself ... that the goal and meaning of all His dealings with the as yet non-existent universe should be the fact that in His Son He would be gracious towards man, uniting Himself with him."[18] As the "subject and object" of this determination, Christ is the election of God's covenant with humanity.[19]

One of Barth's theological innovations is to fuse a doctrine of predestination with Christology. In other words, for Barth, God's act of predestination is self-referential. As the electing God, Christ is the "will of God in action" and the "Reconciler between God and man."[20] As the elect man, Christ's "election is the original and all-inclusive election," which "has as its object and content ... the salvation of all men."[21] Christ thus absorbs both the positive and negative aspects of a traditional doctrine of predestination. In Christ, God takes upon himself judgment and rejection and exalts humanity to covenant relationship with God. For Barth, "predestination means that from all eternity God has determined upon man's acquittal at His own cost." Thus, "predestination is the non-rejection of man ... because it is the rejection of the Son of God."[22]

## THE ELECTION OF THE COMMUNITY

It is within the context of the election of Jesus Christ that Barth treats the election of humanity. Ultimately, the love of God in Jesus Christ is aimed teleologically at "the election of the many (from whom none is excluded)."[23] However, the biblical narrative does not allow us to move directly from the election of Christ to the election of universal humanity or that of individual persons. Rather, according to Scripture, there is a "mediate and mediating" election of the community that forms the "natural and historical environment of Jesus Christ," whose commission is to point beyond itself "to the fellowship of all men in face of which it is a witness and herald."[24] The elect community forms the "inner circle" around Jesus Christ that has

---

18. Barth, *Church Dogmatics* II/2, 101.
19. Ibid., 102.
20. Ibid., 104–05.
21. Ibid., 116.
22. Ibid., 167.
23. Ibid., 195.
24. Ibid., 196.

been chosen to summon the whole world to faith in Christ. The election of the inner circle takes place within the election of Jesus Christ, and the outer circle's awareness of its own election is "mediated, conditioned and bounded by the election of the community."[25]

The unity of the elect community is grounded in the unity of Christ, though it is likewise twofold in nature. As Christ is both the "son of Abraham and David, the Messiah of Israel" and the "Head and Lord of the Church," so the elect community consists of Israel ("in the whole range of its history in past and future, *ante* and *post Christum natum*") and the church (of Jews and Gentiles, "from its revelation at Pentecost to its *fulfil*-ment by the second coming of Christ").[26] Furthermore, the twofold nature of the elect community reflects the judgment and exaltation of Christ's own election. Just as Christ as the crucified Messiah of Israel witnesses to the judgment that God takes upon himself, so Israel, "the people of the Jews which resists its divine election," exhibits "the unwillingness, inca-pacity and unworthiness of man with respect to the love of God" and the "justice of the divine judgment on man borne by God Himself."[27] Israel thus represents the "passing form" of the community of God, merely hearing the promise of God but not putting faith in it.[28] Likewise, "as Jesus Christ the crucified Messiah of Israel shows Himself in his resurrection to be the Lord of the Church," so the church as the "coming form" of the com-munity (which emerges as the old form passes away) "can recognize and confess the divine mercy shown to man," not merely hearing the divine word but believing it.[29]

Further corresponding to the election of Christ, Israel represents the elect man (who turns away from the electing God) while the church rep-resents the electing God (who turns toward the elect man). As Christ's election is the election to death and to life, so "Israel's determination is the praise of the mercy of God in the passing, the death, the setting aside of the old man, of the man who resists his election and therefore God."[30]

---

25. Ibid., 197.
26. Ibid., 197–98.
27. Ibid., 198.
28. Ibid., 233–36.
29. Ibid., 199.
30. Ibid., 260.

Israel discloses that God takes upon himself "the frailty of the flesh, suffering, dying, death, in order to take it away from man, in order to clothe man instead with His glory."[31] Israel's history of suffering reveals the depth of human need, and therefore the depth of divine mercy that cannot be thwarted. Though Israel, through Christ, has already passed from death to life, it refuses to accept and actualize this reality. Israel persists in a "perverse" and "cheerless" service, existing as "the personification of a half-vulnerable, half-gruesome relic, of a miraculously preserved antique, of human whimsicality."[32] However, even and especially in this way Israel testifies to the mercy of God who took on and accepted this flesh, snatching it from ruin.

The church, on the other hand, is "the perfect form of the one community of God,"[33] reflecting God's mercy in turning to and electing humanity. It does this, however, as it recognizes its unity and interrelationship with Israel. Even as the church "waits for the conversion of Israel,"[34] it confesses the unity of God's mercy that embraces the one elect community. The church bears witness to the life that follows death, to freedom for the captives and to glad tidings for the sick, distressed, and wayward. As the church recognizes its preexistence in Israel and its ongoing interrelationship with Israel, it welcomes "the positive confirmation of the election of all Israel," and "it will be glad to have in its midst Christians from the Jews also."[35]

Despite the Jews' resistance to their election and the church's calling on the ground of its election, both Israel and the church are elect in Christ: "We cannot, therefore, call the Jews the 'rejected' and the Church the 'elected' community. The object of election is neither Israel for itself nor the Church for itself, but both together in their unity. ... What is elected in Jesus Christ (His 'body') is the community which has the two fold form of Israel and the Church."[36] Israel's specific service within the elect community is to witness to the judgment from which God has rescued humanity, and to reveal the

---

31. Ibid., 261.
32. Ibid., 263.
33. Ibid., 264.
34. Ibid., 213.
35. Ibid., 267
36. Ibid., 199.

fact that God elects fellowship with an obdurate people that has everything to receive from Him.[37] To the extent that Israel refuses to "enter the Church" and become obedient to its election, it creates a schism in the midst of the community of God, acting as though "it had still another special determination and future beside and outwith the Church."[38] Israel's obstinacy is displayed in its upholding the synagogue, "even though the conclusion of its history is confirmed by the fall of Jerusalem."[39]

However, even in its inaccurate hearing of God's word and resistance to its election, Israel is a witness to God's sovereign election in that God's mercy overcomes humanity's revolt. As God chooses humanity for communion with himself "He does this by electing flesh and blood from Judah-Israel to be His tabernacle and the Church of Jews and Gentiles to be His sanctuary, to declare to the world His gracious turning."[40] Thus, Israel and the church—together in their unity and differentiation—are the "mediate and mediating object of the divine election."[41]

Barth's treatment of the election of the community is accompanied by a running exegesis of Romans 9–11.[42] Even as Paul expects and waits for the conversion of the Jews, he insists that Israel has not been written out of the people of God. With regard to Romans 10:2, Barth explains that even though Israel's zeal stems from unbelief, "[the members of the synagogue] are the people of the true God and that the true God is their God is not effaced by their guilt. It cannot be effaced at all because it is based on God's election."[43]

---

37. Ibid., 206.

38. Ibid., 208. See also ibid., 262–63.

39. Ibid., 208. For Barth, the term "Synagogue" is used to designate post-biblical Judaism that does not yield to Christ. It is consistently portrayed in negative terms, offering a foil to the truly obedient community and life. The synagogue is a "Synagogue of death" that has "proved unserviceable in relation to what God willed," persisting in "unbelief" and "resistance" (ibid., 264, 280–81, 287).

40. Ibid., 211.

41. Ibid., 201.

42. While Barth's exegesis is rich and thought-provoking, in the words of Geoffrey Bromiley, "The expositions of Romans 9–11, even admitting the difficult nature of the passage, are not always clear, are hard to follow in relation to the general theme, and do not in every case have the necessary cogency" (Geoffrey W. Bromiley, *Introduction to the Theology of Karl Barth* [Grand Rapids: Eerdmans, 1979], 97).

43. Barth, *Church Dogmatics* II/2, 243.

Further, commenting on the proscription against boasting in 11:17, Barth writes the following with regard to the people of Israel:

> It is incontestable that this people as such is the holy people of God: the people with whom God has dealt in His grace and in His wrath; in the midst of whom He has blessed and judged, enlightened and hardened, accepted and rejected; whose cause either way He has made His own, and has not ceased to make His own, and will not cease to make His own. They are all of them by nature sanctified by Him, sanctified as ancestors and kinsmen of the one Holy One in Israel, in a sense that Gentiles are not by nature, not even the best of Gentiles, not even the Gentile Christians, not even the best of Gentile Christians, in spite of their membership of the Church, in spite of the fact that they too are now sanctified by the Holy One of Israel and have become Israel. Each member of the people of Israel as such still continues to participate in the holiness which can be that of no other people, in the holiness of the natural root who because He is the Last and therefore also the First is called Jesus. This holiness the Gentile Christian has to respect in every Jew as such without exception.[44]

With regard to the law, Barth explains that Israel's obedience to the law is grounded in its relationship to God: "The Law itself can be kept and fulfilled only in this relationship and apprehension, i.e., only in faith."[45] However, according to Barth's reading of Romans, this is precisely what Israel lacked. Specifically, Israel "did not want to rely on the promise, on the mercy of God, but on itself, on its own willing and running in the direction of the promised fulfilment. ... Therefore, having all, it lacked all."[46]

Israel's self-reliance is evidenced by its refusal to accept Jesus Christ, the one to whom the law points and through whom the law is fulfilled: "The Jew who now in his zeal for God has rejected and crucified Jesus Christ ... remains all too faithful to his way of work-righteousness, of storming

---

44. Ibid., 287.
45. Ibid., 241.
46. Ibid.

heaven and hell, and therefore of active unbelief."[47] According to Barth, to fulfill the righteousness required by the law is tantamount to confessing Jesus Christ as Lord.[48] The "apostolic message of God's mercy actualised in Jesus Christ does not speak of any new revelation. And again, the one old revelation of God in which Israel participates is as such the message which is proclaimed by the apostles."[49] In other words, that the law is summed up by faith in Christ is not an addition to Israel's understanding of the law. The Synagogue, therefore, "does not have to choose between the authority to which it knows and declares itself to be responsible and another newly arisen and not in any sense obligatory quantity. It has to choose between fulfilment and non-fulfilment in face of the authority recognised by itself. That it chooses non-fulfilment is its guilt—the guilt of unbelieving Israel."[50] Again, as Barth explains concisely: "The demand addressed through the Law to the Jews had found its final point in the demand for confession. What God requires from Israel is that along with the Church, being merged in the Church, and thus by attesting itself as Israel and establishing its election, it should confess Jesus as Lord."[51]

However, as Barth has insisted all along, Israel's disobedience confirms rather than nullifies its election. The "concentration and consistency" of Paul's use of Scripture is meant to demonstrate that "the meaning of [Israel's] election is that in the very act of becoming guilty towards God it must genuinely magnify His faithfulness."[52]

## THE ELECTION OF THE INDIVIDUAL

While the traditional Christian doctrine of predestination has always considered primary the private relationship between God and individual human beings,[53] Barth explains that this aspect of election must be viewed through the lens of the election of Jesus Christ and of the elect community. Barth does not wish to do away with individual election, for Christ's

---

47. Ibid., 247.
48. Ibid.
49. Ibid.
50. Ibid.
51. Ibid., 250.
52. Ibid., 258–59.
53. Ibid., 306.

election as the original election affords lasting validity to "individualism."[54] Likewise, Barth grounds the election of the individual in the oneness of God.[55] Indeed, for Barth, we must understand "the election of the 'individual' as the *telos* of the election of the community."[56] The community is the necessary medium for the election of the individual, but ultimately "there are no predestined families and no predestined nations—even the Israelite nation is simply the first (transitory) form of the community—nor is there a predestined humanity. There are only predestined men—predestined in Jesus Christ and by way of the community. It is individuals who are chosen and not the totality of men."[57]

However, Barth nuances the definition of the individual, adding a negative dimension that God overcomes in the act of election. According to the shadow side of individualism, the individual acts as though their election is freestanding and exists outside the context of community. This "sinful and fatal isolation ... is the essence of man's godlessness."[58] In the act of election, God overturns this self-willed isolation; in fact, "it is this very man, godless in his negative act, wantonly representing the rejected man, who is the predestinate."[59] The elect person is thus called to act upon their election, to hear and believe the word of God and to be converted away from godless isolation. This calling consists of joining with the community of God as lights in the world and witnesses to the mercy and grace of God.[60] Thus "the elect as such are His community: Israel and the Church; the race of those who share in His election and who by their faith may execute, attest and confirm His election and calling."[61]

The witness of the elect testifies to the fact that Jesus Christ "is the Rejected, as and because He is the Elect. In view of His election, there is no other rejected but Himself."[62] In Christ, humanity's rejection of God is

---

54. Ibid., 310.
55. Ibid., 314.
56. Ibid., 311.
57. Ibid., 313.
58. Ibid., 316.
59. Ibid., 317.
60. Ibid., 345.
61. Ibid., 351.
62. Ibid., 353.

precisely that which is rejected. "The rejected man exists in the person of Jesus Christ only in such a way that he is assumed into His being as the elect and beloved of God; only in refutation, conquest and removal by Him; only in such sort that as he is accepted and received by Him he is transformed, being put to death as the rejected and raised to his proper life as the elect, holy, justified and blessed."[63] The elect person is called to awaken the "dormant people of God in the world," to open and enlarge the circle of election, to proclaim to the rejected that their rejection has been overcome.[64]

Those who persist in their rejection of God also witness to God's election. The rejected "is the man whose offence is so great that there neither is nor can there be conceived anything greater—except the compassion of God."[65] Those who reject God witness to that which is denied and overcome by the gospel. Their witness testifies to the futility of their disposition, for "the form of the rejected is in every respect one which yields and dissolves and dissipates."[66] Those who reject God and seek to be their own masters have no future, "but the purpose of the divine election of grace is to grant to this man who in and of himself has no future, a future in covenant with God."[67] The determination of the gospel is that the reluctant and indirect witness of the rejected should become the willing and direct witness to the election of Christ and his community.[68]

As Barth considers the unique witness of the rejected, he offers a lengthy exposition of Judas Iscariot.[69] In the character of Judas, we see that "the New Testament does not seek or find the rejected at a distance, but in the closest conceivable proximity to Jesus Christ Himself."[70] Judas was a disciple who shared with Jesus lineage from the tribe of Judah, and whose confession of Christ was sincere. But, as the one who rejected and

---

63. Ibid., 453.

64. Ibid., 418–19.

65. Ibid., 455.

66. Ibid., 457.

67. Ibid.

68. Ibid., 458.

69. For a thorough exegesis and assessment of Barth's use of Judas, see Katherine Sonderegger, *That Jesus Christ Was Born a Jew: Karl Barth's "Doctrine of Israel"* (University Park: Pennsylvania State University Press, 1992), 83–133.

70. Barth, *Church Dogmatics* II/2, 458.

betrayed Jesus, he is also "the great sinner of the New Testament."[71] For Barth, Judas was a genuine disciple who yet did not "devote himself prodigally to Jesus,"[72] who reserved for himself final authority as to the way of discipleship. According to Barth's reading, Judas represents the Jewish people, for "when he reserves something for himself, and therefore in principle everything, in face of Jesus in this characteristic fashion, he merely does that which Israel has always done in relation to Yahweh."[73] Indeed, "there never was a time when Israel … was willing to trust [God] and therefore dedicate itself wholeheartedly and unreservedly to Him."[74] As Judas rejects and betrays Israel's Messiah, he "does only what the elect people of Israel had always done towards its God, thus finally showing itself in its totality to be the nation rejected by God."[75]

Barth correlates the suicide of Judas (as recorded in Matt 27:5) with the destruction of Jerusalem, which Barth understands to be, in essence, Israel's suicide as embodied in "the revolt against the Romans and particularly in the defence of Jerusalem against Titus in A.D. 70."[76] As a result of his betrayal, "this Judas must die, as he did die; and this Jerusalem must be destroyed, as it was destroyed. Israel's right to exist is extinguished, and therefore its existence can only be extinguished."[77]

However, the power of divine deliverance overthrows Judas' (and Israel's) rejection. That the New Testament continues to describe Judas as "one of the twelve" demonstrates that "his election excels and outshines and controls and directs his rejection: not just partly, but wholly; not just relatively, but absolutely. … This very man, who is wholly rejected, is elect."[78] Likewise, "Israel could not destroy the God-given promise by its unfaithfulness, or reverse or nullify the mission to all people which had been entrusted to it. Israel has fulfilled and vindicated the meaning of its

---

71. Ibid., 461.
72. Ibid., 462.
73. Ibid., 464.
74. Ibid.
75. Ibid., 505.
76. Ibid., 470.
77. Ibid., 505.
78. Ibid., 504.

existence by giving rise to Jesus Christ."[79] As Barth explains, "What alone justifies the Jewish tradition, the utterly disobedient Israel which rejects the fulfilment of its promises and the grace of God manifested towards it, is that it has always the role of the chosen people of God which finds its true fulfilment in the Church."[80] Even to the extent that Israel, as a "past and rejected people," has not "arisen to new life in the Church, it is still true that with its evil human 'tradition' it was the instrument by which the Church of Jesus Christ was built, by which even for Israel itself the light of hope was placed on the candlestick. The divine 'tradition' which the Church of Jesus Christ proclaims in its confession is the hope of Israel, the promise of its election, which always outlasts and excels and surpasses its rejection."[81]

## THE COMMAND OF GOD
## IN BARTH'S THEOLOGY

### THE COMMAND OF GOD

In volume II/2, Barth's treatment of "The Election of God" is immediately followed by his exposition of "The Command of God." Because God is only known and knowable in the person of Jesus Christ, to talk about God is necessarily to talk about humanity as well. The divine-human covenant is part and parcel of the doctrine of God, and this covenant is characterized by God's gracious election. However, humanity's election is teleological; it is directed toward humanity's service as a witness to God. Therefore, an exposition of the election of God must immediately be followed by an exposition of the question, "What is it that God wants from humanity?"[82] In Barth's words, "It is in and with man's determination by God as this takes place in predestination that the question arises of man's self-determination, his responsibility and decision, his obedience and action."[83] This tight connection between election and command leads Barth to reject the common antinomy between gospel and law. For Barth, the one word of God is both

---

79. Ibid., 505.
80. Ibid., 484.
81. Ibid., 506.
82. Ibid., 510.
83. Ibid., 511.

gospel and law; "it is first Gospel and then Law."[84] As he puts it, the content of the word of God is gospel while its form and fashion is law.[85]

Accordingly, for Barth, "election itself and as such demands that it be understood as God's command directed to man; as the sanctification or claiming which comes to elected man from the electing God in the fact that when God turns to Him and gives Himself to him He becomes his Commander."[86] For Barth, the dogmatic task is the ethical task; election and the call to holiness (enacted through obedience to God's command) are inseparable. Barth's actualistic understanding of God undergirds his actualistic anthropology. Just as God reveals himself through his acts, "it is as he acts that man exists as a person."[87] The question of good and right action is thus "his life question, the question by whose answer he stands or falls. ... The command of God is therefore the truth from which—whether he knows and wants to know it or not—man derives, and which he will not evade."[88]

As the elect man, Jesus Christ is the ethical man and the answer to the ethical question. Just as Jesus Christ is both the electing God and the elect man, "He is also the sanctifying God and sanctified man in One. In His person God has acted rightly towards us. And in the same person man has also acted rightly for us."[89] Gospel and law unite in the person of Christ. As Barth explains, "Jesus Christ Himself as the Gospel, revealed, proclaimed, offered to man and affecting him, is always clothed in the Law, hidden in the manger and the swaddling clothes of the commandments, His divine commanding."[90] Jesus Christ is the full revelation of both "the Gospel which reconciles us with God" and the law that "really binds and obligates us."[91] For Barth, it is this law alone to which theological ethics clings.

As both gospel and law, Jesus Christ deposes humanity from being the judge of good and evil. The good is the command issued and obeyed by

---

84. Ibid.
85. Ibid.
86. Ibid., 512.
87. Ibid., 516.
88. Ibid.
89. Ibid., 539.
90. Ibid., 563.
91. Ibid., 539.

Jesus Christ—further discernment of good and evil is neither necessary nor permitted.[92] To the extent that ethics goes beyond this point, it evades the grace of God and thus enacts a sinful derailment from its rightful task. Theological ethics cannot appeal to any sort of human reasoning, for any attempt to discern ethical behavior from a source other than God's command in Christ is anathema to the ethical task.[93] For Barth, "there is no good which is not obedience to God's commands."[94] Accordingly, humans do good insofar as they hear and obey the word of God, as they act as those called to responsibility before God. The necessary starting point of theological ethics is that "all ethical truth is enclosed in the command of the grace of God,"[95] which speaks with universally binding force.

The command of God makes a total and complete claim upon humanity, and "we can know of no human action which does not stand under God's command, of no human existence which does not respond in one way or another to God's command, which has not the character of obedience or disobedience to God's command. We do not know any human action which is free, i.e., exempted from decision in relation to God's command, or neutral in regard to it."[96] Each person is confronted with the command of God and called to accountability before it. Human beings are contingent beings; they do not stand by themselves. For Barth, "the man to whom the Word of God is directed ... is not an independent subject, to be considered independently. In virtue of the death and resurrection of Jesus Christ—whether he knows and believes it or not—it is simply not true that he belongs to himself and is left to himself, that he is thrown back on himself. ... He exists

---

92. "The question of good and evil has been decided and settled once and for all in the decree of God, by the cross and the resurrection of Jesus Christ. Now that this decision has been made, theological ethics cannot go back on it. It can only accept it as a decision that has been made actually and effectively. It can only attest and confirm and copy it" (ibid., 536).

93. Because Barth grounds humanity in the person of Jesus Christ, he disallows for any sort of non-theological ethics. In Barth's words, "In so far as a non-theological ethics has for its content a humanity which is grounded in itself and discovers and proclaims itself, theological ethics will have to deny the character of this humanity as humanity and consequently the character of this ethics as ethics. ... There is no humanity outside the humanity of Jesus Christ or the voluntary or involuntary glorifying of the grace of God which has manifested itself in this humanity" (ibid., 541).

94. Ibid., 541.

95. Ibid., 527.

96. Ibid., 535. See also ibid., 662.

because Jesus Christ exists. He exists as a predicate of this Subject, i.e., that which has been decided and is real for man in this Subject is true for him."[97]

For Barth, the foundational principle of theological ethics is that the command of God is an event.[98] The command of God is not a reality that is, but a reality that occurs. It is "not in any sense static but active, not in any sense general but supremely particular."[99] It is here that Barth's actualistic ontology connects to his conception of human obedience.

In light of God's command, we must release all that we have held onto as static construals of obedience or faithfulness. According to Barth,

> When we honestly ask: What are we to do?, we approach God as those who are ignorant in and with all that they already know, and stand in dire need of divine instruction and conversion. We are then ready, with a view to our next decision, to bracket and hold in reserve all that we think we know considering the rightness and goodness of our past and present decisions, all the rules and axioms, however good, all the inner and outer laws and necessities under which we have hitherto placed ourselves and perhaps do so again. None of these has an unlimited claim to be valid again today as it was valid yesterday. None of them is identical with the divine command.[100]

For Barth, the church must always search the Scriptures anew, not relying upon past readings or conclusions. The church "sickens and dies when it is enslaved by its past instead of being disciplined by the new beginning which it must always make in the Scriptures."[101] The same holds true for the individual, who cannot accept yesterday's instruction and conversion as adequate for obedience today: "The principle of necessary repetition and renewal, and not a law of stability, is the law of the spiritual growth and continuity of our life."[102]

---

97. Ibid., 539.
98. Ibid., 548.
99. Ibid.
100. Ibid., 646.
101. Ibid., 647.
102. Ibid.

While the command of God is dynamic rather than static, it is not without definite content. According to Barth, God's command can be summed up "by saying that what God wants of us and all men is that we should believe in Jesus Christ."[103] The extent to which we are bound to Jesus Christ determines whether or not it is the command of God that binds us. The command of God claims us completely, and in every way it claims us for Christ.

> The command of God requires that I should do this and not do that. But within this limitation it is distinguished from other commands by the fact that in itself it is unlimited, that in and with all its individual demands it demands myself—myself for Jesus, my subordination to this name and its law. ... In its specific requirements and prohibitions, it demands everything, the totality of my life. It demands my active acknowledgment 'that I am not my own, but the property of my faithful Saviour Jesus Christ.' It demands my life as that of a limb of His body, of which He is the Head.[104]

Humanity cannot regard the claim of God with a "reserved and distant attitude," nor can it take a "leisurely interest" as a mere spectator. Rather, "to be in Jesus Christ is to be oneself the new creature fashioned by Him, to belong to Him as a member of His body."[105]

For Barth, the command of God "is not at all an empty form to which we have to give specific content (appropriate to this or that moment of our lives) by our action and the accompanying judgment of our ethical reflection. The command of God is an integral whole. For in it form and content, general prescription and concrete application are not two things, but one."[106] The command of God confronts us concretely, addressing us in the particularity of "each momentary decision and epitomising the totality of each momentary requirement." Furthermore, the command of God "does not need any interpretation, for even to the smallest details it is self-interpreting."[107] To the objection that God has not really given such a clear and definite command, Barth responds by declaring again that in

---

103. Ibid., 583. See also ibid., 609.
104. Ibid., 610.
105. Ibid., 656.
106. Ibid., 663.
107. Ibid., 665

God's self-revelation in Jesus Christ, we have the ethical command in its fullness: "Because God has given us Himself ... He has also given us His command."[108] The God who has revealed himself to humanity "is present to the world and each individual, and confronts him in the smallest of his steps and thoughts as his Commander and Judge."[109] It is not a matter of whether God speaks, but of whether we hear.

As Barth exegetes Scripture, the dominant form of God's command is "purely concrete and related to this or that particular man in this or that particular situation. It consists in what God wills that he should do or not do in a specific situation."[110] We are led astray to the extent that we seek to universalize or generalize these concrete commands; they are to be understood in all their historical particularity and uniqueness. We cannot seek the biblical witness to God's command in "lists of universal religious-moral-juridical rules" and "legal codes that are valid regardless of space and time."[111] Barth is concerned that we not replace the immediate command of God with a set of universal rules, principles, and codes. Rather, we must always affirm that "in the command of God we are face to face with the person of God, with the action and revelation of this person, with God Himself."[112] Thus even the person who lives in complete obedience to the law can be living without regard to God's command.[113] For Barth, "to obey God's command is to accept this invitation to live as those who belong to Him."[114]

Barth believes obedience to the law is dependent on one's disposition before God, not whether or not one carries out the law's specific decrees. For example, with regard to the Ten Commandments (which Barth considers

---

108. Ibid., 669–70.

109. Ibid., 669.

110. Ibid., 672.

111. Ibid. According to Geoffrey Bromiley, "If Barth cannot deny the existence of embracing commands both in the Old Testament and the New, he regards these as cables, so to speak, along which God transmits his specific commands to individuals. God does not speak apart from the cable, which summarizes his commands; but along this cable there is a specific wire through which he issues a specific command" (Bromiley, *Introduction to the Theology of Karl Barth*, 104).

112. Ibid., 676

113. Ibid., 686.

114. Ibid., 738.

to be "only the peak points of a whole series of special decrees and ordinances"[115]), Barth writes the following:

> To keep the Ten Commandments is to take up the position which
> they outline and define, and in this—the only possible—position to
> wait for the specific commands of God for which the proclamation
> of the Law prepares us, to be constantly obedient to His call. The
> man who does this is righteous and will live. The man who does
> not transgresses all the Ten Commandments and the whole Law,
> however precisely his conduct keeps within the limits defined by
> the Ten Commandments. For without living obedience to the living
> God, he does not in fact stand in the place to which he is directed
> by the commandments.[116]

Barth concludes volume II/2 with an exposition of the command of
God as the judgment of God, declaring that God's justification of human
beings is God's strongest protest against and overruling of human sinfulness. Though we are called to live our lives in obedience to God's command
revealed in Jesus Christ, our attempts at self-justification are proven to be
"utterly filthy rags."[117] The command of God reveals our inability to obey it,
for "as God's command is given to us, what we do and do not do is shown
in different ways and to differing degrees, but at bottom in every respect,
to be apostasy, treason and revolt."[118] However, God's grace is supremely
revealed in that he does not leave humanity in its state as "recreant and
rebel," as "enemy and opponent of God."[119] Rather, in Jesus Christ, God "has
openly confessed and avowed our apostasy. He has borne our guilt, the
suffering of the righteous wrath of God on our behalf. This is what God
has done for us by giving us His own Son as our Brother."[120] Justification
thus reveals and chastises our wrongdoing while simultaneously annulling it. The name of Jesus Christ "represents and includes our name, His

---

115. Ibid., 684.
116. Ibid., 686.
117. Ibid., 745.
118. Ibid., 752.
119. Ibid., 749.
120. Ibid.

person our person, both in what He suffers and in what He does, in what He undergoes both as condemnation and as justification."[121]

In volume II/2 of the *Dogmatics*, Barth treats the command of God as part of the doctrine of God. He follows this through by further reflecting on "The Command of God the Creator" in volume III/4 and "The Command of God the Reconciler" in volume IV/4. Had he written volume V, it would have certainly included a section on "The Command of God the Redeemer" as well. In order to further flesh out Barth's doctrine of the command of God and its significance in the overarching structure of his thought, let us move on to review the command of God as Barth presents it in volumes III and IV of the *Church Dogmatics*.

## THE COMMAND OF GOD THE CREATOR

Barth begins volume III/4 by distinguishing between "general ethics" (which, characterized by an "upward look," correspond to God's command as the sanctifying claim made upon humanity), and "special ethics" (which, characterized by a "downward look," refer to humanity's activity, the actual effect and consequences of God's command upon human beings).[122] Barth explains what special ethics is not, and it is worth quoting him at length:

> "Special ethics" is sometimes taken to mean the understanding of the command of God as a prescribed text, which, partly written and partly unwritten, is made up of biblical texts in which there are believed to be seen universally binding divine ordinances and directions, of certain propositions again presumed to be universally valid, of the natural moral law generally perceptible to human reason, and finally of particular norms which have been handed down historically in the tradition of Western Christianity and which lay claim to universal validity. The grouping and blending of the various elements in this text may vary, the Bible, natural law or tradition predominating. The essential point is that God's command is regarded as in some sense a legal text known to the ethical teacher and those whom he has to instruct. On this presupposition the task of special ethics consists (1) in expounding the statements of this

---

121. Ibid., 758.
122. Barth, *Church Dogmatics* III/4, 3–7.

law—on the analogy of a country's law—in relation to the pleni-
tude of conditions and possibilities in which human action takes
place, and then (2) in applying it to the individual cases, which
means either assessing what has been done, or making a regulation
or issuing a prohibition, commandment or permission in respect
of future action.[123]

Barth insists that special ethics not degenerate into casuistry, according
to which "the moralist wishes to set himself on God's throne, to distinguish
good and evil," thereby making himself "lord, king and judge at the place
where only God can be this."[124] For Barth, casuistical ethics allows humanity
to stand at a safe distance from God's claim upon it, thus effectively mas-
tering God's command and God himself. Man does this "by claiming that
in a summa of ethical statements compiled by him and his like from the
Bible, natural law and tradition, he can know the command of God, see
through and past it, and thus master and handle it, i.e., apply it to himself
and others, so that armed with this instrument he may speak as law."[125] In
other words, casuistry deposes God and God's radically event-oriented
command, replacing the concrete and specific command of God with a
fabricated interpretation and application of "universal moral truth fixed
and proclaimed with supreme arbitrariness."[126] Casuistry perpetuates the
illusion that what is required is merely individual right actions rather than
the entirety of one's self. For Barth, "God's demand in relation to man is a
demand of man himself: not merely, then, that he should actually will or
do or not will and do this or that which God proposes; but that he should
voluntarily confess what is proposed, making it a matter of his own choice
and decision."[127] Casuistical reasoning all too easily eclipses and dulls this
radical demand.

Barth identifies this impermissible type of casuistry with rabbinic
Judaism, which, from his perspective, understands the command of God
as a "timeless truth" that "can only be made applicable and usable with the

---

123. Ibid., 6.
124. Ibid., 10.
125. Ibid.
126. Ibid., 13.
127. Ibid.

help of some interpretation which is more or less arbitrary even in relation to the texts, and of all kinds of amplifications and additions drawn from the treasures of natural law and tradition."[128] To the extent that Christianity follows rabbinic Judaism in this regard, it betrays a "lack of confidence in the Spirit (who is the Lord) as the Guide, Lawgiver and Judge in respect of Christian action."[129]

Barth repeatedly distinguishes his own method from what he defines as casuistry, insisting that while human deliberation has no place in ethical reflection, God's will is neither capricious nor inconsistent. For Barth, that the commanding God is Father, Son, and Holy Spirit, as well as creator, reconciler, and redeemer "forms" the ethical event.[130] "The history of God and man is obviously the constant factor and therefore the connexion or context of all ethical events."[131] In other words, the outline of the covenantal history between this God and human beings as his covenant partners sets the parameters of the ethical. The God and man made known in Jesus Christ will always be the referent of the divine command: "Where the divine command and human action meet, there always meet the divine Creator and His creature, the divine Reconciler and the sinner upheld by His faithfulness, the divine Redeemer and Perfecter and the child of God with his eternal expectancy."[132] While Barth endorses "practical casuistry" as humanity's reckoning with God's concrete and specific command with its concrete and specific content, he maintains that "theoretical and systematic casuistry" has no place in theological ethics.[133] The command of God sanctifies humanity and sets it free to be responsive to God and responsible before God, and Barth dedicates the rest of volume III/4 to an investigation of the contours of humanity's derivative freedom.

---

128. Ibid.
129. Ibid., 7.
130. See ibid., 18–19.
131. Ibid., 26.
132. Ibid.
133. Ibid., 10–11.

## THE COMMAND OF GOD THE RECONCILER

In volume IV/4, Barth again revisits the command of God within the doctrine of reconciliation. Here he reiterates the directness of God's command and cautions once more against legalism as an attempt to tame the "incontrollable content" of the encounter between God and man.[134] Barth distinguishes between the free command of God and any sort of "general law" that humanity can control and manipulate. He continues with an explication of "a certain form of human life" that corresponds to humanity's true identity as God's covenant partner in Christ.[135] While Barth never completed volume IV, he got so far as to explicate baptism as the beginning of the Christian life. As "the first step of this life of faithfulness to God," a person is voluntarily baptized with water "as the binding confession of his obedience, conversion and hope."[136] This decision follows the "direct self-attestation and self-impartation of the living Jesus Christ,"[137] which Barth describes as baptism with the Holy Spirit. Barth's exposition of baptism is characteristically Christocentric: "Christmas day is the birthday of every Christian."[138] Baptism represents humanity's participation in Christ's redemptive act, for in baptism one is given an "actual share" in the life, death and resurrection of Christ.[139]

As we stated at the outset, Barth's doctrine of election and the command of God (ethics) significantly undergird his theological program and are particularly relevant for our specific interest in Barth's theology. Having reviewed these basic contours, we are now positioned to turn more directly

---

134. Karl Barth, *The Christian Life: Church Dogmatics vol. IV, part 4 Lecture Fragments*, trans. Geoffrey W. Bromiley (Grand Rapids: Eerdmans, 1981), 5.

135. Ibid., 42–46.

136. Ibid., 2.

137. Ibid., 31.

138. Ibid., 15.

139. Ibid., 14. Barth rehearses the New Testament imagery regarding the newness that one experiences in the Christian life (i.e., donning new robes, becoming a new man, being given a new heart, experiencing new birth) and points out that Christ is the referent of each of these descriptors. In baptism, it is Christ's robes that are put on, it is his birth that becomes one's own, it is his death and resurrection that one participates in (see Barth, *Church Dogmatics* IV/1, 6–10, 14–17). For further exposition and analysis of Barth's doctrine of baptism, see Daniel Migliore, "Reforming the Theology and Practice of Baptism: The Challenge of Karl Barth" in *Toward the Future of Reformed Theology: Tasks, Topics, Traditions*, ed. David Willis and Michael Welker (Grand Rapids: Eerdmans, 1999), 494–511; John Webster, *Barth's Ethics of Reconciliation* (Cambridge: Cambridge University Press, 1995), esp. chs. 4 and 5.

to assessing Barth's theology in light of Marshall's framing question. In the sections that follow, we will further home in on the facets of Barth's theology that aid us in upholding both the universal, ecclesially mediated saving mission of Christ and the permanent election of Israel, which includes the permanent practice of Judaism.

## THE MISSION OF CHRIST
## IN BARTH'S THEOLOGY

Because Barth's theology is thoroughly Christocentric, and because Marshall's framing question requires us to reflect specifically on Christ's mission (and its ecclesial mediation), we will now turn to a more explicit treatment of Barth's Christology, specifically with regard to the connection between Christ, Israel, and the church. In what follows, we will focus on three primary areas: Christology and Christian witness, the Jewishness of Jesus, and Christ as the fullness of the law.

### CHRISTOLOGY AND CHRISTIAN WITNESS

In volume IV of the *Church Dogmatics*, Barth expounds the full implications of Christology for Christian life and vocation. It is here that Barth's most comprehensive treatment of ecclesiology is found, characteristically taking shape within the sphere of Christology. With regard to the universality of Christ's reconciling work, Barth writes the following:

> [Christ] is simply the Son of God and Man in whose life and death the whole world is reconciled with God, in whose person and work every man is justified before God and sanctified for Him. Since He is the man in whom this has taken place for all men, there is none who exists wholly without Him, who does not belong to Him, to whom—whether he realizes it or not and whatever his attitude to it—He is not present as his Lord and Head in whom decision has already been made concerning him prior to all his own decisions, who is more present indeed than he can ever be to himself.[140]

God's gracious election in Christ claims every human being without exception, and this universal election informs the elect community's task.

---

140. Barth, *Church Dogmatics* IV/3, 604.

The election of Jesus Christ is "the eternal election of the one community of God by the existence of which Jesus Christ is to be attested to the whole world and the whole world summoned to faith in Jesus Christ."[141] While Barth distinguishes between de jure and de facto participation, he includes every human being in the order of reconciliation and maintains that this distinction will be overcome eschatologically.[142]

While the scope of Christ's work is all of humanity, the Christian community is comprised of those who have been awakened to the objective reality of Christ's redemption. "It is therefore the provisional representation of the whole world of humanity justified in Him."[143] God has chosen the church to be the herald of God's self-revelation in Christ and commissioned it to bring the outside world into knowledge of its election. While Christ alone effects reconciliation, "He cannot and will not remain alone, nor can He be solitary in the reconciled world on His way to His future, conclusive and universal revelation. He cannot and will not be the Master without disciples, the Leader without followers, the Head without members, the King without fellows in His people, Himself without His own, Christ without Christians."[144]

The primary concept that characterizes Barth's ecclesiology is witness: "The called man in the biblical sense is in fact a witness in the twofold sense that he has seen and heard the acts of God ... and that he is called to the work of declaration, faithfully, if without any claim, addressing, imparting and proclaiming to others that which he has seen as God's act and heard as His Word."[145] As Barth wrote the *Church Dogmatics*, Matthias Grünewald's

---

141. Barth, *Church Dogmatics* II/2, 195.

142. Barth, *Church Dogmatics* IV/1, 92–93. According to Barth, "When the lordship of Jesus Christ over all creation is manifested, and with it the reconciliation of the world to God that has taken place in him," those who have not yet cried "Our Father" "will not finally fail to do it" (Barth, *The Christian Life*, 101).

143. Barth, *Church Dogmatics* IV/1, 643.

144. Barth, *Church Dogmatics* IV/3, 541.

145. Ibid., 592–93. Barth's ecclesiology of witness has contributed to increased missiological emphasis on the *missio Dei*, a concept that provides a theological anchor for both ecclesiology and missiology. For more on this connection, see John G. Flett, *The Witness of God: The Trinity, Missio Dei, Karl Barth, and the Nature of Christian Community* (Grand Rapids: Eerdmans, 2010). For more on *missio Dei* theology, see David J. Bosch, *Transforming Mission: Paradigm Shifts in Theology Mission* (Maryknoll, NY: Orbis Books, 1991); Darrell L. Guder, *Missional Church: A Vision for the Sending of the Church in North America* (Grand Rapids: Eerdmans, 1998); Lesslie Newbigin, *The Open Secret: An Introduction to the Theology of Mission* (Grand Rapids:

Isenheim Altarpiece hung above his desk, and this painting is paradigmatic of Barth's understanding of ecclesiological witness.[146] In the painting, John the Baptist points to Jesus on the cross and reads the words of John 3:30: "He must become greater; I must become less." It is this figure that the church is to emulate; Christian proclamation is the activity by which the church points beyond itself and declares Christ as the full self-revelation of God.

Thus, for Barth, Christian mission is intimately bound to the work of Christ. The church exists to proclaim the saving work of Christ to which it has been awakened. Ecclesiology is bounded by and circumscribed within Christology. In Barth's words, "All ecclesiology is grounded, critically limited, but also positively determined by Christology."[147] Again, the actualistic nature of Barth's theology is clearly visible here. Just as Christology is event-oriented for Barth ("At the heart of the Christian message is the description of an act of God, or better, of God Himself in this act of His"[148]), so too is ecclesiology ("The Church is a work which takes place among men in the form of a human activity"[149]). Barth once more deconstructs any traces of a gospel/law dichotomy. Without the church actualizing its commission, it is not truly the church. Christ continually poses a question to the church:

> What we are really asked by Him is whether we are men in whose lives He has expressed and shown Himself as Revealer, Prophet and Mediator. And this means concretely whether we act accordingly; whether our being, thinking, willing and speaking derive their bias and orientation from the fact that He has done and still does this, that He is for us light, rule, canon and standard, not just theoretically by way of presupposition or assertion, but in practice; whether we do not merely make ourselves out to be those who know, or more or less seriously believe that we are such, but really exist as such.[150]

---

Eerdmans, 1995); Christopher J. H. Wright, *The Mission of God: Unlocking the Bible's Grand Narrative* (Downers Grove, IL: IVP Academic, 2006).

146. Busch, *Karl Barth: His Life from Letters and Autobiographical Texts*, 116, 408.

147. Barth, *Church Dogmatics* IV/3, 786.

148. Barth, *Church Dogmatics* IV/1, 6. Italics added.

149. Ibid., 650.

150. Barth, *Church Dogmatics* IV/3, 77. Italics added.

Again, the act to which the church is held accountable is the universal proclamation of humanity's standing before God in Christ. The elect community exists as the "subsequent and provisional representation of the calling of all humanity and all creatures to the service of God as it has gone forth in Jesus Christ. The origin and goal of the ways of God ... is the calling of every man and indeed of all creation to the service of God. The function of the community is to follow and yet at the same time precede His universal call."[151]

Marshall's question requires that both the universality and the ecclesial mediation of Christ's saving work be affirmed. The solid connection Barth draws between Christology and ecclesiology links and upholds these twin doctrinal principles. As the above explication makes clear, Barth's theology strongly affirms the christological and ecclesiological dimensions of Marshall's question. Barth's robust Christology safeguards the universality of Christ's saving mission, and the elect community serves as the medium by which all of humanity is awakened to its election in Christ. Thus, not only is the scope of Christ's election universal, but it is necessarily ecclesially mediated.

As we will see, Barth's contribution to answering Marshall's question with regard to Israel and Torah ends up being more equivocal. This facet of Barth's theology is not, however, unrelated to his Christology. In fact, Barth's most significant weaknesses with regard to the second part of Marshall's question arguably stem directly from Barth's christological lens. It is this topic that we will address in the pages that follow.

### THE JEWISHNESS OF JESUS IN BARTH'S CHRISTOLOGY

While maintaining a universal scope and an imbedded ecclesiology, the contours of Barth's robust Christology end up causing the most trouble for his theological understanding of Israel. Though Barth strongly upholds the necessity of Jesus' Jewishness, the manner in which Barth construes this connection ultimately handicaps its effect and implications. In a section of *Church Dogmatics* IV/1 entitled "The Way of the Son of God into the Far Country" (§59), Barth writes the following: "There is one thing which we must emphasize especially. ... From this one thing everything else ...

---

151. Ibid., 793.

acquires its contour and colour, its definiteness and necessity. The Word did not simply become any 'flesh,' any man humbled and suffering. It became Jewish flesh. The Church's whole doctrine of the incarnation and the atonement becomes abstract and valueless and meaningless to the extent that this comes to be regarded as something accidental and incidental."[152] A very strong affirmation indeed. But what theological yield does this doctrine produce in Barth's theology?

Barth reflects on what "flesh" connotes throughout the Bible, ultimately declaring that Israel is the representative of all humanity in its fleshliness.

> "Flesh" in the language of the New (and earlier the Old) Testament means man standing under the divine verdict and judgment, man who is a sinner and whose existence therefore must perish before God, whose existence has already become nothing, and hastens to nothingness and is a victim to death. "Flesh" is the concrete form of human nature and the being of man in his world under the sign of the fall of Adam—the being of man as corrupted and therefore destroyed, as unreconciled with God and therefore lost.[153]

For Barth, flesh is shorthand for humanity in its unrepentant and unredeemed state. Having offered this vivid definition, Barth explains that "we now have a complete outline of what it means that according to the New Testament the Word, or Son of God, was made flesh. To be flesh means to exist with the 'children' of Israel under the wrath and judgment of the electing and loving God. To be flesh is to be in a state of perishing before this God."[154] Israel embodies fallen fleshly existence par excellence.

That Christ took on flesh—Jewish flesh—reveals the depth of God's love for and mercy upon sinful humanity, whose plight is summed up in the history of Israel. "The Son of God in His unity with the Israelite Jesus exists in direct and unlimited solidarity with the representatively and manifestly sinful humanity of Israel. ... He accepts personal responsibility for all the unfaithfulness and deceit, the rebellion of this people and its priests and kings."[155] That Jesus is Jewish guarantees that the grasp of God's electing

---

152. Barth, *Church Dogmatics* IV/1, 166–67
153. Ibid., 165
154. Ibid., 174–75.
155. Ibid., 172.

love is universal, reaching out even to the most resistant and obstinate—i.e., Israel. Barth's consistently negative portrayal of Israel thus informs his understanding of Jesus' Jewishness as God's thoroughgoing rejection of human waywardness. After graphically describing Israel's perversity, resistance, and wretchedness, Barth makes explicit that "this was and is the flesh that God accepted and took upon Him."[156] In other words, just as Israel's witness is construed in negative terms, so Jesus' Jewishness is construed in negative terms, thus magnifying the boundlessness of God's grace.

Barth includes in this discussion an explanation of the role of suffering, both in the life of Israel and in the life of Jesus. As "the obedient Son and servant of God," Jesus is the one "who essentially and necessarily suffers."[157] In his suffering, Jesus takes upon himself the suffering of Israel that inevitably results from its status as God's chosen people. According to Barth, Israel's history "had to be a history of suffering … not in spite of the fact but because of the fact that it was the history of the chosen people of God, because it was inevitable that there should be revealed in the people chosen and loved and blessed by God not only the fall and disobedience of man, but the scorching fire of the love of God, and the breaking and destruction of man on God."[158]

Elsewhere in the *Dogmatics*, Barth uses the image of the burning bush to describe Israel's suffering: "The burning bush of Exod. 3:2 cannot be consumed. But the unconsumed bush must burn. This bush is Israel. And the flame which burns it but does not consume it is the God of Israel, the Holy God."[159] Israel's suffering is the result of God's commitment to refine Israel and set it apart from the other nations. This is the necessary suffering that Jesus assumes by virtue of his incarnation in Jewish flesh. As Barth explains,

> If the Old Testament history was the type, this history has been
> an additional attestation of its fulfilment in the one Israelite Jesus.
> The Son of God in His unity with this man exists in solidarity with
> the humanity of Israel suffering under the mighty hand of God. …
> He does not suffer any suffering, but their suffering; the suffering

---

156. Barth, *Church Dogmatics* II/2, 263.

157. Barth, *Church Dogmatics* IV/1, 166.

158. Ibid., 174.

159. Barth, *Church Dogmatics* II/1, 366.

of the children chastised by their Father. ... He stands under the wrath and judgment of God, He is broken and destroyed on God. It cannot be otherwise. It has to be like this. His history must be a history of suffering.[160]

Barth thus links the suffering of Jesus with the suffering of Israel, using it to highlight the Jewish Jesus' solidarity with his people Israel. Nor does Barth limit this assessment of Israel's suffering to the history of Old Testament Israel; rather, according to Barth, "we can and must think of the history of the Jews right up to our own day."[161] Because Jesus has taken upon himself the suffering of the Jewish people, anti-Semitism is tantamount to blaspheming the gracious and efficacious work of God. In *The Church and the Political Problem of Our Day* (1939), Barth writes, "He who rejects and persecutes the Jews rejects and persecutes Him who died for the sins of the Jews—and then, and only thereby for our sins as well. He who is a radical enemy of the Jews, were he in every other regard an angel of light, shows himself, as such, to be a radical enemy of Jesus Christ. Anti-Semitism is sin against the Holy Ghost. For anti-Semitism means rejection of the grace of God."[162]

Because Barth grounds the election of Israel within the election of Christ, Israel is not ultimately at liberty to determine its own destiny. Israel's unfaithfulness has been definitively overruled by God in Christ, and any attempt to hold Israel liable for its obduracy effectively denies the power of God. In this way, Israel's rejection confirms and magnifies its election. What Barth says of the condemned man in volume IV/3 equally applies to the rejected Israel:

Thou art no longer the man of sin whose figure and role thou dost still assume. That man is set aside and overcome. He is dead. Thou canst be that man no longer, not just because thou has put him to death, but because thou hast done so in My death and passion. I have lived and died for thee. In Me thou becomest and art another

---

160. Barth, *Church Dogmatics* IV/1, 175.

161. Ibid., 175.

162. Karl Barth, *The Church and the Political Problem of Our Day* (New York: Charles Scribner's Sons, 1939), 51.

man justified before God and sanctified for Him: thou in Me as the
Son of God and Man who exists in thy place as thy Saviour, Head
and Lord; thou as My brother and therefore a child of God, who has
acted and decided and spoken through Me, as thine.[163]

This account of Jesus' Jewishness and Jesus' suffering on Israel's behalf
safeguards against any justification for anti-Semitism, and Barth's biblical exposition of these profound theological concepts carried a powerful
message into the concrete context in which he wrote. Barth's unyielding
declaration of Jesus' solidarity with Israel was spoken in the midst of Nazi
Germany during one of history's most violent and virulent chapters of
Jewish persecution. In fact, Barth delivered *The Church and the Political
Problem of Our Day* as a lecture in Switzerland a few short weeks after
*Kristallnacht*, the infamous night of Nazi destruction of Jewish homes and
synagogues. Barth was one of the leading voices of Christian opposition to
Hitler's regime, and his uncompromising critique came at a remarkably
high personal and professional cost.

While we cannot overlook these positive aspects of Barth's Christology
in solidarity with Israel, Barth's overwhelmingly negative construal of Jesus'
Jewishness eclipses an entire array of implications with regard to Jesus'
own identity. Unfortunately, what Barth gains in one hand, he loses from
the other. The manner in which Barth grounds the election of the community in the election of Christ disallows for the election of Israel—which
historically precedes the incarnation—to adequately inform Christology.
On account of Christ's overarching and all-encompassing election, the
actual historical narrative of God's covenanting with humanity—beginning with Israel—is not given full expression.[164] In the words of Kendall
Soulen, "Covenant history becomes a reality that exists extrinsically to
human history in Jesus Christ alone. In the end, covenant history seems

---

163. Barth, *Church Dogmatics* IV/3, 463.

164. Interestingly, Mark Kinzer's theology (which we will evaluate in chapter 4) has
been accused of the exact opposite error. In the words of David Guretzki, "Kinzer favours the
chronological priority of God's election of Israel in the history of salvation over [the] theological priority of God's election of Jesus Christ as the ground and culmination of the covenant"
(David Guretzki, "Karl Barth on Mark Kinzer's 'Non-Supersessionist and Post-Missionary
Ecclesiology': Yes! and No!" [paper presented at the Canadian Evangelical Theological
Association, Carleton University, Ottawa, May 23, 2009, 6]).

to collapse and disappear into the figure of Jesus Christ."[165] Barth offers a theologically powerful understanding of Israel's existence in Christ, but he lacks an adequate conception of Christ's existence in Israel. Here Barth's dehistoricized Christology yields an anemic portrayal of Jesus' Jewishness. Barth's configuration of Jesus vis-à-vis Israel is bound together with Barth's understanding of the law, and it is to Barth's christological account of the law that we now turn.

## CHRIST AS THE FULLNESS OF THE LAW

As Marshall maintains, to talk about Israel requires talking about Torah as Israel's covenantally circumscribed prescription for faithfulness. Barth's contention that the law is the form of the gospel leads him to strongly affirm the law and its teleological function. For example, in volume II/1 Barth offers a lengthy exposition of the Levitical Holiness Code. Because God chooses Israel to be his holy people, God's command that Israel be holy is "simply the command of self-preservation."[166] In other words, Israel persists as the people of God by mirroring God's holiness in its collective life. Through obedience to the commandments, Israel does not achieve any sort of freestanding holiness; in Barth's words, "The keeping of the Holiness Code cannot even remotely signify anything which might be construed as a meritorious righteousness of works."[167] Rather, the commandments are the means by which Israel cleaves to God, the one and only source of holiness.

The Holiness Code reminds man that "all along the line God's own holy will is dealing with him, and that he, intrinsically unholy man, is saved by it, not because he sanctifies himself, but because in obedience to these commands he submits himself to the holiness of God."[168] God inscribes his

---

165. R. Kendall Soulen, *The God of Israel and Christian Theology* (Minneapolis: Fortress, 1996), 94. According to Soulen, Barth is to be lauded for fundamentally recasting the canonical narrative so as to "expose and correct aspects of the semi-gnosticism latent in the deep structure of the church's standard canonical narrative." However, Barth ultimately "subordinates his unprecedented vision of covenant history to a christocentric account of Christian doctrine that stands in direct continuity with … the standard canonical narrative in its classical form" (Soulen, *The God of Israel*, 81, 93). For a deeper engagement with Soulen's thought, see ch. 3, Renouncing Supersessionism, below.

166. Barth, *Church Dogmatics* II/1, 364.

167. Ibid., 365.

168. Ibid.

name on Israel "with His own independent curves and lines in personal, everyday, popular life," such that "the divinity of the love of God is in few other passages of the Bible so distinctly manifest as in that Book which is so often misunderstood and regarded as obscure, useless and imprisoned within the limitations of its period, the Book of Leviticus."[169] God's electing and sanctifying love for Israel is reflected in Israel's obedience to the commandments. In God's commitment to molding Israel, God delimits that which accords with Israel's service to God and that which is contrary to Israel's destined holiness. As the commandments explicitly chart out the path to abiding in God's holiness, "there is sin only where man transgresses the commandments of God."[170]

It is this image of the law that informs Barth's understanding of Christ as the fullness of the law. Christ is "the meaning, the authority, the fulfiller and the way to fulfilment of the Law, He is Himself the righteousness before God."[171] Thus, to live in obedience means to believe in Christ, the "necessary expression" of which involves "outward obligations and commitments."[172] As Barth reads Romans 10:5–10, the one who fulfills the law is the one who confesses with his mouth that "Jesus is the Lord, i.e., that this very man whom the Law intends and proclaims, who is set before the chosen people by its Law as the aim and essence of all that God wills from it and with it, has all the attributes of true Godhead, and therefore, since these attributes can belong to no other beside God, is the true God Himself."[173] Expounding Romans 10:10, Barth notes both the inward and the outward dimensions of obedience to the law: "Let elected man make his election sure in this twofold performance—by the faith of his heart his dignity as elected man, by the confession of his mouth the salvation that falls to him on the ground of this dignity."[174]

The one who believes in and confesses Christ "will satisfy the righteousness required in the Law. He is a true Israelite."[175] Thus, to the extent that

169. Ibid.

170. Ibid.

171. Barth, *Church Dogmatics* II/2, 245.

172. Ibid., 248.

173. Ibid., 247.

174. Ibid., 248.

175. Ibid.

it rejects Christ, "Israel transgresses and breaks its own Law. ... It fails, not with regard to a new revelation, but with regard to the one Word of its God spoken to it and heard by it from the first."[176] In this way, Christ is the one "who from the first has secretly been the meaning, fulfilment and authority of the Law, and who has now been revealed as all this."[177] Along these lines, Barth eschews any assertion that "in and with Christ the Law given to the people of Israel by its God was antiquated, superseded, set aside and abrogated."[178] As he exegetes Romans 9–11, Barth wonders, "where in all these chapters (but also in all the rest of the Pauline theology) do we find the slightest indication that the apostle of the Church regarded the Law of Israel as a gift of God cancelled and invalidated by Christ?"[179] Christ does not supersede the law; rather, he is the fullness of the law.

The manner in which Barth reorients the law around Christ radically redefines what obedience to the commandments looks like. Because Christ is the true fabric and substance of the law, the Torah observance of the Jewish people (i.e., the synagogue) is categorically disallowed to actually count as obedience. In fact, it becomes the opposite. According to Barth,

> In all its works Israel omits this one work which in the last resort is the only counterpart of its mission and endowment. All its works, therefore, the temple cultus and service of the Law, become sin and guilt. ... With all its zeal to be Israel, to become worthy of and to participate in its promise, by failing to believe it has failed to do the one thing in which it could be active and attest itself as Israel. ... By its attitude to Jesus Christ, it has proved that it wished to rely on itself, to push on to the fulfilment of the promise by its own willing and running.[180]

The eloquent explanation of the Holiness Code and its specific commandments melts away into confession of Christ, which has become tantamount to fulfillment of the law. Now that Christ has been revealed, believing in and witnessing to him constitutes the content of the law. The

---

176. Ibid., 245.
177. Ibid.
178. Ibid., 244.
179. Ibid.
180. Ibid., 242.

specific stipulations of Israel's covenantal life with God are subsumed into this one overarching act—knowing Christ and making him known.

If we return to Marshall's central question, we begin to clearly see the disconnect in Barth's theology. To put it succinctly, Barth essentially severs Jewishness from Judaism, both with regard to Christ and true obedience to the law. That Christ is the fullness of the law apparently leaves no room for the ongoing practice of the Holiness Code in all of its sanctifying detail. Confession of Christ replaces obedience to Levitical law, and failure to acknowledge Christ comprises disobedience to the Torah. As far as we can discern from Barth's theology, there is no sense in which Jesus himself conformed to Jewish practice, nor any indication that he taught his Jewish followers to do likewise.

As Katherine Sonderegger explains,

> In Barth's account of the earthly Jesus, the Royal Man, there is little about Christ's teaching and observing and ratifying of Israel's Law. ... There is much about 'Divine command,' much about Divine instruction and direction, much about Jesus' obedience to God's will and much about the famous, living voice of God, the *Deus dixit*. And all these of course are in the neighborhood of Israel's Torah; but they are self-consciously event-oriented, dynamic versions of what Israel and Jews of all ages call the ordinances, statutes and precepts of the Divine covenant with his people.[181]

While Barth safeguards the Jewishness of Jesus as an essential feature of his Christology, he fails to reckon with the practical implications of this claim.

While there is much debate about what constituted Judaism (or, more properly, Judaisms) in the first century, this question cannot be answered without recourse to Jewish practice. In his description of Judaism during the period of 63 BCE–66 CE, E. P. Sanders explains,

> Judaism's most distinctive point ... was the extension of divine law to all the areas of life. ... As such it embraced what people did more than what they thought. ... There were theological convictions that were common, but agreement about speculative theology

---

181. Katherine Sonderegger, "Barth's Christology and the Law of Israel" (paper presented at The Center for Barth Studies Conference, Princeton, NJ, June 21–24, 2009), 13.

was not a requirement that was imposed on Jews. Though Judaism went beyond the general ancient concentration on cultic activity, it did not break with the ancient view that religion requires certain behaviour. ... This emphasis on correct action in every sphere of life, technically called "orthopraxy," is a hallmark of Judaism. Judaism, that is, required obedience to the law.[182]

Sanders uses the term "common Judaism" to describe the Jewish beliefs and practices that he claims were normative across the spectrum of first-century Judaism. Along with Jewish practices associated with the temple, Sanders offers a list of daily and weekly obligations that played a very important role in communal and private Jewish life, both in Palestine and in the diaspora. This list includes worship of the one God in synagogue and home, Sabbath observance, circumcision, and dietary laws.[183] It is within the context of these overarching commonalities that Sanders treats the various groups and parties that existed in first-century Judaism. Since the publication of Sanders' book, *Judaism: Practice and Belief, 63 BCE–66 CE*, "the idea that there existed a common Judaism that transcended the well-known parties and sects has become widely accepted."[184]

While we cannot wade into the complexities of what Sanders' perspective means for Jesus' Jewishness, his work makes clear that Jewish identity in the first century cannot be separated from Jewish practice. While Jesus clearly challenged the approach to Torah observance of his contemporaries, he undoubtedly did so out of reverence for the Torah, not disregard of it. In the words of Katherine Sonderegger, "Israel without the Law is not the Israel honored, remembered and sustained by Jews and Judaism to this day, nor ... the Israel Jesus Christ himself came to shepherd, obey, and fulfill in his own covenant righteousness. ... For Christ was and is a bar mitzvah,

---

182. E. P. Sanders, *Judaism: Practice and Belief, 63 BCE–66 CE* (London: SCM Press, 1992), 191.

183. Sanders, *Judaism*, 195–200.

184. Wayne O. McCready and Adele Reinhartz, eds., *Common Judaism: Explorations in Second-Temple Judaism* (Minneapolis: Fortress, 2008), 1. Certainly there are those who reject Sanders' paradigm. See, for example, Jacob Neusner and Bruce Chilton, *Judaism in the New Testament: Practices and Beliefs* (London: Routledge, 1995); Philip S. Alexander, " 'The Parting of the Ways' from the Perspective of Rabbinic Judaism," in *Jews and Christians: The Parting of the Ways, A.D. 70 to 135*, ed. James D. G. Dunn (Grand Rapids: Eerdmans, 1999), 1–25.

a Son of the Commandment, or in the Apostle Paul's words, Christ is the *telos nomou*, the goal and perfection of the Law."[185]

Undeniably, it is only in retrospect that Barth's theology can be faulted along these lines. Though Barth's theology arguably contributed to the renaissance in New Testament studies within which Sanders stands, Barth himself could not possibly have read the New Testament through the lens afforded to us today. While this critique of Barth's thought is only possible in light of the scholarship that has emerged over the past half century, it is precisely this interval that allows us to identify these problematic tenets of Barth's theological framework. Bearing in mind the historical gap between Barth's time and our own, with regard to Marshall's criteria, Barth's Christology does not address the important set of orthopractic particulars embedded within first-century Judaism. According to Sonderegger, a "Torah observant Christology" would serve to advance, deepen, and secure the contribution Barth makes to overcoming supersessionist Christian theology.[186]

As we have seen, the universality and ecclesial mediation of Christ's saving mission is well established in Barth's theology. However, his particular construal of Christ's relationship to Israel and Torah (and Jesus' own Jewish identity) casts its shadow over his perspective on the permanent election of Israel, and perhaps more especially on his view of Jewish practice (i.e., Torah). It is to Barth's treatment of these latter concepts that we now turn.

## THE ELECTION OF ISRAEL IN BARTH'S THEOLOGY

### BARTH'S DOCTRINE OF THE JEWISH PEOPLE (ISRAEL)

With regard to Barth's contribution to an affirmation of the permanent election of the Jewish people and the practice of Judaism, our assessment is characterized by a certain ambivalence. Formally, Israel's election is secure and irrevocable by virtue of Christ's election. Barth goes to great lengths to demonstrate that regardless of Israel's faithlessness toward God, God's

---

185. Sonderegger, "Barth's Christology and the Law of Israel," 14.
186. Ibid., 20.

faithfulness toward Israel does not waver. Israel's obstinacy only serves to magnify God's grace and steadfast love. While this aspect of Barth's theology cannot be disregarded, it is not the whole story of Barth's position.

Marshall's framework implies that the ongoing election of Israel plays a positive role in the plan of God. Hence, for Marshall, "the existence of faithful Jews is not simply an empirical likelihood or a devout hope, let alone an evil God puts up with, but belongs to God's own good and unalterable purposes."[187] While, according to Barth, Israel's election is upheld, Israel's witness is purely negative. In fact, for Barth, this negative witness is the very tenet that secures Israel's election, for it magnifies the free grace of God and the power of God to execute his sovereign will. As we saw above, Israel (as "the people of the Jews") witnesses to the "unwillingness, incapacity and unworthiness of man with respect to the love of God directed to him."[188] In the words of Scott Bader-Saye, "Barth saw in Israel only an example of what not to be as God's people, and therefore, his ear was deaf to the ongoing constructive and faithful witness of the Jewish people."[189] Until Israel enters into the church, its role cannot be other than this negative witness. Here Barth's theology suffers from an overly strict formalism, whereby Israel and the church are assigned unequivocal roles in Barth's theological system. In Geoffrey Bromiley's assessment, "the interrelating of Israel and the church, though thought-provoking, smacks of simplified systematization."[190]

In an essay entitled "Why Was and Is the Theology of Karl Barth of Interest to a Jewish Theologian?," Orthodox Jewish theologian Michael Wyschogrod critiques Barth on precisely this point. After praising Barth for being "perfectly clear about the election of the Jewish people, especially their continuing election after the crucifixion,"[191] Wyschogrod indicts Barth with the claim that

---

187. Bruce D. Marshall, "Elder Brothers: John Paul II's Teaching on the Jewish People as a Question to the Church," in *John Paul II and the Jewish People: A Jewish-Christian Dialogue*, ed. David G. Dalin and Matthew Levering (Lanham, MD: Rowman & Littlefield, 2008), 122.

188. Barth, *Church Dogmatics* II/2, 198.

189. Scott Bader-Saye, *Church and Israel after Christendom: The Politics of Election* (Eugene, OR: Wipf & Stock, 2005), 76.

190. Bromiley, *Introduction to the Theology of Karl Barth*, 97.

191. Michael Wyschogrod, "Why Was and Is the Theology of Karl Barth of Interest to a Jewish Theologian?" in *Abraham's Promise: Judaism and Jewish-Christian Relations*, ed. R. Kendall

reading Barth one would gain the impression that there is nothing but faithfulness on God's part and unfaithfulness on Israel's. This is not so. ... Along with the unfaithfulness, there is also Israel's faithfulness, its obedience and trust in God, its clinging to its election, identity and mission against all the odds. True, all of Israel's obedience is tinged with its disobedience but all of its disobedience is also tinged with its obedience. It is true that Israel does not deserve its election but it is also true that its election is not in vain, that this people, with its sin, has never ceased to love its God and that it has responded to God's wrath ... by shouldering its mission again, again searing circumcision into its flesh and, while hoping for the best, prepared for what it knows can happen again.[192]

Katherine Sonderegger echoes this critique. She too does not recognize the historical character and journey of the Jewish people in Barth's formalized description of Israel. In her words, "Barth shows little conceptual room for an Israel that 'rejoices in the Law,' and little place in his historical work for a covenant people that also obeyed the precepts and statutes Moses gave, followed in the traditions of the ancestors, kept holy the Divine Name, and taught their children by the way, at their down-sitting and up-rising to call upon the Name of the Lord, and praise his mighty deeds toward his people Israel."[193]

As these critiques make clear, Barth's account of Israel does not correspond to the reality of Jewish existence, either in biblical or post-biblical times. Likewise, to the extent that the synagogue does uphold covenantal practices, its blindness toward Christ undermines any potential faithfulness. The symmetrical nature of Barth's theology requires him to paint both Israel and the church in idealized terms that do not account for the much more nuanced and complex reality of history. As Stephen Haynes explains,

Just as Barth's attempt to bring "Israel" into the system of his doctrine of election ... is abstract and formal, Barth's attempt ... to explain the history of the Jews and the persistence of anti-Semitism

---

Soulen (Grand Rapids: Eerdmans, 2004), 221.

192. Wyschogrod, "The Theology of Karl Barth," 223-24; see also ibid., 181-82.

193. Sonderegger, "Barth's Christology and the Law of Israel," 18-19.

is dependent on a fictionalized "Jewish history" and a mythicized "Jew." Barth's "Jewish history" is the fate of the Jewish people seen from the perspective of their supposed function in salvation history followed by the rejection of Jesus. Barth's "Jew" is a model of human depravity, of the person who is chosen and called by God, but refuses to respond. Barth's myths of "Jews" and "Jewish history" have little connection with any actual Jewish persons, except that where they are embraced, the myths Barth helps perpetuate can have murderous consequences for Jewish life.[194]

In his book, *Living Letters of the Law: Ideas of the Jew in Medieval Christianity*, Jeremy Cohen coins the term "hermeneutical Jew" to characterize the way in which medieval Christian theologians conceptualized the Jewish people. As Cohen observes, Christian ideas of Jewish existence are derivative of the functions the Jewish people play in Christian theology. Historically, Christians have thus "perceived the Jews to be who they were supposed to be, not who they actually were, and related to them accordingly."[195] The Christian concept of the Jew arose from a particular Christian reading of Scripture that approaches the Jewish people as a foil to Christian exegesis and ecclesial self-understanding. Hence, the creation of the " 'hermeneutical Jew'—that is, the Jew as constructed in the discourse of Christian theology, and above all in Christian theologians' interpretation of Scripture."[196]

That Wyschogrod, Sonderegger, and Haynes do not recognize Barth's description of the Jews in history is evidence that Barth consistently employs the "hermeneutical Jew" in his theological work. In fact, Barth so much as admits that he was not dealing with actual Jews but with a biblically abstracted notion of Israel. In a letter written to Friedrich-Wilhelm Marquardt in 1967, Barth admits to a "gap" in his work, explaining that "biblical Israel as such gave me so much to think about and to cope with that I simply did not have the time or intellectual strength to look more closely at Baeck, Buber, Rosenzweig, etc. as you have now done in such a

---

194. Stephen Haynes, *Prospects for Post-Holocaust Theology*, 71.

195. Jeremy Cohen, *Living Letters of the Law: Ideas of the Jew in Medieval Christianity* (Berkeley: University of California Press, 1999), 2.

196. Cohen, *Living Letters of the Law*, 2–3.

worthy fashion."[197] In the letter, Barth goes on to describe his "totally irra-
tional aversion" to "living Jews (even Jewish Christians)," and to praise
Marquardt for his work in improving upon Barth's attempts. This biblically
dictated worldview, a touchstone of Barth's theology throughout, consistently renders Barth's understanding of Judaism and the Jewish people
problematic. That Barth's exegesis of Romans 9–11 comprises well over
half of his treatment of "Israel and the Church" in *Church Dogmatics* II/2
demonstrates Barth's unwavering commitment to a biblical understanding
of the world outside the Bible, not least the Jewish people throughout the
ages. As Sonderegger explains, "Far from withdrawing Christian confession into a private realm of faith and insider narrative, Barth claimed the
whole world for biblical authority; there is no world occurrence outside
the governance, ruling, and command of God."[198] However, Paul's description of Israel in Romans 9–11 does not describe present-day Jews or Judaism.
Rabbinic Judaism (Barth's "Synagogue") is fundamentally a different religious system than Second Temple Judaism, though Jewish adherents will
no doubt recognize its development out of and derivation from biblical
Judaism. Barth reserved his harshest words of criticism and rebuke for
"the lifeless and joyless synagogue, with no future but destruction, the witness of a people disobedient to their election, stubbornly clinging to their
own religion of achievement."[199] It was precisely the "thought, practice,
and talmudic argument of this system that Barth found so little time for."[200]

As Sonderegger argues, it is Barth's biblical worldview that led him
to unwaveringly condemn rabbinic Judaism. As she explains, according
to Barth, "the self-definition of rabbinic Judaism, the Judaism without
temple worship and priest, cannot be given a full hearing by the Christian
church because that Judaism is unknown to the Bible."[201] Barth did not

---

197. Geoffrey W. Bromiley, ed. and trans., *Karl Barth Letters, 1961–1968* (Grand Rapids:
Eerdmans, 1981), 262. The occasion for the letter is Barth's reading of Marquardt's book, *Die
Entdeckung des Judentums für die christliche Theologie: Israel im Denken Karl Barths* (Munich:
Kaiser, 1967).

198. Katherine Sonderegger, "Response to Indissoluble Unity," in *For the Sake of the World:
Karl Barth and the Future of Ecclesial Theology*, ed. George Hunsinger (Grand Rapids: Eerdmans,
2004), 85.

199. Sonderegger, "Response," 84.

200. Ibid.

201. Ibid., 86.

consider rabbinic Judaism on its own terms, nor allow room for its own self-definition. Rather, "Barth's interpretation of Judaism was constructed from sources within Christianity's resources and received opinions, well outside Jewish self-understanding and analysis."[202] Barth's commitment to viewing history through the lens of Scripture eclipses the complexities of history and disallows any degree of theological ambiguity. His imposition of categories—biblical categories—upon the sweep of history distorts the actual character of history, and, in this case, of post-biblical Israel.[203] This biblical worldview no doubt informs Barth's denouncement of the synagogue's Torah observance, which we will address in the following section.

### BARTH'S DOCTRINE OF JUDAISM (TORAH)

The theological framework that Barth overlays onto the Jewish people (Israel) is equally visible in his understanding and rejection of Jewish practice (Torah). Just as the former is seen most clearly through Barth's doctrine of election, the latter is made explicit in his reflections on ethics. For Barth, that Jesus Christ is God's full self-revelation means that God's will for humanity has been completely disclosed. This dynamic plays out in Barth's understanding of the command of God, which, as we saw above, "does not need any interpretation, for even to the smallest details it is self-interpreting."[204] It is in this way that Barth launches his attack against casuistical ethics, which he sees in its quintessential form in rabbinic Judaism. Because revelation for Barth is an immediate encounter between God and human beings that demands an equally immediate response of obedience, "Barth's ethics is stringently contextual in nature, excluding any reliance on principles, rules or norms that are 'applied' by reason to the ethical context."[205]

Barth assumes that casuistry (and thus rabbinic Judaism) implies a completely closed system that necessarily shuts its ears to the word of God

---

202. Sonderegger, *That Jesus Christ was Born a Jew*, 13.

203. As we will see in chapter 4, Mark Kinzer offers a more nuanced reading of post-biblical Israel's theological status with regard to obedience and disobedience to the command of God.

204. Barth, *Church Dogmatics* II/2, 665.

205. Robert E. Willis, *The Ethics of Karl Barth* (Leiden: Brill, 1971), 439.

spoken into particular cases.[206] According to Nigel Biggar, this understanding of casuistry is a misconception: "Casuistry has not always, or perhaps even usually, pretended to provide an absolute method of deciding what is right. Seldom has it imagined that it could capture cases by the inexorable movement of deductive logic, by the mere application of a technique."[207] Rather, the casuistical method is a dynamic and fluid process by which right action is discerned through both a consideration of fixed rules and openness to new guidance. "In other words, the casuistical process is not a one-way movement from principles through rules to cases, but a dialectic in which rules provide ready-made guidance with respect to morally familiar cases while being open to adaptation in the face of unfamiliar ones."[208] According to Biggar, "The elements of this dialectical kind of casuistry are all present in Barth's ethical thought. But his persistent identification of casuistry as the epitome of ethical rationalism prevented him from bringing them to the fore, and so robbed him of part of what is required for an explicit and coherent account of the relationship between systematic ethical deliberation about right action and the hearing of a command of God."[209] That Barth himself endorses and engages in a form of "practical casuistry" is another issue, which we will examine in a moment.

What Biggar claims with regard to casuistry is also true for Jewish ethics, which are definitely not a closed system as Barth presupposes. Barth's assessment of Judaism from a Christian vantage point precludes him from seeing the more nuanced and theological nature of Jewish ethical deliberation. Barth assumes that rabbinic Judaism disregards the voice of God and replaces it with purely human ethical reasoning. However, as Abraham Joshua Heschel explains, this description does not accord with a Jewish understanding of *halakhah*,[210] according to which "the law is the means, not the end; the way, not the goal. One of the goals is 'Ye shalt be holy.' The Torah is guidance to an end through a law. ... Man created in the likeness of God is called upon to re-create the world in the likeness of the

---

206. See Nigel Biggar, *The Hastening That Waits: Karl Barth's Ethics* (Oxford: Oxford University Press, 1993), 40.

207. Biggar, *Hastening*, 41.

208. Ibid.

209. Ibid.

210. For a definition of *halakhah*, see Introduction, note 45 above.

vision of God."[211] Hence, from a Jewish perspective, just as Israel is unintelligible apart from Torah, so Torah is unintelligible apart from God. As Heschel powerfully explains, "*Halacha* must not be observed for its own sake but for the sake of God. ... We live and die for the sake of God rather than for the sake of the law."[212] Like Barth, Heschel places faith at the center of an obedient life. In fact, Heschel's description of the law sounds remarkably similar to Barth's exposition of the Holiness Code. However, because Barth's Jesus neither follows nor promotes Torah observance, the synagogue and true faithfulness end up being mutually exclusive. For Barth, there is no manner in which traditional Jewish *halakhah* (or Jewish practice more broadly) can comprise obedience to the law.[213]

While faith in God stands at the center of Judaism, ultimately, "not the confession of belief, but the active acceptance of the kingship of God and its order is the central demand of Judaism. ... Thus our relation to God cannot be expressed in a belief but rather in the accepting of an order that determines all of life."[214] Once again, Barth's emphasis on the law as the form of the gospel mirrors Heschel's ordering of Jewish faith and practice. Like Barth, Judaism refuses to separate orthodoxy from orthopraxy. The following passage from Mishnah Berakhot illustrates this point well: "Rabbi Joshua ben Karha said: Why does in our liturgy the section *Hear O Israel* precede the section *And it shall come to pass if ye shall hearken* (which deals with the observance)? So that a man shall first receive upon himself the yoke of the kingship of heaven, and afterwards receive upon himself the yoke of the commandments."[215] Obedience to Torah is part and parcel of a faithful Jewish life, of which God stands at the center. Fundamentally, Barth's thought coheres well with a rabbinic worldview. However, Barth's conception of rabbinic Judaism does not permit him to recognize its high level of convergence with his own framework. Barth's assessment of the synagogue is one-dimensional; it has demonstrated its faithlessness by

---

211. Abraham Joshua Heschel, *God in Search of Man: A Philosophy of Judaism* (New York: Farrar, Straus and Giroux, 1976), 323.

212. Heschel, *God in Search of Man*, 326.

213. As we will see in chapter 4, faithfulness to Torah and faith in Christ need not be viewed as mutually exclusive.

214. Heschel, *God in Search of Man*, 331.

215. Mishnah Berakhot 2:2. Quoted in Heschel, *God in Search of Man*, 333.

rejecting Christ, who is the fullness of the law. Thus any obedience to the statutes of the Torah is categorically excluded from being reckoned as faithfulness to God.

David Hartman's explication of Psalm 119, which tightly correlates God's presence and God's commandments (i.e., Torah), further illustrates Torah observance as a harkening to God's voice. In Hartman's words, "According to the letter and spirit of [Psalm 119], the word of God is interchangeable with God. Torah, therefore, conveys the immediacy of God's presence, as if it were an incarnation of God's will and love. The language of worship, which in other biblical contexts is directed toward God ... is here directed, with no less intensity, toward the commandments."[216] As we saw above, Barth draws an equally strong connection between God's presence and God's command, though he fails to link God's command with Torah, as Hartman does. For Hartman, at the most fundamental level, Torah "embodies the living reality of God."[217] While Barth refuses to decouple gospel and law, the formalism of his system and categories leaves no room for the faith-saturated understanding of Torah that Heschel and Hartman put forth.

The rabbinic emphasis on *halakhah* expresses Judaism's central concern to obey God's command, rather than an attempt to replace the voice of the living God with a static, manmade prescription. Jewish ethics, therefore, has as its goal the very thing Barth most emphasizes: obedience in all circumstances to the command of God. For Barth, obedience precludes any sort of authoritative human interpretation. For Judaism, it requires it. Ultimately, Jewish ethics do not place any less importance on discerning the will of God, though the means of ascertaining God's will in a given situation depart from what Barth allows.

However, according to Jewish understanding, it is precisely God who has authorized human interpretation. Communal deliberation is seen as the divinely sanctioned means by which God's command in a particular context is made known. In Judaism, "the words of God are not read as if their meaning were self-evident. Rather, their meaning is expected to emerge from the ongoing and admittedly fallible process of arguing

---

216. David Hartman, *A Heart of Many Rooms: Celebrating the Many Voices within Judaism* (Woodstock, VT: Jewish Lights Publishing, 2002), 7.

217. Hartman, *A Heart of Many Rooms*, 8.

about the text and of finding ever new and additional meanings in it. Study, innovation (*hiddush*), and interpretation are always linked."[218] This notion poses a conceptual difficulty, for it is often assumed that "seeing a text as ambiguous, complex, difficult, must involve seeing it as creating a distance between the recipient and the author."[219] But this is not the case with rabbinic Judaism. "If there is a fundamental novelty in rabbinic religiosity, it is that the sages saw figuring out what God means by his words as a form of intimacy with God. Judaism is an interpretive tradition, and as Hartman puts it, 'In the interpretive tradition, God never abandons you, because His word is always with you.' "[220] As we saw above, Barth portrays casuistry as an attempt to "master and handle" the command of God, to domesticate its radical and all-encompassing claim upon human beings. However, Jewish ethical deliberation is in the service of discerning and obeying the word of God, the very thing with which Barth is most concerned. What Barth failed to see is that, in Jewish tradition, the process of wrestling with the text in order to ascertain its meaning for a given context is the primary mode of relating to and seeking out God.

The talmudic story told in Bava Metzi'a 59a–59b (referred to as the "Oven of Akhnai") nicely illustrates the divinely sanctioned interpretive authority of the rabbis. The context of the story is a rabbinic dispute about the purity of an oven, and the story reads as follows:

> (A1) We learned there: If he cut it (an oven) into segments and placed sand between the segments, R. Eliezer rules that it is pure and the sages rule that it is impure. And this is the oven of 'Akhnai.
>
> (A2) What is 'Akhnai (=snake)? Rav Yehuda said Shmuel said, "Since they surrounded him with words like this snake and ruled it impure."
>
> (B1) It was taught: On that day R. Eliezer responded with all the responses in the world, but they did not accept them from him.
>
> (B2) He said to them, "If the law is as I say, let the carob [tree] prove it." The carob uprooted itself from its place and went one

218. Hilary Putnam, "Jewish Ethics?" in *The Blackwell Companion to Religious Ethics*, ed. William Schweiker (Oxford: Blackwell, 2005), 163.

219. Putnam, "Jewish Ethics?" 164.

220. Putnam, "Jewish Ethics?" 164; Hartman, *A Heart of Many Rooms*, 11.

hundred cubits. ... They said to him, "One does not bring proof from the carob." The carob returned to its place.

(B3) He said to them, "If the law is as I say, let the aqueduct prove it." The water turned backwards. They said to him, "One does not bring proof from water." The water returned to its place.

(B4) He said to them, "If it (the law) is as I say, let the walls of the academy prove it." The walls of the academy inclined to fall. R. Yehoshua rebuked them. He said to them, "When sages defeat each other in law, what is it for you?"

(B5) It was taught: They did not fall because of the honor of R. Yehoshua, and they did not stand because of the honor of R. Eliezer, and they are still inclining and standing.

(C1) He said to them, "If it is as I say, let it be proved from heaven." A heavenly voice went forth and said, "What is it for you with R. Eliezer, since the law is like him in every place?"

(C2) R. Yehoshua stood up on his feet and said, "It is not in heaven (Deut 30:12)."

(C3) What is, "It is not in heaven?"

(C4) R. Yimah said, "We do not listen to a heavenly voice, since you already gave it to us on Mt. Sinai and it is written there, Incline after the majority (Exod 23:2)."

(D) R. Natan came upon Elijah. He said to him, "What was the Holy One doing at that time?" He said to him, "He laughed and smiled and said, 'My sons have defeated me, my sons have defeated me.'"[221]

Two things in particular are worth noting in this story. First, according to the rabbis, God's giving of the Torah implies that its proper sphere of interpretation is on earth. The quotation from Deuteronomy 30 is used here to indicate that the interpretation and application of Torah rightfully belongs to human beings. Second, the story includes a divine affirmation of this principle. God's laughter is used to indicate his approval of the debate

---

221. Jeffrey L. Rubenstein, *Talmudic Stories: Narrative Art, Composition, and Culture* (Baltimore: Johns Hopkins University Press, 1999), 36–37.

that is taking place, for it represents the sort of wrestling with the text that constitutes faithful Jewish *halakhic* life.[222]

In Barth's ethical framework, this type of ethical reasoning and wrestling is disallowed. According to Robert Willis, "Barth's interpretation of the definiteness of the command ... amounts to nothing less than a total exclusion of the necessity of deliberation in ethics."[223] In the face of God's self-interpreting command, the only possible human response is obedience or disobedience. According to Barth, the human ethical decision "is whether in my conduct I shall correspond to the command which encounters and confronts me in the most concrete and pointed way, whether I shall be obedient or disobedient to it, whether I, for my part, shall meet it according to my election (the election of Jesus Christ) as a believer or an unbeliever."[224] Thus Barth essentially eliminates the intermediate stage that comprises the heart of Jewish ethics, namely the task of discerning how the command of God informs a particular situation.

---

222. It should be noted that this story, oft-quoted to make the precise—and warranted— point we are making, is taken out of context when it is seen as solely focusing on this issue. The story goes on to tell of the way in which R. Eliezer is shamed for his attempts to support his *halakhic* ruling, such that the story in its entirety is about both a legal dispute and human conduct and sensitivity. As Jeffrey Rubenstein explains, "As a whole, the story undoubtedly has great significance for understanding the rabbinic conception of the legal process and related ideas about divine authority and human interpretation." However, this discussion appears "within a story that focuses less on the legal controversy than its aftermath, the interpersonal relationships, emotional harm, and verbal wrong. Moreover, the entire story appears in a *halakhic* and literary context that emphasizes these themes. Ultimately the story focuses on the tension between these two realms, between a legal process that involves interpretation, debate, and decision, on the one hand, and human feelings, emotions, and dignity on the other. ... The sages must negotiate this tension so as to preserve the integrity of the law while treating each other with respect and consideration. The story, then, is not only about the nature of the legal process but about how that process must be conducted" (Rubenstein, *Talmudic Stories*, 47-48). See also Eliezer Berkovits, *Not in Heaven: The Nature and Function of Jewish Law* (Jerusalem: Shalem Press, 2010), 47-48.

223. Willis, *The Ethics of Karl Barth*, 183. John Webster argues that Barth's uneasiness with moral deliberation stems from the threat of "absolutising the activity of moral reflectivity into an inner life untouched by relation to God." According to Webster, "Barth is not (as is sometimes thought) denying any place to moral consciousness—to what he calls 'awareness' ... but he is denying that moral awareness offers us a place to stand outside our history with God, prior to engaging in that history and the command which it issues to us." In other words, Barth does not "make moral action into a mere reflex," but denies "that moral authenticity has its ultimate ground in transcendent moral consciousness" (Webster, *Barth's Ethics of Reconciliation*, 56).

224. Barth, *Church Dogmatics* II/2, 669.

For Barth, God determines right action in every particular situation, for God's command "always confronts us with a specific meaning and intention, with a will which has foreseen everything and each thing in particular, which has not left the smallest thing to chance or our caprice."[225] As James Gustafson explains, for Barth,

> God, and no human being, is the decisive determiner of proper human activity. The image of man is not the self-legislating moral agent exercising reason in the determination of what is right according to some moral principles or ethical guides. ... Man is the hearer of this very precise and objective command of God. ... [Human beings] can fail to hear the command, and they can disobey it when they do hear it. But, again, what is right and good is determined objectively (in relation to human impulses, dispositions, and reasoning) by God; it is not determined by human beings.[226]

In fact, for Barth, to identify God's will with an ethical system is to bring it under human control and thus deny God's freedom.[227] Barth's rejection of casuistical ethics notwithstanding, he himself engages in a form of casuistry as he lays out the practical implications of his own ethical framework. According to Nigel Biggar, "In spite of his unequivocal insistence that God's command is absolutely self-determining, reaching us with an immediacy and definiteness that precludes interpretation, and that the only legitimate kind of ethical reflection is a sort of spiritual self-examination, Barth himself engaged extensively in a systematic form of ethical deliberation about right conduct."[228] Barth maintains that "special ethics," while no doubt focusing upon the sphere of human action, "is not self-contained and self-sufficient. It does not pretend to autonomy. It is not a closed system."[229] As we have already seen, Barth's conception of special ethics is distinguished from casuistry, which Barth construes as necessarily

---

225. Ibid., 663.

226. James Gustafson, *Ethics from a Theocentric Perspective*, vol 2 of *Ethics and Theology* (Chicago: University of Chicago Press, 1984), 30. For a cultural critique of this aspect of Barth's theology, see Graham Ward, *Cultural Transformation and Religious Practice* (Cambridge: Cambridge University Press, 2005), esp. ch. 1.

227. See Biggar, *Hastening*, 9.

228. Ibid., 25.

229. Ibid., 31.

self-enclosed and which he identifies par excellence in rabbinic Judaism. Barth's engagement in "practical casuistry"—always in the service of hearing the command of God—"legitimates the kinds of observations about experience, the uses of biblical teachings and analogies, and the grasping of political and social realities that inform Barth's often richly insightful discussions of all sorts of occasions in which moral action is required: marriage, family, politics, tyranny, capital punishment, and many more."[230]

It is Barth's definition of terms, rather than any sort of reality on the ground, that reinforces the mutually exclusive division between his own ethical framework and that of rabbinic Judaism. Barth effectually creates a straw man out of rabbinic Judaism, and it is this portrayal upon which his false dichotomy rests. Had his evaluation of Jewish ethics not been so thoroughly colored by pre-drawn conclusions about the bankruptcy of rabbinic Judaism, Barth would have seen that his attempt to systematize ethical implications without closing them off to the ever-living command of God is entirely resonant with a Jewish ethical framework. If Barth had attended to post-biblical Israel in all its nuance and complexity, he would have seen that the Jewish pursuit of right action in obedience to God does not completely violate his ethical paradigm. That Barth does not adhere to his own purely formal proscription against human deliberation reveals that his on-the-ground ethics are much closer to Jewish ethics than he is able to recognize.

## CONCLUSION

Having reviewed Barth's christological construal of election, Israel, Torah, and ethics, what can we conclude with regard to Barth's contribution to answering Marshall's question? As we saw above, Barth's doctrine of election and Christocentric ecclesiology strongly uphold the first part of Marshall's framework. The universal scope of Christ's saving work and its ecclesial mediation are strong points in Barth's thought. As the primary referent of God's election, Christ claims each and every human being for inclusion in the elect community. While the church functions as the means by which all of humanity is awakened to its election in Christ, the permanent election of Israel is entirely safeguarded within Barth's thought.

---

230. Gustafson, *Ethics*, 32.

Israel's obedience or disobedience does not ultimately determine its covenantal status before God; rather, Israel's ongoing election is a product of God's gracious and sovereign election of humanity in Christ.

The indelible correlation that Barth draws between Israel and the church chips away at a supersessionist framework, and Jesus' solidarity with the Jewish people precludes the possibility of juxtaposing Christ's faithfulness with Israel's unfaithfulness in such a way as to write Israel out of God's redemptive plans for humanity. Once again, the forcefulness of these claims in the midst of Nazi Germany cannot be underestimated. Along these lines, Barth paves the way for a radically new assessment of the relationship between Israel and the church. Furthermore, Barth's contention that the law is the form of the gospel disallows for any sort of distance between right faith and right action. Barth's actualistic conception of God undergirds his actualistic anthropology, and this construct finds great resonance with a Jewish view of election and ethics.

However, these positive contributions notwithstanding, Barth's thought with regard to the Jewishness of Jesus and Jewish covenantal faithfulness falls short of connecting Israel to Torah in the way Marshall's question requires. Barth's christologically conceived Torah is ultimately incompatible with traditional Jewish *halakhah*, and Jesus' Jewishness serves merely to highlight his solidarity with unfaithful Israel. Barth's Jesus apparently stands outside the realm of Jewish covenantal practices, and such practices are condemned wholesale as disobedience in light of Judaism's widespread rejection of Christ. Because the Torah's *telos* is faithfulness to Christ, the sanctifying function of Jewish covenantal life is eclipsed entirely, and post-biblical *halakhah* (hypothetically even when practiced by Jesus-believing Jews) is unambiguously equated with disobedience.

While Barth's account of christological salvation and ecclesiological vocation significantly enrich our attempt to answer Marshall's question, Barth's theology does not leave room for a positive assessment of Judaism or Torah that is not explicitly centered upon Christ, nor even a Jewish expression of Christian faith. As we will see in the next chapter, Jewish theologian Franz Rosenzweig provides a helpful complement to Barth on these issues. Rosenzweig offers a model in which Jewish existence and observance furthers God's kingdom, rather than modeling the very disobedience that God overcomes in Christ.

**2**

# "THE SPROUTING OF OUR REDEMPTION": FRANZ ROSENZWEIG'S THEOLOGY OF JUDAISM AND CHRISTIANITY

## INTRODUCTION

As we saw in the last chapter, Karl Barth's robust Christology and teleologically universal ecclesiology offer a strong affirmation of the first half of Marshall's question (namely, the universal, ecclesially mediated saving mission of Christ). However, while Barth formally upholds the permanent election of Israel, his consistent denouncement of the "Synagogue" and his insistence on the negative nature of Israel's witness leave us with a more equivocal assessment with regard to the second part of Marshall's question (namely, the affirmation of Israel's ongoing election, which necessarily includes the ongoing practice of Judaism). It is with Barth's theological strengths and weaknesses in mind that we now turn to Franz Rosenzweig, seeking to discover how his significant contributions can further resource our project at hand.

With regard to modern Jewish thought and Jewish perspectives on Christianity, Franz Rosenzweig's contribution is among the most novel, luminary, and formidable. Emmanuel Lévinas hails Rosenzweig's configuration of the theological puzzle pieces as "unprecedented in the history of thought."[1] According to David Novak, Rosenzweig's incorporation of

---

1. Emmanuel Lévinas, "Foreword" in *System and Revelation: The Philosophy of Franz Rosenzweig*, by Stéphane Mosès, trans. Catherine Tihanyi (Detroit: Wayne State University Press, 1982), 14.

Christianity into his theological system is "very much unlike anything before in the history of Judaism."[2] Stéphane Mosès agrees: "The formal symmetry that Rosenzweig establishes between Judaism and Christianity is unheard of in the orthodox theologies of these two religions."[3] Rosenzweig's influence upon a generation of Jewish and Christian thinkers is nearly impossible to exaggerate. Like Barth, Rosenzweig has served as a pioneer in the emerging intellectual tradition that seeks to expound the indelible connection between Judaism and Christianity, a connection without which neither can be properly understood. Rosenzweig's thought provides a wealth of resources in our attempt to answer Marshall's question.

Having assessed Barth's theology in light of Marshall's question, our engagement with Rosenzweig will pay particular attention to the ways in which Rosenzweig offers a helpful complement to Barth. As we shall see, with regard to Marshall's question, the aggregate of Rosenzweig and Barth is indeed greater than its parts. Once we have delineated the contributions Rosenzweig offers to our theological venture, and the way in which Rosenzweig's thought interfaces with Barth's, we will be prepared to engage and assess a host of post-Holocaust thinkers who extend and build upon the work of both Barth and Rosenzweig (see chapters 3 and 4). The generation that followed Barth and Rosenzweig took their thought and extended it in remarkable ways, clarifying key points and developing ideas that remain incipient in the work of these two pioneers. Before we can turn to this new generation of Jewish and Christian thinkers, we must once again traverse the terrain from which they mined their theological resources. As we saw with Barth in the last chapter, so we shall discover with Rosenzweig in this chapter: both thinkers lay out novel theological frameworks whose full significance and influence is merely beginning to dawn.

This chapter will offer an overview of Rosenzweig's magnum opus, *The Star of Redemption*, with particular emphasis placed on his complementary construal of Judaism and Christianity. We will then assess the explicit contribution Rosenzweig's thought makes to answering Marshall's question, highlighting places where Rosenzweig's theology addresses the weaknesses

---

2. David Novak, *The Election of Israel: The Idea of the Chosen People* (Cambridge: Cambridge University Press, 1995), 100.

3. Mosès, *System and Revelation*, 219.

we saw in Barth's treatment of Israel and Torah. Finally, we will point the way forward to the constellation of post-Holocaust thinkers whose thoughts will occupy us in the following two chapters.

## JUDAISM AND CHRISTIANITY
## IN ROSENZWEIG'S THEOLOGY

### OVERVIEW OF *THE STAR OF REDEMPTION*

*The Star of Redemption* offers a philosophical system[4] that both critiques German Idealism and gives voice to Rosenzweig's own existential experiences. It is here that Rosenzweig offers his most thorough and sustained treatment of Judaism and Christianity, describing these two traditions as parallel yet distinct trajectories toward redemption, both refracting truth but neither exhaustively possessing or representing it. Rosenzweig's theology is not easily classifiable, and the complexity of his ideas mirrors the complex texture of his life and its events.

*The Star of Redemption* is notable for its tight, systematic, and architectonic structure. The book is divided into three parts, and each part has three books. The work as a whole deals with three fundamental elements (God, world, man) and three movements in the relationship between these elements (creation, revelation, redemption).[5] The first part deals with the three primary elements in their primordial state and corresponds to the

---

4. In a seminal essay entitled "The New Thinking" (1925), Rosenzweig wrote the following: "I cannot describe the *Star of Redemption* any more accurately than this critic has done with pregnant brevity: it is indeed not meant for the daily use of every member of every family. It is in general not a 'Jewish book,' at least not in the sense that the buyers, who were so angry with me, think of a Jewish book; for while it deals with Judaism, it deals with it no more comprehensively than it deals with Christianity, and barely more comprehensively than it deals with Islam. Nor does it claim to be a philosophy of religion. How could it do this, given that the word 'religion' does not even occur in it! Rather, it is merely a system of philosophy.

"Nevertheless, [it is] a system of philosophy that gives the reader, the expert as well as the lay reader, the fullest right to be displeased—namely, a philosophy which does not want to bring about a mere 'Copernican Revolution' of thinking, after which he who has performed it sees all things upside down, although they are still the same things he had seen before, rather a philosophy which wants to bring about the total renewal of thinking" (Franz Rosenzweig, *Philosophical and Theological Writings*, trans. and ed. Paul W. Franks and Michael L. Morgan [Indianapolis: Hackett, 2000], 110).

5. It is noteworthy that the three primary chapters of Barth's theological narrative are creation, *reconciliation*, and redemption. That Barth's system has reconciliation at its center (in contrast to Rosenzweig's placement of revelation at the center of his system) presupposes that something in the divine-human covenant has gone awry; there is need for God and

movement of creation (past); the second part tracks the trajectory by which the three elements come to be related to one another and corresponds to the movement of revelation (present); and the third part expounds the way in which the intricate and reciprocal interrelations between the three elements take concrete form and ultimately usher in redemption (future). It is in part 3 that Rosenzweig deals explicitly with Judaism and Christianity, assigning each a function, vocation, and task in the movement from revelation to redemption. The sections build one upon the other, and the obscurity of the book's first half is clarified by the increasing lucidity of the second half.

In parts 1 and 2, Rosenzweig uses the image of the Star of David—two triangles overlaid upon one another, with the points of the upright triangle representing God, world, and man, and the points of the downward-pointing triangle representing creation, revelation, and redemption. Rosenzweig's star imagery shifts in the third part, and here he employs the idea of a celestial star, with Judaism representing the star's inner burning core and Christianity representing the rays that emanate outward from the star, carrying its light and heat to its surroundings. Having briefly overviewed the structure of *The Star of Redemption*, let us now delve more deeply into part 3 of the *Star*, wherein Rosenzweig fleshes out the relationship between Judaism and Christianity and their respective redemptive vocations.

### EXPLICATION OF PART 3 OF *THE STAR OF REDEMPTION*

The final third of *The Star of Redemption* deals with redemption—the process by which man, awakened to revelation, loves his neighbor and thereby the world, thus completing the system. It is here that man's commission is actualized. Although redemption lies primarily in man's hands[6] (via his love

---

humanity to *be reconciled*. Barth makes clear throughout that what necessitates reconciliation is humanity's sin and disobedience, exemplified par excellence in Israel.

6. For Rosenzweig, the interaction between God and man is different in redemption than in creation or revelation. In redemption, "it might happen that man interferes violently in the sovereignty of divine power and love; for *Redemption is after all not directly God's work or action*; but just as God gave to Creation the power to grow in itself organically, so, too, in his love, he gave the soul freedom for the action of love" (Franz Rosenzweig, *The Star of Redemption*, trans. Barbara E. Galli (Madison: University of Wisconsin Press, 2005), 285; italics added). Unless otherwise noted, all quotations from *The Star of Redemption* are taken from this translation.

of the nearest and his prayer for the farthest), man cannot force the kingdom; he cannot choose the day and the hour when it comes.[7] Humanity's redemptive work must keep pace with the organic growth of the kingdom; it cannot hasten ahead and force the kingdom nor can it lag behind and forestall the kingdom

## The Fire or Eternal Life

In part 3, book 1, entitled "The Fire or Eternal Life," Rosenzweig begins to delimit the role of Judaism in ushering in redemption, employing the image of the burning core of a star. The opening paragraph is worth citing at length:

> Praised be he who has planted eternal life in our midst. The fire burns in the heart of the Star. It is only out of the fire of the center that the rays shine forth and flow outwards irresistibly. The heart of the fire must burn without ever stopping. Its flame must eternally nourish itself. It does not want nourishment from anywhere else. Time must roll past it without power. The fire must beget its own time. It must beget itself eternally. It must make its life eternal in the succession of generations, each of which begets the following one, as it itself again will bear witness to the preceding one. The bearing witness takes place in the begetting. In this connection with the double meaning and single effect of begetting and bearing witness, eternal life becomes real. Past and future, otherwise strangers to each other, the one drawing back when the other's turn comes—here they grow into one: the begetting of the future is a direct bearing witness to the past.[8]

---

7. See ibid., 283–315. According to Mosès, "It is essential, in order to understand the idea of Redemption in Rosenzweig, to keep in mind that Redemption is not arbitrary, that it cannot suddenly occur at any moment of time" (Mosès, *System and Revelation*, 156). Rosenzweig identifies two types of prayer that do not align with the *kairos* of the kingdom. The first is the "sinner's prayer," which remains too focused on the self and not enough on the other, thus lagging behind love and not hastening toward redemption. The "zealot's prayer" misses the *kairos* of the kingdom in the opposite manner. This prayer, "in wanting to hasten the future of the Kingdom so that it might come ahead of time, seeks forcibly to seize the Kingdom," yet ultimately also has the effect of delaying the kingdom (Rosenzweig, *The Star of Redemption*, 293).

8. Rosenzweig, *The Star of Redemption*, 317.

This passage lays out the central concept that Rosenzweig will spend the rest of the section unpacking. "Eternal life" is the term that Rosenzweig uses to describe the existence and vocation of the Jewish people. They embody—already in time—the presence of eternity. Like the burning core of a star, their existence must continue to burn without reference to the outside. This fire burns according to its own time, and the continual begetting of new generations connects past and future, essentially creating the eternal present. The Jewish people bears witness to eternity by being what it is and thus serving as a testimony to the world that lives according to natural and human time. The Jewish people's vocation is characterized by a prescribed inwardness, and it is within this inwardness that it lives out the commission of love of neighbor.

The rays that emanate outward—that is, Christianity—exist only by virtue of the burning core; they are utterly contingent upon it. Their life is the product of its life. The core, however, exists without regard to the rays, which add nothing to its fundamental understanding or essence. It remains indifferent to and unaffected by them. Its commission, its means of bearing witness to the world, is to continue its life through the begetting of new generations, to perpetuate itself.

Rosenzweig explains that it is by virtue of this community existing as a "community of blood"[9] that it experiences eternity. Time is no threat to this community, for its very existence is by nature trans-generational: "For it alone time is not an enemy to be restrained, over which perhaps, perhaps even not—but it hopes that—it will be triumphant, but child and grandchild. ... In the natural propagation of the body it has the guarantee of its eternity."[10] While this community shares with other societies the cyclical return of foundational events, for the Jewish people, "this reactivation of original events does not have as essential function the reliving of a primordial time but, rather, the anticipation of an eschatological time."[11] In other words, for this community, past events are merely portents of future realities.

---

9.  Ibid., 317–24.
10. Ibid., 317–18.
11. Mosès, *System and Revelation*, 174.

The Jewish people's bodily existence and perpetuation is not threatened by time as a result of its unique relationship with land, language, and law.[12] The Jewish people are postured against historical time and geographical and linguistic rootedness, sharpening the tangible contrast between this people and the other peoples of the world. Rosenzweig says of the Jewish people, "Our life is no longer interwoven with anything external, we have taken root in ourselves, without roots in the earth, eternal wanderers therefore, yet deeply rooted in ourselves, in our own body and blood. And this rooting in ourselves and only in ourselves guarantees our eternity for us."[13]

The Jewish people's proleptic experience of eternity is most clearly evident in the cycle of the Jewish year.[14] Consistent with what we have already said about the Jewish people's relationship to time, the holidays and liturgy in Judaism do not merely commemorate past events, but more importantly point forward toward the redemptive reality, which the holidays merely intimate and suggest. Through the structure of the year, the Jewish people live out the dramatic progression of creation, revelation, and redemption.[15]

The Sabbath is the smallest building block of the Jewish year, for it "grants existence to the year. ... Only in the expiring sequence of Sabbaths is

---

12. See Appendix 1 for further explanation of the Jewish people's relationship to land, language, and law in Rosenzweig's thought.

13. Rosenzweig, *The Star of Redemption*, 324.

14. The way in which, for Rosenzweig, the Jewish holidays form the life of the Jewish community will become relevant again in chapter 4. As we will see, Mark Kinzer is likewise concerned not merely with a set of ideas but with the concrete fundamentals of building a particular community.

15. The following chart, found in Mosès, *System and Revelation*, 188, is a helpful visual representation of the Jewish liturgical year:

| Creation | Sabbath | Audience | Gathering of individuals |
|---|---|---|---|
| Creation Revelation: Revelation Redemption | Passover Feast of Weeks (Shavuot) Feast of Booths (Succot) | Meal | Community of the people |
| Redemption | New Year (Rosh Hashanah) Day of Atonement (Yom Kippur) | Greeting | Universality of persons |

the year made round into a wreath."[16] The Sabbath is the holiday of remembering creation, for its institution coincided with God's day of rest after having finished creating the earth.[17] Just as the seeds of revelation are already planted in the reality of creation, the Sabbath too points forward to the holidays of revelation, as well as redemption. But because the Sabbath represents creation and not redemption, with its conclusion comes the re-entry into the workweek, into the work of sowing the seeds of redemption: "Outside the sanctuary it is a matter of again finding the road into the everyday. Upon the alternation of holy and ordinary, of seventh day and first, of fulfillment and beginning, of old man and child, the year is built, life is built. The Sabbath is the dream of perfection, but only a dream."[18]

For Rosenzweig, the three pilgrimage festivals—Passover,[19] Shavuot[20] and Succot[21]—celebrate revelation, for they "form an image of the people's

---

16. Rosenzweig, *The Star of Redemption*, 329.

17. "And just as the Creation is not exhausted in the fact that the world was created once long ago, but is first completely fulfilled in its renewal of every morning, so the Sabbath as the holiday of Creation cannot be a holiday of once a year, but must be renewed through the entire cycle every week as the same holiday and yet as a different one every week by means of the weekly portion" (ibid., 330).

18. Ibid., 332–33.

19. Though Passover commemorates creation, it includes a strong chord of Israel's teleological orientation. The freedom celebrated by the Jewish people during the Passover Seder points forward to the freedom of all people that will characterize redemption. "The reading out of the Song of Songs points to Revelation; the distant view of Redemption is made accessible by the prophecy of Isaiah on the sprouting of the root of Jesse, who will strike the earth with the staff of his mouth on the day when the wolf and lamb will dwell together and the earth will be filled with the knowledge of the Lord like the waters cover the sea; but the root will rise, a banner for the peoples, and pagans will follow it. And this is the most profound meaning of the parting words that the partakers of the evening meal of liberated men say: 'Next year in Jerusalem' " (ibid., 338).

20. This middle holiday of the holidays of revelation represents revelation proper, and therefore "stands as the moment of the present between the long everlasting was of the past and the eternal coming of the future" (ibid., 338). The holiday celebrates the giving of the Torah at Sinai, whereby the Jewish people accept the Ten Commandments and thus their corporate vocation. In this moment they are completely consumed by their intimacy with God; the rest of the world fades from consciousness.

21. Succot (Judaism's redemptive holiday within the holidays of revelation) reminds the Jewish people that they are not allowed to linger too long in the sweetness and solitude of their revelational tryst. They "must leave [their] clandestine solitude of a twosome with ... God and go into the world" (ibid., 339). Succot's temporary dwellings permit the Jewish people to experience a foretaste of the rest that redemption promises while not allowing them to forget "the ephemeral nature of all human settlement, the fragility of all institutions, the impossibility of ever attaining the absolute completion of history" (Mosès, *System and Revelation*, 195). Succot reiterates Israel's relationship to the land and its ontological state of perpetual exile.

destiny as the bearer of Revelation."[22] Similar to the Sabbath holiday, the festivals of revelation also re-enact the drama of creation, revelation, redemption, for "in Revelation, also revealed are Creation and Redemption, the former because it took place for the sake of Revelation and hence in the strict sense is directly Creation of Revelation, the latter because Revelation teaches how to wait for it."[23] However, because these three festivals embody the celebration of revelation proper, "they are only apparently holidays of remembrance; in truth, the historical in them is a fully compact present."[24]

For Rosenzweig, the Days of Awe constitute the holidays of redemption. Here the Jewish people transcend their particularity through the recognition that all of humanity constitutes a universal community, and they pray "for the day where everything created sinks to its knees and forms one single covenant to do God's will with a whole heart."[25] The Days of Awe "place the eternal Redemption into the midst of time," and the "judgment that is otherwise set into the end of times here is placed immediately into the present moment."[26] Here man confesses his guilt before God, and miraculously experiences God's forgiveness: "God inclines his countenance, the God who loves man before his sin as afterwards, the God whom man in his need can call to account as to why he abandoned him, the God who is compassionate and merciful, patiently full of unmerited clemency and full of faithfulness, who keeps his love to the two-thousandth generation and forgives wickedness and defiance and guilt and pardons him who returns."[27] For Rosenzweig, Yom Kippur represents the absolute height of all religious experience. It is on this day that eternity really does break into history, and the end that is otherwise only anticipated takes place in the present.

Having expounded this mystical event in which the Jewish people encounters redemption already in time, Rosenzweig goes on to further contrast this people with the peoples of the world. Because the Jewish people exist as an eternal people, they do not experience the "growing" that other peoples undergo as they journey toward completion.

---

22. Rosenzweig, *The Star of Redemption*, 335.
23. Ibid., 335–36.
24. Ibid., 336.
25. Ibid., 343–44.
26. Ibid., 344.
27. Ibid., 347.

However, though the Jewish people already inhabit eternal life, they must wait for the nations of the world to join them: "Waiting and wandering are affairs of the soul; only growing falls on the side of the world. And the eternal people forgo precisely this growing. Its peoplehood is already at that place to which the peoples of the world only aspire. Its world is at the goal."[28] Here the Jew embraces his particularity as a member of the eternal people, and does not concern himself with the growth of the world: "The Jew's myth leads him by leading him into his people, and at the same time under the countenance of his God who is the God also of the nations; for the Jewish people, no discrepancy applies between that which is most their own and that which is the highest, for it love for itself turns immediately into love for the neighbor."[29]

*The Rays or the Eternal Way*

Rosenzweig's depiction of Christianity describes the trajectory of the rays that emanate from the heart of the star, whose destiny is eternity but whose course leads through time. Christianity, represented by these rays, cannot free itself from historical time but must instead master time. Christianity achieves this mastery by organizing time into epochs, thus conferring meaning upon the fleeting passage of time. The time between Christ's birth and his second coming forms one great epoch, during which beginning and end are always equidistant from the ever-central present: "So Christianity, by making of the moment into an epoch-making epoch, gets power over time. From Christ's birth on there is now only still the present. Time does not bounce off Christianity like off the Jewish people, but fleeting time is captured and must now serve as an imprisoned slave."[30]

While God has withheld the Jewish people from the progression of history by charting their course "over the river of time," the Christian exists within and beside the historical advancement of worldly time.[31] The

---

28. Ibid., 348.

29. Ibid., 349.

30. Ibid., 360–61.

31. Ibid., 359–60. Rosenzweig uses the image of a river to orient Judaism and Christianity with regard to time. The following passage clearly lays out Rosenzweig's framework along the lines of this image: "This is the vitality of a life in the moment: that it is life in time, lets itself be carried off from the past and calls to the future. Thus live men and peoples. From this life God withheld the Jew by arching the bridge of his Law heavenwards over the river

Christian is not captive to the rushing flow of unoriented time, but neither is she entirely outside of time. Her existence in time is situated alongside the progression of secular time, whose beginning and end are uncertain. The Christian knows from whence her existence stems and to whither it heads, but she cannot but be in between these points. As long as the river of historical time continues to flow, the Christian will always be between beginning and end. For her beginning and end are equally near, and her current location is "entirely center, entirely between, entirely way."[32]

The Christ event provides orientation for time, where everything before Christ's birth is past, the last judgment is future, and "in between stands a single hour, a single day, the Christian world time in which everything is middle, everything equally light as day."[33] Historical time responds to this orientation, acting as the "obedient bookkeeper"[34] of Christianity's steps, having unlearned its confidence in itself: "The taking over of time by Christian eternity is symbolized by the fact that Christianity has imposed its calendar on the Western world. The history of the West begins with the birth of Christ."[35]

Rosenzweig then proceeds to ask how Christianity achieves, maintains, and lives out the mutual participation that binds it together across the ages and across the world. Like Judaism, the collective existence of Christianity is eternal, though its configuration is contrasted to that of Judaism: "Eternal life and eternal way—they are as different as the infinity of a point and of a line. The infinity of a point can only consist in the fact that it is never wiped away; therefore it is preserved in the eternal self-preservation of the blood that continuously begets. The infinity of a line however stops when it would no longer be possible to extend it; it

---

of time under whose arch it now rushes powerlessly into all eternity. The Christian, however, takes up the contest with the river. He lays alongside it the tracks of his eternal way. He who takes this train measures the place of the river he has just seen only according to the distance between the station of departure and that of arrival. He himself is always only on the track and his real interest is only that he is still always on the way, still always between departure and goal" (ibid., 359–60).

32. Ibid., 360.
33. Ibid., 361.
34. Ibid.
35. Mosès, *System and Revelation*, 226.

consists in this possibility of unlimited extension."[36] Whereas Judaism's eternity consists in the prolongation of its inward existence, Christianity's eternity is dependent upon its outward promulgation. For Christianity, mere preservation is not efficacious for eternal existence: "Christianity as eternal way must always spread further. Simple preservation of its continuance would mean for it the renouncing of its eternity and hence death. Christianity must be missionary."[37]

Whereas bearing witness for the Jewish people (as a "community of blood") takes the form of begetting future generations, of "sealing off the pure source of blood from foreign admixture,"[38] Christianity's witness takes a spiritual form, where "the pouring out of the Spirit in the uninterrupted stream of baptismal water from one to the other must establish the mutual participation of bearing witness."[39] Each point must testify to its centrality until a whole series of points makes up an infinite line, and the content of that testimony is faith. For the Jew, to live faithfully is to silently beget future generations, for "he is himself the having of faith."[40] Christian faith cannot merely be in its own existence; it must rely on words, it must be dogmatic, and it must be translatable into every tongue. "A faith that wants to win the world must be faith in something,"[41] and Christian faith is faith in the way. This way is Christ, and all who are united in Christian faith are called to mutual action and issued a common task.

Christianity creates a simultaneity in time that allows people from all over the world to be joined despite the distance that separates them. This simultaneity is what allows the Christian to love his neighbor as himself: "Time is already laid conquered at its feet; love only still has to fly over the separating space. And so it flies over the enmity of peoples and the cruelty of race, the envy of classes and the limitations of age; and so it brings it about that all those who are enemies, cruel, envious, limited behold each other as brother, in the one same central moment of time."[42] Judaism, in

---

36. Rosenzweig, *The Star of Redemption*, 362.
37. Ibid.
38. Ibid.
39. Ibid.
40. Ibid., 363.
41. Ibid.
42. Ibid., 367.

contrast, in order to embody the eternal people, must bridge time, not space. For the Jews, "the moment shows us eternity otherwise: not in the brother who stands nearest us, but in those who stand farthest from us in time."[43]

In the midst of the church's existence in historical time, "the ecclesiastical year weaves the halo of eternity."[44] Here again Rosenzweig traverses the spiritual year, this time with reference to Christian holidays instead of Jewish holidays. For Christians, Sunday is the weekly holiday of creation upon which the year is founded. Rosenzweig contrasts the Christian Sunday to the Jewish Sabbath, assigning deep theological significance to the church's decision to change the holiday from the last day of the week to the first day of the week in an effort "bluntly to distinguish itself from the synagogue."[45] While the Sabbath celebrates creation, it is marked by a rest that points forward to redemption, ever reminding the world that creation is for the sake of redemption. Sunday, on the other hand, "which has seldom taken very stringently the precept of rest,"[46] marks the beginning of the week and thus corresponds to Christianity's orientation toward the beginning: "The Cross is always beginning, always starting-point of the coordinates of the world. As the Christian chronology begins there, so faith, too, always takes a new starting run from there."[47] Christmas, Easter, and Pentecost comprise the Christian holidays of revelation.

Christmas parallels Passover as the formational event that founds a new people, with the birth of Christ corresponding to the birth of the Jewish

---

43. Ibid.

44. Ibid., 374. The following chart, found in Mosès, *System and Revelation*, 251, is a helpful visual representation of the Christian liturgical year:

| Creation | Sunday | Audience | Sacred architecture (space) | Sacrament of the Word |
|---|---|---|---|---|
| Creation Revelation: Revelation Redemption | Christmas Easter Pentecost | Meal | Sacred music (time) | Eucharist |
| Redemption | Lay festivals | Motion | Processions Popular plays (gestuality) | Baptism |

45. Rosenzweig, *The Star of Redemption*, 380.

46. Ibid.

47. Ibid.

people in the exodus. As the central holiday of the holidays of revelation, Easter holds Christianity's foundational moment always before the eyes of the Christian: "Christianity considers only Golgotha and the empty tomb, and not primarily the stable in Bethlehem, to be the beginning of its way."[48] Just as for the Jew the gift of the Torah at Sinai (and not the exodus from Egypt) remains that which presently constitutes the Jewish people, the cross is for the Christian the ever-present reminder of his present orientation and vocation. Though Pentecost remains within the holidays of revelation, it already anticipates redemption, for it indicates "the point where the way of Christianity turns from the narrow path of the Lord and His disciples into the wide highway of the Church."[49] Pentecost represents humanity's acceptance of its vocation to evangelize the nations, for here "the Church, with its command of all tongues, begins its action in the world."[50]

With regard to redemption, Rosenzweig claims that Christianity has no holiday that parallels Judaism's Days of Awe. He notes that Christmas, unlike Easter and Pentecost, does not correspond to any holiday in the Jewish calendar. While Rosenzweig traces analogues between Christmas' meaning and the Jewish holidays of redemption (namely Succot and Yom Kippur[51]), these similarities notwithstanding, Christianity lacks a distinct holiday of redemption. This is because Christianity blurs the distinction, seen so clearly in Judaism, between revelation and redemption.[52] For Christianity, Christ's incarnation, crucifixion, and resurrection already signal the arrival of redemption, such that anticipation of the future kingdom is overshadowed by the heralding of Christ's already

---

48. Ibid., 387.

49. Ibid., 388.

50. Ibid.

51. In the same way that Succot celebrates "the tent that granted rest to the eternal people during its wandering through the desert," the stable which housed the manger of the Christ child—remembered each Christmas—symbolizes the future redemption that will embrace humanity and the world. Rosenzweig also notes the resonance between Christmas and Yom Kippur in that both serve to draw in those who have otherwise strayed from religion, symbolizing Judaism's capacity for self-preservation and Christianity's capacity for outward expansion. See ibid., 389.

52. "As with us in the idea of Creation and Revelation there is an impulse to be consumed in the ideas of Redemption, for the sake of which alone, after all, everything that preceded it took place, so in Christianity the idea of Redemption is engulfed back into Creation, into Revelation" (ibid., 390).

achieved victory.[53] Rosenzweig also notes that as "part of the mission to the pagans which it presses forward," Christianity participates in secular holidays, thus sowing redemption by "casting its transfiguring light upon the branches of national life."[54]

Rosenzweig's exposition of the Christian liturgical year includes a discussion of three Christian sacraments: the word, Eucharist, and baptism. The sermon, which is heard in common each week on Sunday (the Christian holiday of creation), "takes the individual by the hand and guides him on the way that leads to mutual participation."[55] The Eucharist, which occupies a central role in Christian worship and represents the Christian's participation in the life, death, and resurrection of Christ, corresponds to revelation. Finally, the sacrament of baptism holds redemptive significance, even though (in Rosenzweig's exposition) it takes place at the beginning of one's life. This further highlights "the fundamental opposition between Christian eternity as a perpetual return to the origin and Jewish eternity as a constant tensing toward the future."[56]

The Christian experiences the ecclesiastical year, but world history surrounds him as well, and he "lives at the intersection of two orders, he is always at the crossroads."[57] While Rosenzweig describes the Jewish year as a circle, the Christian year represents a spiral, ever approaching the redemption that Judaism, through its liturgical life, already experiences. Christianity does not resolve this tension between "eternity and time, Church and the world,"[58] but rather lives in the crux of these two worlds "that seem otherwise reciprocally to cancel each other."[59] In Mosès' words, "this crossroad is at the same time the Road of the Cross."[60]

---

53. In fact, it is before the manger of Christ (and the Mass which celebrates Christ's sacrifice) that the Christian kneels, whereas for the Jew kneeling is reserved only for the day that most clearly points forward toward redemption and the world to come.

54. Rosenzweig, The Star of Redemption, 391.

55. Ibid., 379. This is most evident in Protestantism, which elevates the sermon as the chief sacrament.

56. Mosès, System and Revelation, 259.

57. Ibid.

58. Rosenzweig, The Star of Redemption, 398.

59. Ibid., 399.

60. Mosès, System and Revelation, 259.

*The Star or Eternal Truth*

In this last book of *The Star of Redemption*, Rosenzweig expounds the truth that transcends Judaism and Christianity but is manifested by both in their respective existences and vocations. It is here that he explains the way in which Judaism and Christianity serve as necessary counterweights for one another, each preventing the other from falling into the dangers that perpetually tempt it. God, who is truth, is only fully made known in the *eschaton* when the deep division of Judaism and Christianity is finally and ultimately reconciled. Only God sees the whole and experiences the *telos* toward which each is heading.

Whereas we know God as the one who directly acts upon the world through creation and directly acts on humanity through revelation, God's participation in redemption is different. God experiences redemption rather than directly effecting it: "Redemption is [God's] day of rest, his great Sabbath, to which the Sabbath of Creation only points beforehand."[61] Following God's initiatory action toward the world in creation and toward humanity in revelation, redemption is made manifest via the direct interaction between humanity and the world. According to Rosenzweig, the primary actor in the work of redemption is humanity.

Even as God makes himself known in revelation, humanity "verifies" that revelation by carrying out its intended vocation. Judaism and Christianity each verify truth in their own way. The Jew is born into his vocation and can no more escape it than he can escape his very self. His identity is "as an inner home that he may as little get rid of as the snail its house, or to use a better metaphor: a magic circle from which he can as little escape as can his blood from circulation, just because, like and with this latter, he carries it everywhere he may ever walk or stand."[62] His rebirth comes in the form of his recognizing the corporate nature of his vocation; that he does not respond alone, but as a part of his people.

For the Christian it is otherwise. "*Christianus fit, non nascitur.*"[63] The Christian's awakening to vocation happens individually, at the moment when their pagan nature receives the orientation of revelation. For the

---

61. Rosenzweig, *The Star of Redemption*, 406.

62. Ibid., 418.

63. Ibid., 419. Translation: "A Christian is made, not born."

Christian this rebirth comes as a surprise and a radical reorientation, whereas for the Jew it comes as an awakening to that which he already is. The Christian's identity is not intrinsic to his being as is the Jew's: "That which is naturally Christian has being outside of him in worldly and ecclesiastical institutions; he does not carry it around within him."[64] Whereas the foundation of Christian identity lies in Christ, the Jewish people itself constitutes the foundation of its existence.

This fundamental contrast between Judaism and Christianity corresponds to their respective vocational trajectories. Just as rebirth for the Christian leads him away from his former self, "Christian life leads the Christian into the outside. The rays shine continually until all that is outside is filled with the rays."[65] For the Jew, however, rebirth is a leading back into one's identity upon their first birth (and into an entire story into which that birth occurred), and thus "Jewish life becomes remembrance and deepening and filling with a glow that which is innermost."[66] Once again, these separate paths will endure until the *eschaton* wherein alone truth will be united.

As Christianity goes about its task of converting the pagans away from "the old gods, the old world, the old Adam,"[67] it is always susceptible to three related dangers. The first is succumbing to a "deification of the Spirit, or rather … a spiritualization of God, which would, on account of the Spirit, forget God himself."[68] As Mosès explains, this danger involves the "temptation of flight into pure contemplation," which empties the idea of God of its "concrete richness."[69] Christianity's second danger pertains specifically to man and is characterized by "a deification of man and a humanization of God."[70] In its rightful attempt to bridge the divisions by which the pagans are separated, Christianity is always in danger of unrightfully bridging the gap that separates man from God. The third danger facing Christianity, which specifically pertains to the world, is "deification of the world or

---

64. Ibid.
65. Ibid., 420.
66. Ibid.
67. Ibid., 421.
68. Ibid., 422.
69. Mosès, *System and Revelation*, 274.
70. Rosenzweig, *The Star of Redemption*, 423.

secularization of God, which, on account of the all in all would forget the One above all."[71] Christianity is tempted to rely upon its own strength—rather than God's providence—to unify God's kingdom and usher in redemption.

The Jewish people, as the "glowing embers" whose inwardness characterizes their vocation, are likewise susceptible to three dangers. While Judaism understands God as both "our" God and the king of the world, the first Jewish temptation is to magnify God's intimacy with the Jewish people to the necessary and complete exclusion of the rest of the world and its peoples: "Paganism, which was embraced by the ways of Christianity that radiate outwards and radiate back into a unity, is left behind here, entirely outside. ... Jewish feeling has put Creation and Revelation entirely into the most intimate space between God and His people."[72] The Jewish people's second danger entails forgetting that the ultimate redemption upon which they wait applies to all humanity; they instead act as though it exists for them alone. Judaism's third danger similarly entails the Jewish people's inwardness causing them to forsake the rest of the world. For the Jew, the law, which creates order in this worldly life, serves to bridge this world and the world to come. The Jew's immersion in the law leads to a willful ignorance and indifference regarding the pagan world that has embraced Christianity, and hence a forgetfulness that the law is not the universal human track to the world to come. Judaism "collects into one the entire world ... which grows toward Redemption, and squeezes it into the cozy domestic space between the Law and its, the Law's, people."[73]

The dangers of Judaism and Christianity stem from their separate but corollary tasks and foundations.

> Christianity, by radiating outwards, is in danger of evaporating into isolated rays far away from the divine core of truth. Judaism, by growing inwards, is in danger of gathering its heat into its own bosom far distant from the pagan world reality. If there the dangers

---

71. Ibid., 424.

72. Ibid., 426.

73. Ibid., 429. It is significant to note that in Rosenzweig's description of the Jewish dangers, he draws a correlation between God-world-man and God-Israel-Torah. As described in the introduction to this study, the latter triad is the basis of all Jewish theology.

were spiritualization of God, humanization of God, making God into the world, then here it was denial of the world, disdain for the world, mortification of the world ... All three of these dangers are the necessary consequences of the inwardness turned away from the world, as those dangers of Christianity are the consequences of self-renunciation turned toward the world.[74]

Here Rosenzweig reflects on the most profound difference between the Jewish man and the Christian man. The Christian always begins as a pagan, and thus must renounce his former self in order to become a Christian; the Jew, on the other hand, is born Jewish and thus must live ever deeper into himself in order to be a Jew.

Rosenzweig concludes *The Star of Redemption* with a short section entitled "Gate," where he explains that, while redemption will not be completely ushered in until the gods of paganism are fully exposed and deposed, it has already taken root in Judaism and Christianity. The transtemporal life of the Jewish people manifests redemption, such that "Revelation is actually already Redemption."[75] Likewise, the birth of the "second Adam," to whom redemption belongs from the very beginning, reveals that "Creation is really already Redemption."[76] When the seeds of redemption that have been planted in our midst grow into their fullness, truth will finally be unveiled and all creation will recognize the universal orientation upon which it is grounded.

Having reviewed the contours of Rosenzweig's theology, focusing especially on his construal of the relationship between and the respective vocations of Judaism and Christianity, we may now assess his thought with regard to Marshall's question. What can Rosenzweig contribute to an affirmation of both the universal, ecclesially mediated saving mission of Christ and the ongoing election of the Jewish people, lived out and expressed through the practice of Judaism? Let us address each part of Marshall's question in turn.

---

74. Ibid., 429–30.
75. Ibid., 442.
76. Ibid.

## CHRISTOLOGY AND ECCLESIOLOGY
## IN ROSENZWEIG'S THEOLOGY

As we saw above, Rosenzweig's description of redemption encompasses all of reality. Redemption is the completion of the system, the full interaction and interpenetration of God, world, and man, such that God becomes "all in all."[77] Redemption is a future, eschatological reality that is proleptically breaking forth into the present via Judaism and Christianity. Since the existence and life of the Jewish people already manifests redemption in time, Judaism's vocation is to preserve itself as a means of bearing witness to the world. By contrast, Christianity's vocation is to carry redemption (which for Christianity is embodied in Christ, the "new Adam"[78]) to the ends of the earth. In Rosenzweig's words, the Christian "does not rest until the image of the Crucified One cloaks the whole world."[79]

Rosenzweig asserts that the redemption made manifest through Judaism and Christianity includes and holds significance for all people, whether they are aware of it or not. Just as for Barth, the "recipients and bearers of the Christian message ... dare to make the statement, that God is the One who is with them as God, amongst men who do not yet know this,"[80] so too for Rosenzweig the "rising star of Redemption, ... whether one believes in it or does not, is in any case meant as a fact."[81] In Rosenzweig's theology, the Christian's task is to give to the world the firm orientation of revelation.[82] For both Barth and Rosenzweig, the Christian commission is conceived of as awakening the world to a reality that applies to each and every person, including (and especially) those who are as of yet unaware of their participation in God's coming kingdom. Thus Rosenzweig, like Barth,

---

77. Ibid., 434.

78. Ibid., 442.

79. Ibid., 368.

80. Karl Barth, *Church Dogmatics* IV/1, 4.

81. Rosenzweig, *The Star of Redemption*, 444–45.

82. In Rosenzweig's words, "After revelation there is an actual, no longer relativized Up and Down in nature—'heaven' and 'earth' ... and an actually fixed Earlier and Later in time. Thus: in 'natural' space and in natural time the middle is always the point where I simply *am*; in the revealed space-time world the middle is an immovably fixed point, which I do not displace if I change or move myself: the earth is the middle of the world, and world history lies before and after Christ" (Franz Rosenzweig, " *'Urzelle'* to the *Star of Redemption*," in *Philosophical and Theological Writings*, 50).

safeguards the universal scope of redemption and casts Christianity as the agent of redemption's outward spiral.

Rosenzweig's thought thus corresponds to Marshall's requirement that redemption be "universal" and "ecclesially mediated." However, Rosenzweig never explicitly equates redemption with "Christ's saving mission." While Christianity's vocation figures prominently in his theological system, Rosenzweig nowhere puts forth a well-developed Christology. It is clear that Christianity is founded on Christ, though it is only by loose implication that Christianity's mission is issued by Christ and patterned after Christ's own mission.

Rosenzweig's lack of explicit Christology is explained at least in part by the phenomenological approach he takes to both Judaism and Christianity. As Mosès explains, "The fact that, in the third book of the *Star*, Judaism and Christianity are described from the outside, through the forms of their social lives, and not from the inside through the specific structures of their religious consciousness (their theology, their dogma, their sacred texts), bears witness to Rosenzweig's drive for systematic understanding. Judaism and Christianity are described here less as two particular religions than as two categories of being. As such, they have roots deep into the logical foundations of the system."[83] Rosenzweig is less interested in the precise doctrinal formulations that inform orthodox Judaism and Christianity and more interested in how these two religious entities function with regard to moving God, world, and man toward final redemption.

In this way, Rosenzweig is a quintessentially Jewish thinker. His emphasis on orthopraxy far outweighs his discussion of orthodoxy. As we will see, this feature of his theology offers a rich contribution to addressing Marshall's concern regarding the significance of faithful Jewish life. Not surprisingly, the type of christological clarity and fullness offered by Barth (and sought by Marshall) is difficult to find in Rosenzweig's thought. Rosenzweig's Christology plays an instrumental role in the overarching redemptive vocation of Christianity. There is a connection between Christology and Christianity's task, but comprehending Rosenzweig's system does not depend on its apprehension. Rosenzweig's christological statements are scattered throughout his theological system, and they must

---

83. Mosès, *System and Revelation*, 220–21.

be teased out and parsed if we desire to explore Christ's identity and mission according to Rosenzweig. Their ad hoc character notwithstanding, as we will see, it is rather remarkable that Rosenzweig—a Jewish theologian—offers such rich and textured christological formulations. As we work to uncover Rosenzweig's Christology, we will focus on three points in particular: the connection between Christology and Christianity's redemptive vocation, the Jewishness of Jesus, and the juxtaposition between Christ and the Jewish people.

## CHRISTOLOGY AND CHRISTIANITY'S REDEMPTIVE VOCATION

Rosenzweig's first implicit reference to Christ comes in his description of revelation as that which tears God, world, and man out of their isolation. The God that Rosenzweig describes in part 1, book 1 is the "mythical" god, who is disconnected from man and world. According to Rosenzweig, since the time of "the great philosophers" of antiquity, humans have been striving to bridge this gap by elevating "man and world into the sphere of the divine."[84] According to this attempted deification, love and yearning never lead downward from God to man and the world, but always lead upward from man and the world to God. According to Rosenzweig, this attempt to bridge the human and the divine has the effect of diminishing God, for it merely paints God in man's image. The god to whom man reaches in the heavens that man storms cannot be but a distorted and anemic god. A bridge from below can at best result in a god who loves in response to man. According to Rosenzweig, "It may be that man loves [God]; but his love, God's love for man, could be at most an answer to the love of man, the just reward then, and not the free gift which extends its blessings beyond all norms of justice, not the original divine power that makes choices without constraints, or even anticipates all human love and makes the blind see and the deaf hear."[85]

But if God only loves in response to man's attempt to reach God, how can this divine love ever be universally lavished upon all? God's love could only ever be granted to the "perfect one," and never to the "hardened one." This merit-based construct restricts the love of God, which also must reach

---

84. Rosenzweig, *The Star of Redemption*, 47.
85. Ibid.

those who "murmur against him." For Rosenzweig, "it is precisely these lost ones, these hardened ones, those uncommunicative ones, that is to say the sinners, whom the love of God had to seek, a God not merely worthy of being loved, but who himself loves, independently of the love of men; no, it is just the reverse: a God who is the very One who awakens the love of man."[86] In order for this initiatory divine love to become real, "the infinite God would have to become so finitely near to man, so face to face, a named person to a named person, that no reason of the rational ones, no wisdom of the wise ones could ever admit."[87] However, it would likewise require that "the abyss between the human-worldly and the divine ... be recognized and acknowledged so deeply, so really, and as ... impossible to leap across by all the ascetic powers of man and all the mystical powers of the world."[88] In other words, the love of God must be bestowed upon all of humanity regardless of merit and in such a way that God's sovereignty is upheld, as well as the distinction between God and human beings.

This passage is merely one of the many in which Rosenzweig subtly weaves in biblical references (in this case, specifically New Testament references), alluding to concepts but never explicitly naming them. That Rosenzweig describes orthodox Christology in this depiction of divine love could easily be missed. Rosenzweig's indirect reference to the dual nature of Christ, who exists as both fully human (having condescended to humanity) and fully divine (never blurring the distinction between God and humanity) is no doubt intentional. It is noteworthy that this is the description of divine love that Rosenzweig offers before he ever actually describes revelation proper, which he will not do for another 120 pages. Does this passage in part 1, book 1 of the *Star* cast a christological shadow over all that follows? We cannot answer this question definitely; it must hang in the air merely as a question. It is, however, significant that Rosenzweig's entire construal of redemption in part 3 of the *Star* is divided among three descriptive headings—"Life," "Way," and "Truth"—which

---

86. Ibid. Compare with Luke 19:10 ("for the Son of Man came to seek and to save the lost") and Jesus' words in Matthew 9:13b ("for I have not come to call the righteous, but sinners").

87. Rosenzweig, *The Star of Redemption*, 47. Compare with 1 Corinthians 1:18-19: "For the message of the cross is foolishness to those who are perishing, but to us who are being saved it is the power of God. For it is written: 'I will destroy the wisdom of the wise; the intelligence of the intelligent I will frustrate.'" In verse 19, Paul is quoting Isaiah 29:14.

88. Rosenzweig, *The Star of Redemption*, 48.

correspond to Judaism, Christianity, and Truth (which transcends both). This is yet another unmistakable christological allusion.[89]

Likewise, Rosenzweig's entire explication of revelation as God's love and command to do likewise bears much more resemblance to a Christian framework than a Jewish framework.[90] The tight correspondence between love of God and love of neighbor strongly resembles Jesus' proclamation of the "greatest commandment" in the Synoptic Gospels.[91] While Jesus quotes the Torah in his response to his questioner, the Jewish tradition has not consistently paired these two loves in the way that has become fundamental for Christian theology. Similarly, as we saw above, Rosenzweig concludes his book on revelation with the phrase "as he loves you, so shall you love."[92] While William Hallo finds here an allusion to the Babylonian Talmud, Shabbat 133b ("Become like him; as he is generous and merciful, be thou generous and merciful"),[93] it is equally likely that this is an allusion to Jesus' words in John 15:12 ("My command is this: Love each other as I have loved you").[94]

Just as Jesus models both divine and human love in John's gospel, Rosenzweig's implicit Christology consistently incorporates the theme of

---

89. See Jesus' words in John 14:6: "I am the way and the truth and the life. No one comes to the Father except through me."

90. As David Novak explains, "For Rosenzweig, the direction of the human creature in response to God's love is not facing back to God but, rather, facing out into the world to claim it for God. The human coming out of his or her seclusion with God is the act of *imitatio Dei* that replicates God's coming out of his own seclusion" (Novak, *The Election of Israel*, 98; see Rosenzweig, *The Star of Redemption*, 222–23).

91. See Matthew 22:34–40, Mark 12:28–34, and Luke 10:25–28. Matthew's version reads: "Hearing that Jesus had silenced the Sadducees, the Pharisees got together. One of them, an expert in the law, tested him with this question: 'Teacher, which is the greatest commandment in the Law?' Jesus replied: ' "Love the Lord your God with all your heart and with all your soul and with all your mind" [Deut 6:5]. This is the first and greatest commandment. And the second is like it: "Love your neighbor as yourself" [Lev 19:18]. All the Law and the Prophets hang on these two commandments.' "

92. Rosenzweig, *The Star of Redemption*, 220.

93. William W. Hallo's translation of *The Star of Redemption* includes an "Index of Jewish Sources," in which this citation is listed. See Franz Rosenzweig, *The Star of Redemption*, trans. William W. Hallo (Boston: Beacon Press, 1972), 429.

94. The complete unity between Jesus and the Father emphasized in John 14–15 provides the backdrop for Jesus' love command. As one commentator explains, "A unity of love bonds the Sender and the Sent One. ... Inasmuch as the Father loves Jesus, Jesus commands his disciples to become part of that oneness by abiding in his love" (Francis J. Moloney, *The Gospel of John* [Collegeville, MN: Liturgical Press, 1998], 421).

Christ's dual nature. When Rosenzweig describes the nature of the ekklesia (part 3, book 2), he describes Christ as paradoxically the Lord of the church, but also a member. This description occurs in the context of Rosenzweig's discussion of the "brotherliness" that characterizes the Christian community, in which Christ bridges (rather than erases) the differences that exist among Christians. The unity of the Christian community is founded on Christ, who "is both beginning and end of the way, and consequently content and goal, founder and Lord of the covenant, as well center of the way and hence everywhere present where two are together in his name."[95] While it is Christ's transcendence that guarantees his presence among his followers, his imminence gives that presence intimacy and immediacy; Christ himself is a "brother of his covenant."[96] Again, Rosenzweig does not explain but rather presumes the Christian theological concepts he is clearly employing.

Christian brotherhood is enabled by Christianity's creation of a simultaneity in time that joins together people all over the world by bridging the distance between them. While, as we saw above, Christianity is not transtemporal (as Judaism is), the Christ-event effects Christianity's mastery over worldly time. Having wielded the flow of time, Christianity enables the Christian to love his enemy as his neighbor. This description of Christianity's love of neighbor offers an entrée into the way in which Rosenzweig's Christology grounds his understanding of Christian life and mission. Again, Rosenzweig offers a classically Jewish flourish on Christian discipleship, distinguishing it by a set of practices rather than a set of beliefs. According to Rosenzweig, "To be a Christian does not mean: to have accepted any dogmas; but to live one's life under the rule of another life, the life of Christ and, once this has happened, then to live one's own life solely in the effect of the power flowing from there."[97] To be a Christian means to live in yielded discipleship to Christ, rather than merely to cognitively assent to a set of propositional truths.

---

95. Rosenzweig, *The Star of Redemption*, 365. Compare with Matthew 18:19–20: "Again, truly I tell you that if two of you on earth agree about anything they ask for, it will be done for them by my Father in heaven. For where two or three gather in my name, there am I with them."

96. Rosenzweig, *The Star of Redemption*, 365.

97. Ibid., 295.

This does not imply that Rosenzweig disregards doctrine or dismisses its significance. Rather, for Rosenzweig, doctrine is the servant of discipleship.[98] According to Rosenzweig, the life of Christ is "the dogma of Christianity" and the "only content" of Christian doctrine.[99] The connection between christological doctrine and the Christian life can be seen through Rosenzweig's explication of baptism. According to Rosenzweig, six of the seven traditional Catholic sacraments correspond to redemption,[100] in that they "seek out man in decisive hours and relationships of his natural, moral, social path through life."[101] However, baptism subsumes the five remaining redemptive sacraments into itself; baptism, for Rosenzweig, is the redemptive sacrament. Through baptism, the course for the Christian's life and vocation is established. Accordingly, Christianity spreads by "the pouring out of the Spirit in the uninterrupted stream of baptismal water from one to the other," further establishing the "mutual participation of bearing witness."[102]

It is in baptism that the Christian takes upon himself the redemptive task of Christianity's proliferation, which is connected to a confession of Christ. Christian doctrine thus stems from baptism, which continually produces new Christians. In each and every baptism, "the adoration of the divine child is renewed."[103] According to Rosenzweig, "this is the only way by which that placing of oneself under the life of Christ nevertheless for all that exacts to some degree dogmatic conclusions: the presupposition that that life is unique in the world and its effects can proceed only from him and hence, apart from unimportant, conscious certainties of individuals, only from him in their unconscious vitality in a unique, continuous river."[104]

Correlatively, the Christian's identity is grounded in Christ, not in himself. "That which is naturally Christian has being outside of him in worldly

---

98. This aspect of Rosenzweig's thought mirrors the tight connection Barth draws between gospel and law (i.e., between election and ethics).

99. Rosenzweig, *The Star of Redemption*, 295.

100. As we saw above, the exception is the Eucharist, which is the sole sacrament of revelation.

101. Rosenzweig, *The Star of Redemption*, 397.

102. Ibid., 362.

103. Ibid., 397.

104. Ibid., 295.

and ecclesiastical institutions; he does not carry it around within him."[105]
The Christian finds this lasting identity in Christ, such that becoming a
Christian entails a complete rebirth: "The Christian man, innately, or at
least on account of birth—is a pagan ... So the way of the Christian must
be a way of self-renunciation, he must always go away from himself, give
himself up in order to become Christian."[106] That one must turn outward
in order to become a Christian points us again to the Christian vocation,
which is likewise outward-facing. The correlation between Christian
identity and Christian vocation grounds in part the connection between
Christianity's task and the person and mission of Christ. We will recall
that the phrasing of Marshall's question inherently links these two concepts. While Marshall assumes that the church's universal scope is part
and parcel of Christ's saving mission, for Rosenzweig, this connection is
at best implied.

As we have seen thus far, Rosenzweig's theology makes loosely-thread
associations at precisely the point where Barth's theology was most force-
fully cohesive. Barth's robust Christology grounds his understanding of the
church's mission, whereas for Rosenzweig, Christianity's vocation functions almost independently from any sort of explicit Christology. While
Rosenzweig does make christological assertions, they do not necessarily
and consistently undergird his ecclesiology. Here Rosenzweig's theology
stands in stark contrast to that of Barth, for whom Christology necessarily informs every other theological locus, including ecclesiology. It is
extraordinary, nonetheless, how skillfully and thoroughly Rosenzweig
weaves orthodox Christology into the entirety of his theological system.
This degree of christological reflection is a radical novelty in the world
of Jewish thought, and it is no doubt among the factors that has claimed
Rosenzweig as a pioneer in the new Jewish-Christian encounter.

THE JEWISHNESS OF JESUS IN ROSENZWEIG'S CHRISTOLOGY

This marked christological contrast between Barth and Rosenzweig notwithstanding, if we approach the Christology question from another angle,
we discover a surprising congruity between these two thinkers. Like Barth,

---

105. Ibid., 419.
106. Ibid., 430.

Rosenzweig has a severely underdeveloped notion of the Jewishness of Jesus. Functionally, within the respective theological frameworks of Barth and Rosenzweig, this underdevelopment operates in opposite ways. Whereas Barth's formal construal of Israel and the church arguably stems from his lack of attention to Jesus' Jewishness (among other things), the formalism of Rosenzweig's system quite likely informs his relative neglect of this topic. That Rosenzweig never expounds Jesus' self-proclaimed identity as the Jewish Messiah coheres well with Rosenzweig's construal of Judaism and Christianity as two separate religious entities. Because Rosenzweig does not allow for overlap between the two, the link Jesus forms between Israel and the church is not a connection Rosenzweig is apt to make.

While at numerous points throughout the *Star* Rosenzweig hints at Jesus' Jewishness (and Christ's connection to the Jewish people), he never fully fleshes out this connection. A few examples will suffice to illustrate this point. First, Rosenzweig sets up a number of connections between the Christ event and Judaism as he explains the Christian holidays of revelation with reference to Judaism's equivalent holidays. Note the strong parallelism in the following passage:

> The three holiday periods into which for the Christian, too, Revelation enters into the ecclesiastical year, begin with Christmastime, which, placed at the beginning of the liturgical year, is, like the Jewish holiday of freedom, a holiday of the beginning. This beginning, this Creation of Revelation, must here be the fleshly birth, as in the case of the people it must be the becoming-free. The becoming-free of the "firstborn son of God" to form a people and the becoming-flesh of the "only begotten one" to become a man correspond exactly as the people and the single person, world and man, can correspond.[107]

The connection that Rosenzweig draws between the birth of Christ and the birth of the Jewish people, each event playing a mirror role in the Christian and Jewish calendars, is striking. He elaborates on this connection by describing the way in which the reading of the gospel at Christmas parallels the reading of the Haggadah[108] at Passover. Furthermore, Rosenzweig

---

107. Ibid., 385–86.
108. The Haggadah is the liturgical book used during the traditional Passover meal.

draws a parallel between Christ's circumcision (the celebration of which takes place within the traditional twelve days of Christmas) and the covenant of circumcision in Genesis 17, a central event in the formation of the Jewish people. In his words, "The New Year holiday is the holiday of the Circumcision of the Child, with which, according to Jewish interpretation, the membership to the people, which rests immediately and ultimately on the mystery of the birth, [is] publicly announced in the first observance of a commandment."[109]

While Rosenzweig employs these rich connections between Christmas and Passover (and Christ's circumcision and the Genesis 17 covenant of circumcision) to illustrate the parallelism of Judaism and Christianity, he leaves untouched the most fundamental connection that undergirds them all: the Jewishness of Jesus. It is not by chance that the events of Jesus' life parallel the events of the Jewish year (and consistently model obedience to the commandments), though Rosenzweig does not explore this underlying wellspring.

The same parallelism is at work in Rosenzweig's description of Easter and Shavuot (as the central holidays of revelation), where the cross of Christ closely corresponds to the Torah at Sinai. In Rosenzweig's words,

> Just as, for us, too, above all the miracle of Sinai, the gift of the Torah, and not even the Exodus from Egypt, signifies the Revelation which accompanies us constantly as present; we must first of all remember the Exodus, and it is to be as embodied as if we ourselves had been there; but we do not need to remember the Torah; it is present. So for the Christian it is not the manger, but the Cross that is always present; he holds the latter and not the former before his eyes; as is said by us of the Torah, so could be said by him of the Cross, it must be "in his heart so that his steps do not slip."[110]

---

109. Rosenzweig, *The Star of Redemption*, 386. In Christian liturgical history, January 1 (the "Octave of Christmas") has alternatively commemorated either the Circumcision of Christ (based upon Luke 2:21) or the Anniversary/Solemnity of Mary, the Mother of God. See Adolf Adam, *The Liturgical Year* (New York: Pueblo Publishing Company, 1981), 139–42; L. W. Cowie and John Selwyn Gummer, *The Christian Calendar* (Springfield, MA: G & C Merriam, 1974), 31.

110. Rosenzweig, *The Star of Redemption*, 387.

Again, the connection between Christ and the Torah is remarkably tight. Rosenzweig alludes to Psalm 37:31 ("The law of their God is in their hearts; their feet do not slip") with regard to the Torah for Jews and the cross of Christ for Christians. Just as observing the Torah embodies obedience for the Jewish people, accepting the cross embodies obedience for Jesus and his followers.[111]

However, once again, Rosenzweig leaves the parallel elements at a distance from one another. He does not follow the connection to its christological conclusion; in the words of John 1:14, "The Word became flesh and made his dwelling among us." Torah and Christ need not be viewed as separate but parallel, as Rosenzweig suggests. Rather, they have become one and the same. Jesus is the living Torah; to obey him is to obey Torah. This is a key connection for Barth (as we saw in chapter 1), as well as the post-Holocaust theologians we will assess in chapter 3. Finally, it is of inestimable significance for Messianic Jewish theologian Mark Kinzer (see chapter 4).

A second place where we see Rosenzweig drawing a similar parallel between Christ and the Jewish people, though once again not quite bringing the connection full circle, is in a passage describing suffering. At the end of Rosenzweig's description of Christianity (part 3, book 2), there is a section entitled "The Configuring of Suffering." Here Rosenzweig reflects on the unitive power of suffering for Christians, who, unlike Jews, do not start out as a people. In Rosenzweig's words, "The lonely soul of pagan stock, for which the ultimate unity of the We does not circulate in the blood, only discovers this unity facing the Cross of Golgotha. Only under this Cross does the soul know itself to be one with all souls."[112] For this reason, "the way of the Christian is in every moment the Way of the Cross."[113]

Already in the *Star*, Rosenzweig has alluded to Isaiah 53, that classic prophetic passage about vicarious suffering that Jews most often apply to the

---

111. See Jesus' submission in Gethsemane ("Not as I will, but as you will" [Matthew 26:39, Mark 14:36]) and Jesus' command to his disciples in Luke 14:27 ("Whoever does not carry their cross and follow me cannot be my disciple").

112. Rosenzweig, *The Star of Redemption*, 400.

113. Ibid., 399.

Jewish people and Christians most often apply to Christ.[114] In Rosenzweig's discussion of Judaism (part 3, book 1), he applies Isaiah 53 to the Jewish people: "Israel intercedes before [God] for the sins of the peoples, and it is smitten with sickness so that they find healing."[115] In "The Configuring of Suffering," Rosenzweig again alludes to Isaiah 53, here offering a subtle critique of the traditional Christian interpretation of the passage and the suffering servant it describes. This discussion is couched within a comparison between Christian time and Jewish time, wherein Rosenzweig explains that the cyclical nature of the Christian year points toward the "closed circle" of the Jewish year, which participates already in eternity. In Rosenzweig's words, "This great circle of Redemption closes in the year of the eternal people. On it, that always unknown bearer of that prophecy to the peoples which they had to believe was already fulfilled in the vicarious suffering of the individual for individuals, they live to see the enclosed eternity toward which they themselves helplessly extend."[116]

The vicarious suffering of the "individual for individuals" no doubt refers to Christ's suffering—the traditional Christian interpretation of Isaiah 53. The "always unknown bearer of that prophecy" refers to the Jewish people, whom Christians do not recognize as the referents of the suffering servant of Isaiah 53. However, according to Rosenzweig, the Jewish year and its participation in eternity bears testimony to the Jewish people's role as vicarious sufferer. As we saw in Rosenzweig's explication of Jewish holidays, Yom Kippur is the only day on which redemption is actually present in time, and Christianity does not have a parallel holiday of redemption. Yom Kippur is the one day on which the Jew appears before God "in his naked individuality,"[117] outside the context of the collective Jewish community. As the Jew kneels alone before God, without the merit of

---

114. Isaiah 53:4–5 reads: "Surely he took up our pain and bore our suffering, yet we considered him punished by God, stricken by him, and afflicted. But he was pierced for our transgressions, he was crushed for our iniquities; the punishment that brought us peace was on him, and by his wounds we are healed."

115. Rosenzweig, *The Star of Redemption*, 326. With reference to Rosenzweig's theology, Marc Krell explains that "Israel's election by God is predicated on its tenacious suffering not only for its own sake but also for the sins of the world" (Marc A. Krell, *Intersecting Pathways: Modern Jewish Theologians in Conversation with Christianity* [Oxford: Oxford University Press, 2003], 38).

116. Rosenzweig, *The Star of Redemption*, 401.

117. Ibid., 344.

his membership in the community to recommend him, he represents man in general and his sins resonate with the sins of all humanity. The communality that characterizes Jewish existence is eclipsed on this day, and the Jew here expresses his ultimate eschatological unity with the non-Jew. Rosenzweig's earlier interpretation of Isaiah 53 as applying to the Jewish people suffering on behalf of the nations is likely at play in his description of Yom Kippur as well.[118]

This interpretation is reinforced by the very next subsection (with which Rosenzweig concludes this book), wherein Rosenzweig quotes a famous passage by the medieval Jewish philosopher Judah Halevi. In this passage, the effectual death and resurrection of the Jewish people is poetically described as a seed that falls to the ground, seemingly disappears, and yet miraculously gives birth to new life.[119] It is striking that Rosenzweig concludes his discussion of Christianity in the *Star* with this powerful description of the Jewish people.[120]

---

118. The autobiographical undertones of Rosenzweig's treatment of Yom Kippur are noteworthy. In Rosenzweig's thought, Yom Kippur marks the day that both fundamentally links Judaism and Christianity and highlights their deepest distinction. In Rosenzweig's life, Yom Kippur was the day on which he both had his closest brush with Christianity and his final re-conversion to Judaism. For more on this aspect of Rosenzweig's biography, see The Election of Rosenzweig's Theology below.

119. The passage reads as follows: "God has his secret plan for us, a plan that is like his plan for a seed-kernel that falls into the earth and seemingly changes into earth, water and manure, and nothing remains of it by which an eye might recognize it; and it is yet, on the contrary, precisely it that changes earth and water into its own essence and gradually decomposes their elements and transforms and assimilates them to its own matter, and so it forces forth bark and leaves; and when its inner core is made ready, so that the developing likeness of its former seed may enter into a new corporeality, then the tree brings forth the fruit like the one out of which its seed once came: in this way the instruction of Moses attracts each who comes later, truly transforming him in accordance with himself, although seemingly each rejects it. And those peoples are preparation and being made ready for the Messiah, for whom we are waiting, who will then be the fruit, and all will become his fruit and confess him, and the tree will be one. Then they praise and they venerate the root that they once despised, of which Isaiah speaks" (Rosenzweig, *The Star of Redemption*, 401–2; see Judah Halevi, *Book of Kuzari*, trans. Hartwig Hirschfeld [Whitefish, MT: Kessinger Publishing, 2003], 200).

120. It is also noteworthy that Rosenzweig *opens* the chapter on Christianity with a quote from the great medieval Jewish philosopher Maimonides, who argued that Christianity's mission advances Judaism's vocation and goal. Maimonides quotes Zephaniah 3:9 ("Then I will purify the lips of the peoples, that all of them may call on the name of the LORD and serve him shoulder to shoulder") to demonstrate that Jesus of Nazareth served to "prepare the whole world to worship God with one accord" (quoted in Isadore Twersky, ed., *A Maimonides Reader* [Springfield, NJ: Behrman House, 1972], 226). Rosenzweig's treatment of Christianity is thus bracketed by the thought of two of Judaism's greatest philosophical voices.

However, though Rosenzweig points toward an interpretation of Isaiah 53 in which the suffering servant is both Christ and the Jewish people, Rosenzweig does not expound it. Once again, he leaves it hanging, as if merely to suggest a connection that he does not clearly draw. Nor does Rosenzweig make explicit that Halevi's image is precisely the image Jesus uses in John 12 to describe the efficacy of his own death: "Unless a kernel of wheat falls to the ground and dies, it remains only a single seed. But if it dies, it produces many seeds" (John 12:24). As we will see in the following two chapters, post-Holocaust theology and Messianic Jewish theology have built significantly on this dual interpretation of Isaiah 53, whereby Christ and the Jewish people suffer vicariously. The bridge that is used to connect these twin interpretations is, not surprisingly, the Jewishness of Jesus.

## CHRIST AND THE JEWISH PEOPLE

While in the examples just examined, Rosenzweig points toward analogues between Jesus and the Jewish people, in other places, Rosenzweig seems to directly juxtapose the two, creating a mutually exclusive framework that mirrors his portrayal of Judaism and Christianity. As Rosenzweig describes "The Jewish Man" in part 3, book 1, he builds upon his immediately preceding discussion of "Particularity and Universality." Rosenzweig explains the way in which the Jew, who looks around "with surprise when the world seeks to remind him that not everyone experiences the same feeling of being immediately a child of God,"[121] forgets that God "says as well to Egypt and Assyria: 'my people.' "[122] The Jewish people, wrapped in their unique intimacy with God, tend to ignore the fact that God is also the redeemer of the entire world. Within the context of this discussion, Rosenzweig offers the following contrast between the Jewish people (i.e., those who experience a distinct nearness to God) and the Jewish Messiah (i.e., the one through whom universal redemption spreads to all peoples):

> Opposite Israel, the eternally beloved of God, the eternally faithful one and eternally complete one, there stands the one who eternally comes, eternally waits, eternally wanders, eternally thrives, the Messiah. Opposite the man of the beginning, Adam the son of man,

---

121. Rosenzweig, *The Star of Redemption*, 326.
122. Ibid.

there stands the man of the end, the son of David the King; opposite
him who was created out of the stuff of the earth and the breath
of the divine mouth stands the offshoot from the anointed royal
line; opposite the patriarch stands the last offspring; opposite the
first man who is wrapped in the cloak of divine love, there stands
the Last Man, from whom salvation goes to the ends of the earth;
opposite the first miracles there stand the last ones, of which it is
said they would be greater than those first ones.[123]

Several things are striking about this passage. First, while Rosenzweig
is describing the long-awaited Jewish Messiah, he uses quintessentially
New Testament imagery to do so. The phrase "Last Man" (and the contrast
to Adam) has strong Pauline correlates (see especially Rom 5:12–21), and the
reference to "greater miracles" clearly resonates with John 14:12 ("Whoever
believes in me will do the works I have been doing, and they will do even
greater things than these"). Rosenzweig's messianic portrait is overlaid
with telltale christological hues. Second, the Jewish Messiah in this passage poses a stark contrast to the Jewish people as a whole. His vocation
and disposition cut against the inherent (and prescribed) inwardness and
insularity of the Jewish people. While the idea of the Messiah bringing salvation to the ends of the earth derives from Old Testament prophetic texts
(see, for example, Isa 49:6), this concept becomes a central christological
motif in the New Testament (see, for example, Acts 13:47). So Rosenzweig
describes the Jewish Messiah using characteristically christological language, and he paints the Messiah's vocation in contradistinction to the life
of the Jewish people. Finally, according to Rosenzweig's description, the
Jewish Messiah and Christianity both remind the Jewish people that their
unique intimacy with God is not to the ultimate exclusion of the rest of
the world.[124]

This juxtaposition between Christ and the Jewish people is reinforced by Rosenzweig's description of the respective identities of the Jew
and the Christian, as well as his explanation of the two proleptic loci of

---

123. Ibid.

124. On this point, see Rosenzweig's description of Judaism's "dangers" (Rosenzweig, *The Star of Redemption*, 429–30), The Star or Eternal Truth, above.

redemption. As we saw above, with regard to Jewish and Christian identity, the Jew's identity is anchored in himself (and his people), while the Christian's identity is anchored in Christ.[125] This distinction is played out in Judaism's inward-facing vocation and Christianity's outward-facing vocation. While the Christian's vocation is to awaken the world to the orientation of revelation and draw all peoples into the unifying power of Christ's suffering on the cross, the Jewish vocation is carried out without regard to Christ or the nations of the world. Thus, Christ and the Jewish people are once again set up along mutually exclusive lines. There is no overlap and no convergence this side of the *eschaton*. As we have already seen, the future reality of redemption is already breaking into the present in two places: the life of the Jewish people and the person of Christ.[126] While final redemption will only be accomplished when these seeds of redemption fully blossom through the twin vocations of Judaism and Christianity, the dual loci of redemption's proleptic presence again reinforces the juxtaposition between Christ and the Jewish people.

Finally, according to Rosenzweig, there is an aspect of orthodox Christology that betrays a certain underlying paganism. Rosenzweig makes this explicit in his discussion of the opposition between Father and Son within the Christian God. As Rosenzweig explains,

> Only by means of the Son does the Christian dare to approach the Father: only through the Son does he believe he can come to the Father. If the Son were not man, he would be useless to the Christian. He cannot imagine that God himself, the holy God, could condescend to him in such a way as he wishes to unless he would himself become man. The innermost indestructible piece of paganism in every Christian breaks through here. The pagan wants to be surrounded by human gods, it is not enough for him that he is himself man: God too must be man.[127]

---

125. Ibid., 418–19.
126. Ibid., 442.
127. Ibid., 371.

For Rosenzweig, Christianity's latent paganism enhances its ability to carry out its redemptive vocation, for "precisely that 'paganism' of the Christian qualifies him for the conversion of the pagans."[128]

Judaism serves as a check on pagan Christology, lest Christianity unhitch itself from Judaism and spiral out of its redemptive orbit. In the following passage, Rosenzweig describes the way in which Judaism keeps Christology intact: "The historical Jesus must always take back from the ideal Christ the pedestal under his feet upon which his philosophical or nationalistic worshippers would like to set him, for an 'idea' unites in the end with every wisdom and every self-conceit and confers upon them their own halo. But the historical Christ, precisely Jesus the Christ in the sense of the dogma, does not stand on a pedestal; he really walks in the marketplace of life and compels life to keep still under his gaze."[129] In other words, it is Judaism's influence on Christianity that safeguards against a docetic Christology. However, even as Judaism reminds Christianity of Jesus' humanness, it apparently fails to emphasize that Jesus existed not just as any man, but as a Jewish man. Once again, this would have been an ideal place for Rosenzweig to make this connection, yet he leaves it untouched. Jesus is once more portrayed in contrast to, rather than as part of, the Jewish people.

## A WORD ON JEWISH "DUAL-COVENANT" THEOLOGY

As we have seen, for Rosenzweig, the universal reach of Christianity's vocation has one distinct and significant exception: the Jewish people. As Rosenzweig explains in a letter to Rudolf Ehrenberg: "We are wholly agreed as to what Christ and his church mean to the world: no one can reach the Father save through him. No one can reach the Father! But the situation is quite different for one who does not have to reach the Father because he is already with him. And this is true of the people of Israel."[130] Rosenzweig's Christology often juxtaposes Jesus to the Jewish people, for whom he ends up being entirely irrelevant. The Jewish people's identity

---

128. Ibid.

129. Ibid., 437.

130. Quoted in Nahum Glatzer, *Franz Rosenzweig: His Life and Thought* (Indianapolis: Hackett, 1998), 341.

in no way hinges on the person of Christ, just as Judaism's vocation does not hinge on Christianity's.

This aspect of Rosenzweig's thought has led some to categorize him as a "dual-covenant" theologian.[131] As we seek to mine Rosenzweig's theology for resources with regard to Marshall's question, we must address this feature of Rosenzweig's thought. We will recall that, according to Marshall, some Christian thinkers attempt to resolve the tension highlighted in Marshall's question by asserting that "the Jews, or at least some of them, are not really called to life in the Church, or at least not in the same way, or to the same life, that the gentiles are."[132] This dual-covenant stance upholds the ongoing election of the Jewish people and the ongoing practice of Judaism, but denies the universal scope of Christ's salvific mission, at least to the extent that that mission involves universal participation and involvement in the Christian church. According to Marshall, a Christian affirmation of this position involves forsaking Christianity's "most central, identity-forming convictions."[133]

We must bear in mind that the inadequacies Marshall notes about a dual-covenant position are aimed at Christian dual-covenant proponents. These critiques cannot be applied in a one-to-one manner to Jewish thinkers who put forth a similar model. As Marshall points out, a Christian dual-covenant stance undermines orthodox Christology and thus effectually undercuts the Christian faith. Essentially, such an affirmation relativizes Christianity's core tenets.

However, a Jewish affirmation of a dual-covenant model merits an entirely different assessment. For a Jew to endorse Christianity as a fundamental constitutive element of redemption is to in effect relativize Judaism, not Christianity. Especially in light of the hostility that has repeatedly characterized the history between Judaism and Christianity, such a stance is

---

131. See, for example, Gregory Kaplan, "In the End Shall Christians Become Jews and Jews, Christians? On Franz Rosenzweig's Apocalyptic Eschatology," *Cross Currents* 54, no. 4 (Winter 2004): 511–29; Maurice G. Bowler, "Rosenzweig on Judaism and Christianity: The Two Covenant Theory," *Judaism* 22, no. 4 (Fall 1973): 475–81; Emil Fackenheim, *To Mend the World: Foundations of Post-Holocaust Jewish Thought* (Bloomington: Indiana University Press, 1994), 58–90.

132. Bruce Marshall, "Elder Brothers: John Paul II's Teaching on the Jewish People as a Question to the Church," in *John Paul II and the Jewish People: A Jewish-Christian Dialogue*, ed. David G. Dalin and Matthew Levering (Lanham, MD: Rowman & Littlefield, 2008), 123.

133. Bruce Marshall, *Trinity and Truth*, 177.

rather remarkable. As Samuel Sandmel explains, "Though in the Middle Ages an occasional eminent Jewish voice, a Judah Ha-Levi or a Joseph Albo, conceded that certain values existed in Christian practice and thought, by and large the usual attitudes of the two religions to each other were dominated by a sense of grievances."[134] In describing the nature of the Jewish grievances against Christianity, Sandmel poses the following string of rhetorical questions:

> Why should Christians have wanted [Jews] to concede as true that which they did not believe was true? How could Christians have the temerity to asperse the divine Laws of Moses, and to proceed to regard them as abrogated? How could Christians regard Jesus as divine in light of his crucifixion, and at the same time blame Jews, mere men, for the death of a divine being? How could Christians so extend the blame for the death of Jesus that Jews, born centuries later and thousands of miles away, and despite obvious innocence, still were held responsible and guilty? How could a religious system that accused Jews of hypocrisy itself escape that charge when, pretending to kindliness, it limited Jews economically and politically, herded them into ghettoes, and compelled them to wear badges to identify them as unworthy outsiders? How could Christians apotheosize a "prince of peace," in the light of the countless wars of Christendom? What boast could Christians properly make of the alleged superiority of Christianity in view of the demonstrable failure of Christian civilization to live, at least in its relations with Jews, on even a minimum standard of religious principles?[135]

As evidenced by the issues raised in these questions, negative Jewish views of Christianity were based upon a long history of persecution and rivalry. Even in the midst of the twentieth-century resurgence of Jewish-Christian amity, a Jewish endorsement of Christianity and Christian truth claims poses considerable challenges. For example, David Novak, a strong proponent of Jewish-Christian dialogue, does not allow that both Judaism and Christianity can be equally valid and legitimate ways of understanding

---

134. Samuel Sandmel, *We Jews and Jesus* (New York: Oxford University Press, 1973), 6.
135. Ibid., 7–8.

God and participating in redemption. In his words, "The highest form of worship of the Lord God of Israel is either by the Torah and the tradition of the Jewish people or by Christ and the tradition of the Church."[136] Similarly, Orthodox Jewish scholar Meir Soloveichik is wary of a Jewish stance toward Christianity that casually dismisses Jesus' claims to divinity. In an article entitled "No Friend in Jesus," Soloveichik writes the following about Jesus: "If we deny his divinity, then we can respond with nothing short of shock and dismay when we read the words of a man who puts himself in the place of God."[137]

In light of the history between Judaism and Christianity and the consequent widespread Jewish suspicion and negativity toward Christianity, Rosenzweig's thought stands in even sharper relief. Rosenzweig does not denounce Jesus' identity claims or attempt to prove that Judaism is a more true or authentic religious tradition than Christianity. On the contrary, for Rosenzweig, redemption requires the existence of both Judaism and Christianity. To make this claim is to significantly elevate Christianity and the importance of the Christian vocation. While Rosenzweig's theology may be labeled dual covenant because his Christology has no bearing upon the Jewish people, the critique Marshall issues to a Christian dual-covenant approach is scarcely applicable to a Jewish dual-covenant approach. Our assessment of Rosenzweig cannot disregard this distinction. While a Christian dual-covenant position results from a diminished Christology, a Jewish dual-covenant position presents a remarkably high Christology and appraisal of Christianity. Rosenzweig's thought manifests these characteristics par excellence.

Having analyzed Rosenzweig's Christology and portrayal of Christianity's vocation, let us now move on to an assessment of Rosenzweig's theology with regard to the permanent election of the Jewish people and the ongoing practice of Judaism. We will then be in a position to evaluate Rosenzweig's contributions to answering Marshall's question.

---

136. David Novak, "What to Seek and What to Avoid in Jewish-Christian Dialogue," in *Christianity in Jewish Terms*, ed. Tikva Frymer-Kensky et al. (Boulder, CO: Westview, 2000), 5.

137. Meir Soloveichik, "No Friend in Jesus," *First Things* 179 (January 2008), 31.

## THE ELECTION OF ISRAEL
## IN ROSENZWEIG'S THEOLOGY

The contours of Rosenzweig's biography undergird his strong insistence on Jewish election and the necessity of that election being lived out through Torah observance. Rosenzweig, who early on in his life became "a proud heir of the nineteenth century,"[138] identifying himself with the optimism, progress, and faith in reason that pervaded German culture at the time, came to believe that capitulating to Jewish emancipation and Enlightenment culture demanded that one go all the way and become baptized.[139]

However, as it turned out, what he had intended as a journey through Judaism to Christianity turned out to be a life-long journey deeper into Judaism. The Yom Kippur services in 1913 led Rosenzweig to commit himself to Judaism, and he wrote in a letter to Rudolf Ehrenberg on October 31 that conversion to Christianity was no longer necessary, and in fact no longer possible.[140] According to Nahum Glatzer, "Rosenzweig left the [Yom Kippur] services a changed person. What he had thought he could find in the church only—faith that gives one an orientation in the world—he found that day in the synagogue."[141] At this point Rosenzweig decided to immerse himself in Judaism and its sources, though his new dedication to and passion for Judaism did not lead him to leave behind his notion of the importance and profundity of the Christian faith.[142]

---

138. Glatzer, *Franz Rosenzweig*, xi.

139. In a letter to his parents on November 6, 1909, Rosenzweig wrote: "We are Christians in every respect. We live in a Christian state, attend Christian schools, read Christian books, in short, our whole civilization is fundamentally Christian" (Franz Rosenzweig, *Briefe* [Berlin: Schocken Verlag, 1935], 72, quoted in Eugen Rosenstock-Huessy, ed., *Judaism Despite Christianity* [New York: Schocken, 1969], 28).

140. Rosenzweig, *Briefe*, 71, quoted in Rosenstock-Huessy, ed., *Judaism Despite Christianity*, 37.

141. Glatzer, *Franz Rosenzweig*, xviii.

142. In Alexander Altmann's words, "The interesting feature about Rosenzweig's final position, which he reached in October [1913], is the new insight into the compatibility of Judaism and Christianity 'within the same realm.' What he had worked out for himself with regard to the function of the church militant in the history of the world remained true and valid. But, whereas he had previously failed to see any purpose in the life of the synagogue, because of her broken staff and the bandages before her eyes, he now perceived the meaning of the synagogue as well. He recognized that her stern refutation of the pagan world and her uncompromising attitude constituted the only safeguard for the completion of the work of revelation and of the church herself. ... In Israel's seclusion from the world, in its priestly way

Rosenzweig completed *The Star of Redemption* in 1919 and spent the rest of his life perpetuating the vision of Judaism put forth in the *Star*. In the summer of 1920, Rosenzweig turned down the offer of a university lectureship and instead became the head of the *Freies Jüdisches Lehrhaus*, a Jewish adult educational center. His later writings, including his translation of and commentaries on the poems and hymns of Judah Halevi (and notably not Halevi's more technical and apologetic *Kuzari*) and his Bible translation project with Martin Buber reflect Rosenzweig's ongoing dedication to increasing the religious literacy of the Jewish everyman. His commitment to Jewish learning and his passion for the rich rhythms of Jewish life embodied the inwardness in which he declared that Judaism discovers what it truly is. Rosenzweig's theology of the Jewish people and Jewish practice both informed and were informed by his own experiences and convictions.

## ROSENZWEIG'S DOCTRINE OF THE JEWISH PEOPLE (ISRAEL)

In his book *The Election of Israel: The Idea of a Chosen People*, David Novak seeks to retrieve the classic doctrine of the election of Israel, which has been corroded by modern philosophy. In this regard, Novak hails Rosenzweig as "the turning point, the pivotal figure, in modern Jewish thought." In Novak's assessment, "Rosenzweig's insistence on the truth of the original doctrine of the direct election of Israel by God is his greatest significance for contemporary Jewish thought."[143] As we saw above, Rosenzweig's doctrine of election is part and parcel of his doctrine of revelation. For Rosenzweig, revelation is the divinely initiated event that provides human beings with their definitive spatial and temporal orientation vis-à-vis God and humanity.[144] While God's love constitutes God's self-revelation, and this event awakens and anchors humanity, how does this connect to the specific election of Israel? According to Novak, "the connection between revelation to individuals and revelation to a plural community is an especially difficult problem both for Rosenzweig and for his colleague and best

---

of life, it expresses the essence of revelation in an absolute form, unalloyed by any element of paganism" (Alexander Altmann, "Franz Rosenzweig and Eugen Rosenstock-Huessy: An Introduction to Their 'Letters on Judaism & Christianity," in *Judaism Despite Christianity*, ed. Rosenstock-Huessy, 37–38).

143. Novak, *Election of Israel*, 79.

144. See footnote 82 in this chapter.

theological interlocutor, Martin Buber."[145] How does Rosenzweig make the connection between revelation and the election of Israel?

To answer this question, Novak points us to the following passage from the *Star*: "All human relationships, absolutely all, blood relationship, brotherhood, nation, marriage, all are established in Creation; there is nothing that does not exist from all eternity through these roots and which is not already prefigured in the animal kingdom, and yet all receive their own soul only in Redemption, owing to the rebirth of the soul in Revelation. All are rooted in the blood community, which among them is that which is closest in Creation."[146] According to Novak, Rosenzweig "sees the human object of God's electing revelation as already the one who is a social being through creation. As such, this human object is not a lone individual."[147] Because, for Rosenzweig, the Jewish people are the only "blood community,"[148] according to Novak's assessment, "revelation and the Jews are in essence inseparable."[149]

While individuals can be awakened to revelation, it is only the Jewish people who collectively experience revelation as a community. As we saw above, for Rosenzweig, redemption is brought about through Christianity's missionary vocation and Judaism's self-preservation. These respective vocations stem from the distinct communal realities of Judaism and Christianity. For Rosenzweig, the Jewish people alone constitute a "blood community"; Christianity, by contrast, is a "spiritual community."[150] One of the most obvious differences between these two types of communities is their means of self-perpetuation. While spiritual communities "must make arrangements in order to pass the torch of the present on to the future, only the community of the same blood does not have need of making such

145. Novak, *Election of Israel*, 85.

146. Rosenzweig, *The Star of Redemption*, 258–59; see Novak, *Election of Israel*, 87.

147. Novak, *Election of Israel*, 87.

148. Rosenzweig, *The Star of Redemption*, 317. It is worth noting that Rosenzweig's description of the Jewish people as a "blood community" aligns well with Marshall's stipulation that the election of Israel refer to the "*biological* descendants of Abraham, Isaac and Jacob" (see Bruce D. Marshall, "Christ and the Cultures: The Jewish People and Christian Theology," in *The Cambridge Companion to Christian Doctrine*, ed. Colin E. Gunton [Cambridge: Cambridge Uuniversity Press, 1997], 82. Italics added). Marshall relies on the thought of Michael Wyschogrod, who, as we will see in the next chapter, drinks deeply from Rosenzweig's well.

149. Novak, *Election of Israel*, 88.

150. Rosenzweig, *The Star of Redemption*, 362; Mosès, *System and Revelation*, 176–77.

arrangements for the tradition; it does not need to trouble its mind; in the natural propagation of the body it has the guarantee of its eternity."[151] In other words, as we saw above, Judaism's continuation takes the form of begetting new generations.

While Judaism must preserve revelation in its purest form, it is Christianity's task to carry revelation to the ends of the earth. As Novak explains, "Without Judaism Christianity is in danger of being diluted into the paganism of the unredeemed world; without Christianity Judaism is in danger of being marginalized as the religion of an exotic tribe."[152] Because the Jewish people already experience redemption in their collective life, and because their presence is continually necessary to preserve the purity of that revelation which Christianity takes to all peoples, the eternal election of the Jewish people is an integral assumption that undergirds Rosenzweig's entire theological system. The Jewish people's embodiment of eternity in time points the rest of the world toward the future eschatological reality that characterizes redemption.

In Novak's final assessment, however, Rosenzweig's doctrine of the election of the Jewish people is ultimately inadequate. For Novak, the classic doctrine requires that Israel's election not be in any sense instrumental; it cannot be pointed at any other end than election itself.[153] According to Novak, Rosenzweig's portrayal of redemption construes "the election of Israel as the means to a higher end, which is the election of humanity itself."[154] While the election of the Jewish people is an essential component of redemption's realization, redemption—and not the election of the Jewish people—is seen as the goal. For Novak, this will not suffice: "In Rosenzweig's view, election is teleologically derivative, whereas in the classical view it is nonderivative."[155]

However, for our purposes, we must view Rosenzweig's doctrine of the election of Israel otherwise. Because Marshall seeks to uphold both the particularity of Israel's election and the universality of Christ's saving mission, Novak's desiderata would not satisfy Marshall. From the perspective

---

151. Rosenzweig, *The Star of Redemption*, 318.
152. Novak, *Election of Israel*, 100.
153. See ibid., 78.
154. Ibid., 103.
155. Ibid.

of Marshall's question, it is precisely Rosenzweig's ability to keep both of these perspectives in view that is so appealing.

While Novak declares Rosenzweig's "phenomenology of revelation as election"[156] to be his greatest contribution, from the perspective of Marshall's framework, Rosenzweig's novelty is in his ability to maintain the necessity of Israel's election precisely for the realization of universal redemption.

It is here that Rosenzweig's theology also offers its strongest critique of and complement to Karl Barth. As we saw in the last chapter, Barth's construal of Israel's witness is entirely negative. In his words, Israel, "the people of the Jews which resists its divine election," exhibits "the unwillingness, incapacity and unworthiness of man with respect to the love of God" and the "justice of the divine judgment on man borne by God Himself."[157] While Israel's negative witness does not nullify its election, there is no room for Israel's collective life to contribute positively to God's ongoing redemptive purposes in the world. For Rosenzweig, final redemption is ultimately dependent upon the faithful life and self-preservation of the Jewish people, whose very existence continually reminds the world of its provisionality and incompleteness. Judaism essentially relativizes history, and the Jewish people's existence in eternity points the world toward the final redemption that will only be ushered in eschatologically. For Rosenzweig, Judaism's vocation requires its faithful practice of Jewish life, and it is to this that we now turn.

### ROSENZWEIG'S DOCTRINE OF JUDAISM (TORAH)

As we will recall, Marshall's description of Israel's election requires that Israel be distinct from all other peoples, and that the means of that distinction is Torah observance. As we said above, the election of the Jewish people is irreducibly constitutive of redemption in Rosenzweig's system. For Rosenzweig, how does Torah observance figure into Israel's election?

Rosenzweig's opening words of part 3, book 1 ("The Fire or Eternal Life") are "praised be he who has planted eternal life in our midst."[158] These

---

156. Ibid., 101.

157. Barth, *Church Dogmatics* II/2, 198.

158. Rosenzweig, *The Star of Redemption*, 317.

words are taken from the Torah service in Jewish liturgy, specifically the blessing that is recited after the Torah reading. The full blessing reads: "Blessed are You, Lord our God, King of the Universe, who has given us the Torah of truth, planting everlasting life in our midst. Blessed are You, Lord, Giver of the Torah."[159] In the blessing, the precise context of God's having "planted eternal life in our midst" is God's giving of the Torah at Sinai. No Jewish reader would miss Rosenzweig's allusion. In Rosenzweig's thought, the very existence of the Jewish people is inseparable from the gift of the Torah. Election and law are indivisible.

For Rosenzweig, in giving the law God reveals Judaism's path to redemption. The Jewish people's obedience to the law is the outward sign of their inward election; it activates and confirms their redemptive vocation. "We must keep in mind," Rosenzweig writes, "the obvious fact that a Law, that the Law as a whole, is the prerequisite for being chosen, the law whereby divine election is turned into human electing, and the passive state of a people being chosen and set apart is changed into the activity on the people's side of doing the deed which sets it apart."[160] Election's *telos*, therefore, is a pattern of living, not merely the status of having been chosen by God. For Rosenzweig, election is ineffectual if it is not reciprocated through deeds. While redemption depends upon the existence of the Jewish people, that people does not fulfill its redemptive vocation if it does not live out its election through obedience to the commandments.[161]

For Rosenzweig, Jewish life is what gives the Jewish people their anchor in eternity. It is important to note that Rosenzweig's definition of eternity is not an escape from time, or a timeless reality, but rather the "eternal present." According to Mosès, "for Rosenzweig eternity is not a time

---

159. *The Koren Siddur*, trans. Jonathan Sacks (Jerusalem: Koren, 2009), 162.

160. Franz Rosenzweig, *On Jewish Learning*, ed. Nahum Glatzer (Madison: University of Wisconsin Press, 1955), 119.

161. According to Novak, Rosenzweig positions himself between liberal Judaism, which places undue emphasis on Israel apart from Torah, and traditional Judaism, which unduly privileges law over election. In Novak's words, Rosenzweig's "opposition to liberal Jewish thought can be seen in his rejection of its tendency to derive the reality of the Jewish covenant with God from philosophical theology; and his opposition to Orthodox Jewish thought can be seen in his rejection of its tendency to derive the reality of the Jewish covenant with God from law. The true election-revelation-commandment includes each and transcends both. It must be directly experienced as a whole before it can be abstractly analyzed in its parts" (Novak, *Election of Israel*, 94).

indefinitely stretched out forward but rather a total immobilization of the present instant, a state of perfect equilibrium absolutely outside the flow of time."[162] Redemption, for Rosenzweig, is thus the "projection of eternity into time."[163] The Jewish people already live into redemption by preserving Jewish life from one generation to the next. Rosenzweig explains the relationship between Torah observance and time as follows:

> Since teaching of the Holy Law—for the appellation Torah comprises the two, teaching and law in one—therefore lifts the people out of all temporality and historical relevance of life, it also removes its power over time. The Jewish people does not calculate the years of its own chronology. Neither the memory of its history nor the official times of its lawgivers can become its measure of time; for historical memory is a fixed point in the past that becomes more past every year by one year, but a memory always equally near, really not at all past, but eternally present.[164]

Because each Jew in every generation is to "regard the Exodus out of Egypt as if he himself had also gone out,"[165] Jews for all time experience equally the birth of the Jewish people. According to Rosenzweig, "the people's chronology thus cannot be here the calculation of its own time; for it is valid at all times, it is without time."[166] The perpetuation of Jewish life is the scaffolding for the eternity that characterizes Jewish existence.

One of the primary images Rosenzweig uses to convey this concept is the oft-repeated allusion to the "river of time." Here again the contrast between Judaism's vocation and Christianity's vocation is brought into sharp relief. According to Rosenzweig, God withheld the Jew from the life of "men and peoples ... by arching the bridge of his Law heavenwards over the river of time under whose arch it now rushes powerlessly into all eternity."[167] In other words, the law is the means by which the Jewish people live in eternity instead of in time, which is the sphere of all other peoples'

---

162. Mosès, *System and Revelation*, 170.

163. Ibid., 171.

164. Rosenzweig, *The Star of Redemption*, 323.

165. Ibid.

166. Ibid.

167. Ibid., 359.

lives. As we have already seen, Christianity's vocation is not to transcend time but to sacralize it. Hence Rosenzweig's designation of Christianity as "the Way"—it is always between origin and destination.[168]

For Rosenzweig, the Jewish people's obedience to Torah is most clearly illustrated through the Jewish calendar. Consistent with what we have already said about the Jewish people's relationship to time, the holidays and liturgy in Judaism do not merely commemorate past events, but more importantly point forward toward the redemptive reality that the Jewish people uniquely manifest. For Rosenzweig, Yom Kippur is the one day each year on which eternity really does break into history, and the end that is otherwise only anticipated takes place in the present. As Mosès explains:

> The experience carried by the Day of Atonement is fundamentally different from all those characterizing the other moments of sacred time in Judaism. Contrary to the anticipation of utopia, which only ever represents a metaphorical experience of Redemption, the Day of Atonement embodies the immediate experience of an ideal world at the core of reality itself. ... In the course of the festival of Atonement, during the whole of one day, time is suspended. The community of faithfuls lives out, in each one of its members, a spiritual experience located outside historical time.[169]

On Yom Kippur, the Jew embodies most vividly the call to live into eternity.

Just as the Torah is the means by which the Jewish people live into redemption, it likewise characterizes the Jewish people's embodiment of the love that characterizes revelation. As Rosenzweig explains, "God's commandments, at least those of the 'second Table,' which specify the love of the neighbor, have this form without exception: 'Thou shalt not.' They are capable of wearing the clothing of the law only as prohibitions, only as markers delimiting that which is absolutely inconsistent with love of the neighbor; their positive character, their 'thou shalt,' enters exclusively into the form of the one and general commandment of love."[170] Torah is thus the handmaiden of love; its observance serves a greater goal. The connection

---

168. See note 31 in this chapter for a description of Christianity's reciprocal relationship to the "river of time."

169. Mosès, *System and Revelation*, 200.

170. Rosenzweig, *The Star of Redemption*, 232.

that Rosenzweig draws between obedience to Torah and love of neighbor demystifies the commandments and reveals the way in which faithful
Jewish observance discloses God's love to the world. As these illustrations
show, the election of the Jewish people for Rosenzweig is inseparable from
that people's call to obey Torah. Obedience to the commandments is the
means by which Israel lives into its redemptive vocation. Without the law,
the Jewish people's election is ineffectual and its vocation is unattainable.

## CONCLUSION

Before concluding our assessment of Rosenzweig's thought with regard to
Marshall's question, let us make a few general observations with regard to
Rosenzweig's theological contribution. First, for Rosenzweig, Judaism and
Christianity are cooperative rather than competitive. Departing from history's firmly entrenched adversarial model, Rosenzweig portrays Judaism
and Christianity as equals, not rivals. Rosenzweig's phenomenological
approach helps to deflect battles over truth claims by focusing on the
common God and common *telos* of both Judaism and Christianity. This
posture is one of the touchstones of the new Jewish-Christian encounter
and, as we will see in the following chapter, it has gained increasing traction in the post-Holocaust era. Rosenzweig stands out as perhaps the most
significant exemplar of this new perspective.

Second, Rosenzweig's subtle and integrative portrait of Christ lays a
firm foundation for expositing Jewish concepts in christological terms.
The connections Rosenzweig hints at between central tenets of Judaism
and orthodox Christology open entirely new vistas for theological reflection. Rosenzweig paves the way for considering Christianity in Jewish
terms, which is yet another key feature of the new Jewish-Christian
encounter. While Rosenzweig's Jesus never completely dons a Jewish
identity, Rosenzweig unearths a wellspring of resources for understanding God's incarnation in Christ as a part of Israel's larger narrative. Third,
Rosenzweig pioneers a model wherein a full and textured Jewish life can
coexist simultaneously with a robust Christology. Once again sidestepping
an either/or model, Rosenzweig lays the framework for a Christianity that
does not pose a threat to either the idea or the manifold expressions of
Israel's unique covenant with God.

As we assess Rosenzweig's thought particularly with regard to Marshall's question, we see the way in which Rosenzweig's thought serves as a corrective to Barth's even as it highlights Barth's key strengths. In light of the first part of Marshall's question, what does Rosenzweig contribute to an affirmation of the universal, ecclesially mediated saving mission of Christ? For Rosenzweig, Christianity is the means by which God's revelation ripples outward to all nations. Christianity awakens humanity to its status as God's beloved and its commission to love the world in an act of *imitatio Dei*. While the Jewish people pose an exception to the universal scope of the church's mission, it is only because they already possess this awareness and bear witness to revelation in their collective life. While Rosenzweig's portrayal of Christianity is remarkably high from a Jewish perspective, for Marshall, Christ's disconnectedness from and effectual irrelevance to the Jewish people will not suffice. It is here that Rosenzweig's thought underlines Barth's greatest theological contribution. For Barth, humanity's election in Christ reveals its status as God's covenant partner and informs its call to bear witness to God's gracious being-in-act. As we saw, Barth's christologically grounded anthropology and ecclesiology more than satisfy the first part of Marshall's question.

However, Rosenzweig's doctrine of the Jewish people and Jewish practice provides a rich affirmation of the second part of Marshall's question, which is precisely the area where Barth's thought is left wanting. First, for Rosenzweig, the election of Jewish people is a fundamental constitutive element of redemption. While redemption requires both Judaism and Christianity, the entirety of Christianity's vocation depends on the existence of the Jewish people and the revelation and redemption that people carries in its midst. That Christianity's being and mission is anchored within Judaism precludes any sort of theological dismissal or minimization of the election of Israel. Second, Rosenzweig construes Torah as the means by which the Jewish people live out revelation and live into redemption. Torah observance is the actualization of the Jewish people's election; it is Israel's means of loving neighbor and thus perpetuating the love of God. For Rosenzweig, Israel and Torah are inseparable, and the redemptive life of the Jewish people points the world toward its eschatological *telos*.

As we have seen, where Barth's theology leaves the most to be desired (namely, in his assessment of the people of Israel and the practice of

Judaism), Rosenzweig offers a wealth of theological resources. Conversely, while Barth offers a robust affirmation of the universal, ecclesially mediated saving mission of Christ, Rosenzweig's Christology lacks sufficient clarity and universality. Even as Rosenzweig complements Barth's lack, Rosenzweig's lacunae occur precisely where Barth is strongest.

In light of their respective contributions, is it clear that both of these thinkers pioneered new models for understanding the relationship between Judaism and Christianity, and their thoughts represent the burgeoning of an emerging intellectual tradition. The rest of the theologians we will engage in this study stand upon the shoulders of these remarkable theological progenitors, whose work embodies the new Jewish-Christian encounter in its nascent form. Barth and Rosenzweig serve as the theological springboards for the significant developments that have taken place in the post-Holocaust world, and it is these developments that will occupy us in the remaining two chapters of this study.

# 3
—

# "TORAH SHALL GO FORTH FROM ZION": RECONCEIVING CHRISTOLOGY AND ECCLESIOLOGY IN LIGHT OF ISRAEL

## INTRODUCTION

The past two chapters have described and assessed the ways in which Karl Barth and Franz Rosenzweig laid the groundwork for a new era of Jewish-Christian relations. These two pioneers opened new avenues for understanding the relationship between Israel and the church (Barth) and Judaism and Christianity (Rosenzweig) that have been increasingly treaded upon in the post-Holocaust world. In this chapter, we will examine a small constellation of post-Holocaust Jewish and Christian theologians who both build upon and extend the trajectories charted by Barth and Rosenzweig. Each figure addressed here bears a theological resemblance to and has been directly influenced by one or both of our two seminal pioneers. Each theologian is also deeply committed to their religious tradition while resolutely asserting that Judaism and Christianity are only properly understandable with reference to one another. These theologians are among the main theological architects and builders of the new Jewish-Christian encounter.[1]

---

1. As we will recall from the introduction to this study, the new Jewish-Christian encounter is set apart from the broader sweep of twentieth-century, Jewish-Christian dialogue on account of four distinct characteristics: commitment to theological and doctrinal rigor, assessment of the other's tradition in light of one's own, recognition of underlying theological commonality between Judaism and Christianity, and reassessment of one's own tradition in light of the other's. For more detail on these dialogical distinctives, see "The New Jewish-Christian Encounter" in chapter 1.

As we will recall from our initial description, the new Jewish-Christian encounter is not merely a sharing across mutually agreed upon boundaries, but a thoroughgoing reconception of those boundaries and the consequent self-identities of Jews and Christians. This chapter is not intended as a broad overview of twentieth-century Jewish-Christian relations or dialogue. Rather, it is a focused study of a handful of theologians whose innovative work and key influences position them as principal contributors to the new Jewish-Christian encounter. Our lens throughout this chapter will once again be Marshall's framing question,[2] which will guide our assessment of this burgeoning theological tradition and its constituent theologians. Marshall's question captures the novelty of this encounter and calls for a widespread reconfiguration of the theological puzzle pieces, according to which Christianity cannot disregard or overlook the election of Israel and its concomitant implications. The post-Holocaust theologians addressed in this chapter bring us one step closer to answering Marshall's question and pave the way for the theology of Mark Kinzer, a leading Messianic Jewish theologian whose thought will occupy us in the final chapter of this study.

A touchstone of the new Jewish-Christian encounter, already visible in the thoughts of Barth and Rosenzweig, is the recognition of an indelible connection between Israel, Jesus, and the church. Accordingly, this chapter will be structured under the umbrellas of Christology and ecclesiology, particularly the ways in which these two Christian theological loci are being reconceived in light of Israel. In each of these areas, we will explore three key developments. Under the umbrella of Christology, we will look at the renewed emphasis on the Jewishness of Jesus, God's incarnation in the

---

2. We will recall that, according to Marshall, "the discovery that Christians ought to share with Jews a belief in the permanent election of Abraham's children poses a challenge for Christian theology, one which in some respects has not been faced seriously since the second century: how can Christians coherently maintain a commitment both to the permanent election of Israel and to the unsurpassability of Jesus Christ?" (Marshall, "Christ and the Cultures," 91). Because Marshall recognizes the crucial connection between the *election of the Jewish people* and the *practice of Judaism*, a second question follows: How can Christians affirm that "the existence of faithful Jews is not simply an empirical likelihood or a devout hope, let alone an evil God puts up with, but belongs to God's own good and unalterable purposes"? (Marshall, "Elder Brothers," 122). Accordingly, the central question framing this study is: How can Christians affirm both the universal, ecclesially mediated saving mission of Christ *and* the irrevocable election of Israel, which necessarily entails the ongoing practice of Judaism?

Jewish people, and a theology of suffering. Under the umbrella of ecclesiology, we will assess the renunciation of supersessionism, the church as an expansion of God's covenant with Israel, and the reclamation of the doctrine of election. After surveying these key themes and trends, we will evaluate these developments and appraise their contribution to answering Marshall's question.

## CHRISTOLOGY IN LIGHT OF ISRAEL

Christology forms the necessary bridge between the two parts of Marshall's question, and answering Marshall's question requires that Christology be reconceived through the lens of Israel. Christological reformulation along these lines has become a central priority in the post-Holocaust theological world. Christology is increasingly deemed unintelligible to the extent that it is constructed without regard to God's ongoing covenantal relationship with and salvific purposes through the people of Israel. Through a post-Holocaust lens, to extract Christ from his particular context is to avow a spurious Christology.

Among the post-Holocaust thinkers we are treating in this chapter, understanding the person and mission of Christ within the context of God's enduring covenant with Israel is a paramount concern. In the words of Thomas Torrance, Christ must be understood "within the actual matrix of interrelations from which he sprang as Son of David and Son of Mary, that is, in terms of his intimate bond with Israel in its covenant relationship with God throughout history."[3] This claim is increasingly becoming a christological first principle. Accordingly, Christology in the post-Holocaust era has come to place a greater emphasis on the Jewishness of Jesus, and it is here that we will begin.

### THE JEWISHNESS OF JESUS

As we saw in chapter 1, Barth clearly perceived the irreducible centrality of Jesus' Jewishness and expounded the way in which Jesus participated in Israel's life by bearing Israel's burdens and sin. For Barth, the identification between Jesus and Israel was portrayed in purely negative terms: Israel (as

---

3. Thomas F. Torrance, *The Mediation of Christ* (Colorado Springs: Helmers & Howard, 1992), 3.

the epitome of human "fleshliness") represented the basest of all humanity, and Jesus' taking on of Jewish flesh revealed the depth of God's love and concern for humanity. While Barth pointed us toward the significance of Jesus' Jewishness in significant ways, ultimately his thought fell short of capturing the full nuance and richness of this affirmation.

In a corollary though less explicit way, Rosenzweig distilled the subtlety and power of Jesus' Jewishness by casting the Messiah in a thoroughly Jewish light. For Rosenzweig, the Messiah's work is indelibly bound to the Jewish people and both extends and challenges the mission of that people in significant ways. However, Rosenzweig does not explicitly identify Jesus as Israel's Messiah, nor does he directly address the bond between Jesus and the Jewish people. Rosenzweig's messianic construct lays the groundwork for understanding the Jewishness of Jesus, but it does not make the connections that Marshall's question requires.

Barth and Rosenzweig pointed in the direction of a full-fledged affirmation and understanding of Jesus' Jewishness, and the next generation of theologians has built upon the framework they provided. The contributions of these post-Holocaust thinkers enable us to explore anew the significance of Jesus' Jewishness, his embeddedness in the history of God's covenant with Israel, and the ways in which the contours of his life and mission both cohere with and challenge Israel's own mission and self-understanding.

Thomas Torrance, who studied under Barth at the University of Basel and co-edited the English translation of the *Church Dogmatics*, builds upon Barth's contention that Christology must be grounded in a proper understanding of Israel. According to Torrance, to abstract Jesus from his historical context within the covenant people is to hopelessly distort his person and mission. Torrance's entire theological system reflects a deep commitment to holistic modes of thought in which the interrelation of realities is integral to the very constitution of those realities. According to Elmer Colyer, "If we are to really understand realities, Torrance argues, we must investigate them in the nexus of their interconnections, rather than in isolation, for they are what they are by virtue of the relations in which they are embedded."[4] When we apply this principle to Christology,

---

4. Elmer M. Colyer, *How to Read T. F. Torrance: Understanding His Trinitarian and Scientific Theology* (Downers Grove, IL: InterVarsity Press, 2001), 56.

as Torrance does, we must inquire deeply about Jesus' context and environment. Paramount among these concerns is Jesus' relation to Israel.

For Torrance, "apart from Israel, the incarnation of the Word of God in Jesus Christ would have been a bewildering enigma."[5] Torrance therefore issues a call for Christology to be increasingly rethought around Christ's relationship to Israel. In Torrance's words,

> The inextricable interrelation between God's self-revelation in Jesus and his self-revelation through Israel, and thus the permanent authoritative patterns of understanding which God has forged for us in Israel, require to be re-assessed and appreciated by us today in a much deeper way than ever before. We have tried to understand Jesus within the patterns of our own various cultures so that in the West and the East we have steadily gentilised our image of Jesus. We have tended to abstract Jesus from his setting in the context of Israel and its vicarious mission in regard to divine revelation. ... That is to say, we detach patterns of thought from their embodiment in Israel as they presented in the Old Testament Scriptures, or even in the New Testament, and then schematise them to our own culture, a western culture, a black culture, an oriental culture, as the case may be. ... The continued attempt to make Jesus relevant to modern ways of thought has had the effect of obscuring him, for all the time we have been engaged in plastering upon the face of Jesus a mask of different gentile features which prevents us from seeing him and understanding him as he really is, as a Jew—and certainly prevents our brethren the Jews from recognising in this stylised Christ which we equate with "the historical Jesus" the Messiah whom they are still expecting. The time has come for us to enlist the aid of the Jews in helping us to interpret Jesus as he is actually presented to us in the Jewish Scriptures.[6]

In statements such as this, Torrance hedges against unwittingly employing the category of the "hermeneutical Jew,"[7] and notably calls upon the

---

5. Torrance, *Mediation*, 18.

6. Ibid., 19–20.

7. See Jeremy Cohen, *Living Letters of the Law: Ideas of the Jew in Medieval Christianity* (Berkeley: University of California Press, 1999), 2; see The Election of Israel in Barth's Theology in chapter 1.

Jewish people themselves to aid Christians in fully comprehending the Jewishness of Jesus. While Torrance builds on Barth's Christology, he also works toward overcoming Barth's tendency to view Judaism through a purely Christian lens and consequently distort Jesus' relationship to Israel.

For Torrance, Israel serves as the mediator of revelation and reconciliation to all humanity and thereby the locus of the "prehistory" of Christ. In Israel, God reveals himself and crafts a people whose communal life reflects the appropriate response to that divine self-revelation. This process is not without intense and sustained strife, as God continually shapes and molds this people for their mediatory role. Torrance explains the suffering that characterizes Israel's existence along these lines: "To be the bearer of divine revelation is to suffer, and not only to suffer but to be killed and made alive again, and not only to be made alive but to be continually renewed and refashioned under its creative impact. That is the pre-history of the crucifixion and resurrection of Jesus in Israel."[8] In Israel, we see the manifestation and dynamic of divine revelation's encounter with humanity. Due to the "innate resistance of the human soul and mind resulting from the alienation of man from God,"[9] Israel's repeated rebellion against God seems to be inversely proportional to God's favor lavished upon Israel. However, this process merely reveals the inevitable encounter of divine self-revelation with humanity, intensified in Israel on account of God's unprecedented intimacy with this particular people.

It is this conflict between innate human waywardness and the demands of divine revelation that reaches its climax in Jesus: "Throughout his earthly life Jesus embodied this fearful tension, repeating the conflict between God and humanity represented in Israel, grappling with the root of evil in the human heart in enmity toward God, uncovering and decisively overcoming it in life and in atoning sacrifice on the cross."[10] In this way, Jesus' unique bond to Israel is to be understood. Torrance reminds us that "there developed especially in Latin theology from the fifth century a steadily growing rejection of the fact that it was our alienated, fallen, and sinful humanity that the Holy Son of God assumed, and there was taught instead the idea

---

8. Torrance, *Mediation*, 11.

9. Ibid., 10.

10. Colyer, *How to Read*, 67–68. See Torrance, *Mediation*, 29–31.

that it was humanity in its perfect original state that Jesus took."[11] This is a dangerous christological blunder, for such a move detaches Christ's atonement from its prehistory in Israel that serves as the key to proper understanding. In Christ, the conflict between humanity's hostility toward God and God's commitment to humanity reaches its zenith, and God finally overcomes that hostility by making it his own and suffering its consequences: "Thus it is through the weakness of the man on the Cross and on the ground of reconciliation wrought out there that God meets, suffers, and triumphs over the enmity entrenched in human existence and history."[12] While this event begins a new chapter in the relationship between God and humanity, it by no means undoes God's everlasting covenant with Israel. Despite—and on account of—Israel's widespread rejection of Christ, Israel continues to play a mediating role between humanity and God: "If the Jew, caught up in man's conflict with God through the vicarious role God has put on him, could not but react as he did, he was acting in our place and representing our rejection of God's self-giving, so that divine reconciliation might come to us as well and be grounded in the depths of our being."[13] Thus, even in its deepest rejection of God, Israel represents all of humanity, and it is on account of Israel's rejection that God heals the waywardness of all human beings.

Likewise, the suffering that Israel continues to endure is, for Torrance, constitutive of Israel's ongoing work of mediation. Israel participates in the suffering of Christ wherein divine-human reconciliation is accomplished. Here, Torrance assigns separate but complementary roles to Israel and the church (or, in his words, the "Jewish Church" and the "Christian Church") in terms of their respective witnesses to divine reconciliation. While the Christian Church's life stems from the reality of the resurrection, Israel (the "Jewish Church") continues to exist under the shadow of the crucifixion. The Christian Church's perspective is "governed by the triumphant vindication of the Servant in which the emphasis falls upon the concept of atonement as a finished work," while the Jewish Church's perspective is "governed by the baffling role of the Servant in continuing to bear the

---

11. Torrance, *Mediation*, 40.
12. Ibid., 31.
13. Ibid., 35.

disgrace of God's people in which the emphasis falls upon the concept of atonement as divinely prolonged into history."[14] While Christians bear witness to the reconciliation already accomplished by Christ, Israel continues to participate in the ongoing working out of that reconciliation. Thus, Christ (and his atoning work) can only be properly understood in light of his connection to Israel, and the mysterious sufferings of Israel can only properly be understood in light of Israel's deep connection to and participation in Christ.[15] In the conclusion of this chapter, we will assess Torrance's thought in relation to Barth's and in light of Marshall's question.

Jesus' relationship to Israel has become an increasingly popular topic among post-Holocaust Jewish thinkers as well. Jewish theologian Will Herberg, who was deeply influenced by Barth and Rosenzweig and attempted to both follow and critique each of them, portrays the relationship between Jesus and Israel in a manner similar to Torrance.[16] Just as Torrance sees Israel and Jesus as mutually informing hermeneutical keys, Herberg assesses both Israel and Jesus under the common umbrella of covenant, describing the way in which Jesus enables gentiles to participate in Israel's covenantal blessings. For Herberg, covenant is the "central category of biblical thinking."[17] The centrality of covenant implies that there is "no such thing as a direct and unmediated relation to God; this relation must in some way be mediated through one's covenant status."[18]

While individuals can only gain access to God through standing in a covenant, that covenant is distinct for Jews and for gentiles. For Jews, being among the flesh-and-blood people of Israel constitutes one's covenantal status. In Jewish liturgy, prayers are offered on the merits of the patriarchs. For gentiles, who would otherwise not have access to covenant

---

14. Ibid., 37.

15. We will explore this connection further in Theology of Suffering in this chapter.

16. For a detailed biography of Herberg and an explication of the impact of Barth and Rosenzweig upon his thought and work, see Harry J. Ausmus, *Will Herberg: From Right to Right* (Chapel Hill: University of North Carolina Press, 2009).

17. Will Herberg, "Judaism and Christianity: Their Unity and Difference," in *Jewish Perspectives on Christianity*, ed. Fritz A. Rothschild (New York: Crossroad, 1990), 243. Along these lines, Herberg quotes Paul Ramsey: "Never imagine that you have rightly grasped a biblical idea until you have reduced it to a corollary of the idea of 'covenant' " (Paul Ramsey, "Elements of a Biblical Political Theory," *Journal of Religion* 29, no. 4 [1949]: 258).

18. Herberg, "Judaism and Christianity," 246.

relationship with God, Christ provides the means by which they too may enter into covenant standing before God. Christ accomplishes this by functioning as the "one-man Israel," offering the covenant blessings of relationship with God to the nations: "To be a Jew means to meet God and receive his grace in and through Israel; to be a Christian means to meet God and receive his grace in and through Christ."[19] Christ makes God's covenant with Israel accessible to those who are not by birth included in this covenant. Christology, therefore, can only be understood against the backdrop of God's covenant with Israel.

As we will see below,[20] Herberg draws a tight correlation between covenant and commandment, arguing that *halakhah*[21] is the means by which the Jew "affirms, maintains, and ever renews his belonging to Israel, the People of God."[22] However, Herberg does not discuss whether Jesus himself lived a *halakhic* life, and he thus leaves unexplored the implications of this important inquiry. Nonetheless, Herberg sees Jesus' existence within the people of Israel as central to his life and mission. It is only by virtue of Jesus' membership in the people of Israel that he is able to extend the mechanism of covenant relationship with God to the gentiles. Christ as the "one-man Israel" presupposes that the incarnation is the climax of a process that was already underway within the people of Israel; rethinking God's incarnation in Christ in light of Israel leads to a reconception of the very idea of incarnation, and it is to this idea that we now turn.

### GOD'S INCARNATION IN THE JEWISH PEOPLE

As we saw in the previous two chapters, the incarnation of God in Christ is a mainstay of Barth's theology, whereas incarnational theology is essentially absent from Rosenzweig's implicit Christology. Here, Barth and Rosenzweig are representative of their respective traditions; the incarnation is a weight-bearing theological beam in Christianity, whereas Jewish thought has consistently rejected the claim that God became incarnate in the person

---

19. Herberg, "Judaism and Christianity," 247; as we will see in the following chapter, Herberg's construal of Christ as the "one-man Israel" significantly undergirds the thought of Messianic Jewish theologian, Mark Kinzer.

20. See Christianity as God's Expanded Covenant with Israel below.

21. For a definition of *halakhah*, see Introduction, note 45 of this study.

22. Herberg, "Judaism and Christianity," 250.

of Jesus. This well-entrenched theological disagreement notwithstanding, a number of post-Holocaust Jewish thinkers have nuanced the divergence by arguing that the core issue is not the idea of God becoming incarnate in the material world, but the specific claim that Jesus is God incarnate. Neither Barth nor Rosenzweig explicitly address Jewish antecedents of the Christian doctrine of incarnation (including God's incarnation in the Jewish people), yet the treatment of this topic by post-Holocaust theologians provides a fascinating bridge between Jewish and Christian theology.

Elliot Wolfson, who has published several essays on the work of Franz Rosenzweig and wrote the introduction to the newest English translation of *The Star of Redemption*,[23] explains:

> It may be valid to conclude ... that the particular expression of incarnation in Christianity, the union of the divine and the human in the body of Jesus, is an idea that has neither precedent in the ancient Israelite religion nor parallel in any of the varieties of Judaism in late antiquity that were contemporaneous with the emerging religion. *This does not mean that the doctrine of incarnation in general is antithetical to Judaism.* On the contrary, the idea of incarnation unique to Christianity should be viewed as a "particular framing" of the conception of incarnation that was idiomatic to a variety of Judaic authors who represented God as a person.[24]

Wolfson reminds us that the Hebrew Bible contains a number of depictions of God in anthropomorphic form, or embodied in space and time, and that the ontological reality of these accounts need not be reduced to merely linguistic anthropomorphization. With regard to Jacob's struggle in Genesis 32, Wolfson writes that "in some cases the anthropomorphisms

---

23. See Elliot R. Wolfson, "Facing the Effaced: Mystical Eschatology and the Idealistic Orientation in the Thought of Franz Rosenzweig," *Zeitschrift für Neure Theologiegeschichte* 4 (1997): 39–81; Wolfson, "Light Does Not Talk but Shines: Apophasis and Vision in Rosenzweig's Theopoetic Temporality," in *New Directions in Jewish Philosophy*, ed. Aaron W. Hughes and Elliot R. Wolfson (Bloomington: Indiana University Press, 2009), 87–148; Wolfson, "Introduction to Barbara Galli's Translation of Rosenzweig's *Star*," in Franz Rosenzweig, *The Star of Redemption*, trans. Barbara E. Galli (Madison: University of Wisconsin Press, 2005), xvii–xx.

24. Elliot R. Wolfson, "Judaism and Incarnation: The Imaginal Body of God," in *Christianity in Jewish Terms*, ed. Tikva Frymer-Kensky et al. (Boulder, CO: Westview, 2000), 240. Italics added.

in Hebrew Scripture do imply an element of incarnation."[25] Wolfson goes on to discuss "God occupying space as an incarnate form"[26] with regard to the tabernacle and temple, angels, and the Torah. According to Wolfson, "in rabbinic Judaism of the formative and medieval periods, based on biblical precedent, an anthropomorphic conception of God is affirmed. These anthropomorphic characterizations are not to be taken simply as figurative or metaphorical."[27]

Building on the notion of divine anthropomorphism, Michael Wyschogrod[28] claims that the Hebrew Bible is rife with anthropomorphic imagery of God, making manifest what Wyschogrod refers to as "diluted incarnation" that can serve to "narrow, though not eliminate, the gap between [Judaism and Christianity] on the issue of incarnation."[29] Wyschogrod explains that, in a manner analogous to God's presence in the temple, God indwells the Jewish people themselves: "The people of Israel and the Temple in Jerusalem are God's dwelling places in the world. When the Temple is out of commission, God's presence on the Temple Mount is reduced though not absent. But then his presence in the people of Israel is increased."[30]

For Wyschogrod, God's indwelling the Jewish people is God's primary mode of self-manifestation on earth; God's presence in the tabernacle and temple is secondary to and derivative of the people of Israel as God's chosen people: "Just as the prophets prophesy only because of Israel, so God was present in the Tabernacle, the Temple and on Mount Sinai only because

---

25. Ibid., 242.

26. Ibid., 243.

27. Ibid., 253.

28. Wyschogrod has drunk deeply at the well of both Barth's and Rosenzweig's thought, and their influence upon him can be seen clearly in the following essays: "Franz Rosenzweig's *The Star of Redemption*," in *Abraham's Promise: Judaism and Jewish-Christian Relations*, ed. R. Kendall Soulen (Grand Rapids: Eerdmans, 2004), 121–30; "Why Was and Is the Theology of Karl Barth of Interest to a Jewish Theologian?" in ibid., 211–24; "A Jewish Perspective on Karl Barth," in *How Karl Barth Changed My Mind*, ed. Donald McKim (Grand Rapids: Eerdmans, 1986), 156–61. Also of interest are the following articles: Shai Held, "The Promise and Peril of Jewish Barthianism: The Theology of Michael Wyschogrod," *Modern Judaism* 25, no. 3 (October 2005): 316–26; R. R. Reno, "The Carnal Reality of Revelation," *First Things* (August 26, 2010). Available at firstthings.com/web-exclusives/2010/04/the-carnal-reality-of-revelation.

29. Wyschogrod, "Incarnation and God's Dwelling in Israel," in *Abraham's Promise*, 168.

30. Ibid., 175.

of Israel. To put it more accurately, he dwells in these places *because* he dwells in and with the people of Israel. It is Israel, the people of the cove-nant, who are the dwelling place of God in this world."[31] The Jewish people represent God in the world, such that "he who touches this people, touches God and perhaps not altogether symbolically."[32]

With regard to Christ, Wyschogrod boldly asserts that "the divinity of Jesus has been unanimously rejected by all Jewish (and Muslim) authors as incompatible with true monotheism and possibly idolatrous."[33] However, similar to Wolfson, Wyschogrod explains that such a rejection cannot be based on a categorical rejection of the idea of incarnation: "It must be emphasized that the Jewish objection to an incarnational theology cannot be based on a priori grounds, as if something in the nature of the Jewish concept of God made his appearance in the form of humanity a rational impossibility."[34] Rather, Christianity appropriates an idea that is funda-mentally at home in Judaism and applies it to a specific context that Judaism rejects. In Wyschogrod's words, "The Christian teaching of the incarna-tion of God in Jesus is the intensification of the teaching of the indwelling of God in Israel by concentrating that indwelling in one Jew rather than leaving it diffused in the people of Jesus as a whole."[35]

Following from this assessment, Wyschogrod critiques Christian incar-national theology for its attempt to separate Jesus from the context of his people. Citing passages from Matthew, Wyschogrod reminds us that Jesus describes his mission as pertaining to "the lost sheep of the house of Israel," instructing his disciples not to enter gentile areas.[36] Thus, Wyschogrod's words to Christian theologians: "Jesus must not be separated from the Jewish people because he did not wish to separate himself from them."[37] In the long history of Israel's election, God indeed called some to be proph-ets, priests, kings, etc., but the significance of these figures can only be

---

31. Michael Wyschogrod, "A Jewish Perspective on Incarnation," *Modern Theology* 12, no. 2 (April 1996): 208. Italics added.

32. Ibid., 208.

33. Ibid. 197–98.

34. Ibid., 204.

35. Wyschogrod, "Incarnation and God's Dwelling in Israel," 178.

36. See Matthew 10:5–6; 15:24.

37. Wyschogrod, "A Jewish Perspective," 206.

understood when properly contextualized within the larger body of Israel. These leaders and intercessors "each had their significance only as they came out of Israel and returned into it as sons of the nation God had elected and which he had sworn not to abandon."[38] For Wyschogrod, the same orientation must be true for Jesus.

Wyschogrod thus takes issue with Christian incarnational theology on two reinforcing fronts. As we have seen, Wyschogrod claims that ascribing divinity to a human being is a fundamental affront to monotheism. However, a parallel claim that seems at least as central in Wyschogrod's argument is that even if a human being (in this case, a member of the house of Israel) were to be considered divine, they could not be so apart from the people to which they belong. The attempt to separate Jesus from his flesh-and-blood community is apparently as heretical as ascribing divinity to him. In Wyschogrod's words, "If we are prepared to take seriously the implanting of Jesus in his people, if the Israel that gave birth to him and whose boundaries (spiritual, geographic, linguistic, intellectual, etc.) he never left is more than just a backdrop to the drama, a backdrop from which Jesus is to be distinguished rather than into which he is to be integrated, if all this is to change, then what is true of Jesus must in some fundamental way also be true of the Jewish people. And that includes the incarnation."[39]

Torrance offers a similar critique of any Christian incarnational theology that does not recognize God's incarnation in the Jewish people. According to Torrance, this breakdown is the result of dualistic thinking that attempts to skirt the issue of God taking on the material aspects of Israel's existence. In Torrance's words:

One of the most startling features about the Old Testament Scriptures is the way in which they represent the Word of God as becoming physically implicated with Israel in the very stuff of its earthy being and behaviour. Divine revelation did not just bear upon the life and culture of Israel in some tangential fashion, rippling the surface of its moral and religious consciousness, but penetrated into the innermost centre of Israel and involved itself in the concrete actuality and locality of its existence in time and space, so that in

---

38. Ibid.
39. Ibid., 207.

its articulated form as human word it struck home to Israel with incisive definiteness and specificity. That is something which we find difficult to understand when we operate with a dualist frame of thought at the back of our minds, for it makes us want to detach the religious concept of Israel from the particularity of its physical existence and history in space and time, and to peel away from divine revelation what we tend to regard as its transient physical clothing. That would be a fatal mistake.[40]

To spiritualize God's presence in Israel inevitably leads to a skewed understanding of the incarnation, for the two cannot be understood apart from one another. God's incarnation in the person of Jesus is the full manifestation of God's presence on earth, but God's indwelling the Jewish people is the ineradicable context of God's self-revelation in Christ. As we will see in the next section, the parallelism of God's presence in Israel and Jesus offers at least part of the explanation for the affliction that has characteristically accompanied the Jewish people. If Christ's incarnation must be situated within God's incarnation in the Jewish people, then Christ's atonement is only intelligible in its connection to Israel's suffering, and vice versa. It is this connection that we will explore in the pages below.

THEOLOGY OF SUFFERING

As we have seen, both Barth and Rosenzweig offer powerful reflections on the suffering of the Jewish people and its connection to the Messiah's own affliction. For Barth, Jesus takes upon himself the suffering of Israel, thus revealing his steadfast solidarity with the wayward people of God. Rosenzweig's exposition of Isaiah 53 treats the Jewish people's suffering on behalf of the nations in conjunction with the parallel vicarious suffering of Christ. Here again Barth and Rosenzweig serve as forerunners to post-Holocaust Jewish and Christian theology, in which the connection between the suffering of the Jewish people and the suffering of Christ has received considerable attention.

Scholars, authors, poets, and artists have found themselves at a loss when trying to express the horrors that befell the Jewish people during the

---

40. Torrance, *Mediation*, 15–16.

Holocaust, an event that highlighted and surpassed the long and treacherous history of Jewish persecution. It goes without saying that the magnitude of the Holocaust and its effect on the Jewish people cannot be exaggerated. Holocaust survivor Ignaz Maybaum refers to the Holocaust as the third *churban*, defining *churban* as "a catastrophe which makes an end to an old era and creates a new era."[41] He lists only three such events in Jewish history—the destruction of the first temple, the destruction of the second temple, and the Holocaust. Elie Wiesel recounts being a child in Auschwitz and watching a rabbinical tribunal put God on trial and find God guilty of crimes against humanity. In the face of burning children, all theological anchors suddenly fail. In Wiesel's words, "Auschwitz negates all systems, opposes all doctrines."[42]

As survivors and scholars have attempted to put words and images to the horrors that befell the Jewish people during the Holocaust, one concept has continually come to the fore—the crucifixion. Marc Chagall (1887–1985)—hailed as "the quintessential Jewish modernist artist of the twentieth century"[43]—produced over one hundred paintings and sketches depicting Jesus-figures and crucifixion scenes. His earliest crucifixion scene (*Crucifixion*) was sketched in 1908 and this became a central motif of Chagall's art during and after the Holocaust. While interpretation of this aspect of Chagall's work varies widely,[44] it is clear that Chagall repeatedly used crucifixion images to represent the suffering of the Jewish people. In Chagall's words, "For me, Christ has always symbolized the true type of Jewish martyr. That is how I understood him in 1908 when I used this figure for the first time. ... It was under the influence of the pogroms."[45]

As Jewish persecution intensified, Chagall repeatedly reached for crucifixion imagery in his work: "His series of crucifixion paintings and

41. Ignaz Maybaum, *The Face of God after Auschwitz* (Amsterdam: Polak & Van Gennep, 1965), 32.

42. Elie Wiesel, "Art and Culture after the Holocaust," in *Auschwitz: Beginning of a New Era? Reflections on the Holocaust*, ed. Eva Fleischner (New York: Ktav, 1977), 405.

43. Matthew Hoffman, *From Rebel to Rabbi: Reclaiming Jesus and the Making of Modern Jewish Culture* (Stanford: Stanford University Press, 2007), 207.

44. That Chagall often painted himself into his crucifixion pieces—either as the artist painting the scene, the man on the cross, or the lone survivor in the midst of crucified Jews and decimated villages—contributes to the multiplicity of interpretations. See Hoffman, *From Rebel to Rabbi*, esp. ch. 5.

45. Cited in Ibid., 218.

sketches from 1938 to 1944 ... graphically incorporated a Christological depiction of Jewish suffering during the war that explicitly identified the image matrix of Christ's passion with the contemporary victimization of Europe's Jews."[46] Chagall's crucifixion pieces incorporate a number of tell-tale Jewish symbols that serve to reclaim the cross as an image of Jewish suffering. Throughout these paintings, we see the figure on the cross wrapped in a *tallit* (prayer shawl), wearing *tefillin* (phylacteries), wearing a yarmulke, surrounded by animals associated with the Jewish sacrificial system, connected to a host of suffering Jews who surround the cross, and depicted amid traditional images of the Akedah (binding of Isaac).

In these paintings, we see a crucified Christ who "appears utterly powerless, unable to abate the landscape of Jewish suffering that practically engulfs him," as the crucifixion becomes "the archetypal visual symbol of Jewish suffering."[47] Chagall's paintings weave Christ on the cross into the fabric of Jewish existence, "suggesting that ascending and descending the martyr's cross was a continual act, not just one isolated event."[48] In *Exodus* (completed in 1966), Chagall depicts Christ on the cross embracing the entire Jewish nation at Sinai, perhaps alluding to the Jewish people's suffering vocation that began at its inception.[49] Chagall beheld this collective suffering his entire life and thus repeatedly depicted the crucified Christ in an unmistakably Jewish manner: "Chagall was utilizing powerfully rooted Jewish symbols along with the crucifixion—which he and others established as a Jewish symbol—as part of his quest to find a meaningful visual representation of the plight of Europe's Jews during World War II."[50]

Similarly, Ignaz Maybaum (who draws extensively on the work of Rosenzweig[51]) interacts at length with the cross as the paradigmatic image

---

46. Ibid., 243. See Appendix 2(A) for a reproduction of Chagall's *White Crucifixion*, painted in 1938.

47. Hoffman, *From Rebel to Rabbi*, 246, 250.

48. Ibid., 249.

49. See Appendix 2(B) for a reproduction of Chagall's *Exodus*.

50. Hoffman, *From Rebel to Rabbi*, 249.

51. Maybaum makes repeated references to Rosenzweig's work, and Maybaum described his *Trialogue between Jew, Christian and Muslim* (London: Routledge, 1973) as "a kind of commentary on Franz Rosenzweig's *The Star of Redemption*," which he regarded as "a *Guide for the Perplexed* of contemporary Jewry" (Nicholas de Lange, ed., *Ignaz Maybaum: A Reader* [New York: Berghahn Books, 2001], xxii).

of Jewish suffering and attempts to correct the connotations the cross has taken on in the Christian world. In his words,

> Christianity presented the man on the cross as a glorified tragic hero and obscured the fact that he was a persecuted Jew hanging on a Roman gallows. Christianity made this pagan and cruel monstrosity respectable, representing it through the symbol of the Cross as the Christian tragedy. ... The Cross, as the poetic symbol of suffering, hides the truth. Auschwitz is the truth, the truth which reveals such monstrosity that the word tragedy becomes a white-washing lie. ... The Cross was the smug symbol of a religion which lived in Concordat with Hitler. Auschwitz is the uncompromising *ecce homo*, behold the suffering man. Auschwitz cries out that mankind is threatened by monstrosity when man ceases to be what the Jew is: man, the messenger and witness of God.[52]

Not only does Maybaum draw a parallel between the cross of Christ and the suffering of the Jewish people, he seeks to reclaim the cross—an image that has been co-opted and corrupted by Christian piety—as the rightful image of Jewish suffering. Wiesel agrees: "A symbol of compassion and love to Christians, the cross has become an instrument of torment and terror to be used against Jews. ... Born in suffering, Christianity became a source and pretext of suffering to others."[53]

While Maybaum places the Holocaust on par with the destruction of the first and second temples, he notes one significant difference: "It says in the liturgy of the synagogue, in reference to the first and second *churban*, albeit centuries after the event: 'because of our sins.' After Auschwitz Jews need not say this. Can any martyr be a more innocent sin-offering than those murdered in Auschwitz? The millions who died in Auschwitz died because of the sins of others. Jews and non-Jews died in Auschwitz, but the Jew-hatred which Hitler inherited from the medieval church made Auschwitz the twentieth century Calvary of the Jewish people."[54] The vicarious nature of Christ's suffering on the cross is thus applied to the suffering of the Jews

---

52. Maybaum, *The Face of God after Auschwitz*, 48.
53. Wiesel, "Art and Culture after the Holocaust," 406.
54. de Lange, ed., *Ignaz Maybaum: A Reader*, 158.

during the Holocaust. According to Maybaum, while the Holocaust did not happen as a result of Jewish sin, the Jewish people must recognize God's judgment in this catastrophe and cannot walk away unchanged: "God sat in His judgment seat, and our old ideals and ideologies have been condemned. Whether we are Orthodox or Liberals or belong to the Reform Movement, whether we are Zionists or non-Zionists, we must not remain after the Day of Judgment what we were before."[55]

According to Maybaum, just as in the days of Jerusalem's captivity, in the Holocaust, God was pronouncing judgment over a chapter in history that could only have led to greater evil. Maybaum recounts that after the destruction of Samaria in 722 BCE the Jewish people, with the help of their prophets, had "the religious strength to celebrate God's victory over an evil, decadent chapter of history and to confess as suffering victims, with no co-operation with the real leaders, their share in the sins of the condemned age."[56] Likening the Holocaust to Amos' "day of the Lord," Maybaum describes the way in which God pronounced judgment on humanity's pride in humanistic and utopian ideas of progress, on human beings' independent dream of "a happy playground for their creative enterprise, forgetting the Creator, the maker of man and of history."[57] For this reason, the Jewish people, who contributed to—though were not exclusively responsible for—the pre-Auschwitz state of affairs, can find their future only in a return to God—"Jewry has a religious future or none at all."[58]

Leora Batnitzky speaks to this vacillation we see in Maybaum's thought regarding the theological connection between Israel's sin and Israel's suffering. Batnitzky sets up the dual models of suffering as a result of sin and suffering as a necessary part of chosenness, explaining that "much of the Jewish tradition stresses the view of suffering as the just chastisement of the beloved child gone astray," but that "in the modern period, and especially after the Holocaust, many Jewish thinkers ... reject the connection between suffering and sin altogether, while nonetheless retaining the intimate connection between suffering and chosenness."[59] In this way,

---

55. Ibid., 155.

56. Ibid., 168.

57. Ibid.

58. Ibid., 154.

59. Leora Batnitzky, "On the Suffering of God's Chosen: Christian Views in Jewish Terms," in *Christianity in Jewish Terms*, 207.

Isaiah 53 is a close parallel to the binding of Isaac in Genesis 22, a text that became a central heuristic lens for the Jewish people during the medieval period: "Like the early Christian interpretation of Isaiah 52:13–53:12, Jewish communities in the Middle Ages understood their suffering as intimately linked to the suffering of God's beloved son, in this case Isaac. The Jewish community's suffering under this interpretation is not retributive. It is not a sign of God's rejection of the Jewish people. Rather, like Isaac, the Jewish community is the favorite of the father, who, for the sake of the will of God, is sacrificed precisely because of its beloved status."[60]

The Jewish people, according to Maybaum, will usher humanity into a new chapter in history. While Maybaum emphasizes the Jewish people's need to reform and draw near once again to God, the role of the Jewish people goes deeper than the effort exerted on their part to refuse the historical attitudes that led to the Holocaust: "The innocent who died in Auschwitz, not for the sake of their own sins but because of the sins of others, *atone for evil*; they are the sacrifice which is brought to the altar and which God acknowledges favourably. ... Their death purged western civilization so that it can again become a place where men can live, do justly, love mercy, and walk humbly with God."[61] Here Maybaum makes clear that the role of the Jewish people is, after all, more than simply correcting destructive and erroneous patterns of human thought and behavior. Something about the suffering of the Jewish people is actually atoning.

Maybaum wrestles with the idea of vicarious suffering, using Christianity and Islam to mark opposite poles and describing Judaism's struggle to identify itself somewhere along the spectrum. In his interpretation, Christianity embraces the efficacy of vicarious suffering—epitomized in the death of Christ—while Islam unambiguously rejects it:

> Chapter 53 and other texts from the book of the so-called Second Isaiah preach the message of vicarious suffering. In Western Jewish thought from Geiger to Baeck the text 'to be a light to the nations' (Isaiah 49:6) was explained as the Jewish contribution to mankind. Yet today, after the Holocaust, the third *churban*, during which six million Jews were tortured and murdered, there are second

---

60. Batnitzky, "On the Suffering of God's Chosen," 209.
61. de Lange, ed., *Ignaz Maybaum: A Reader*, 168. Italics added.

thoughts. We are not so sure now about the doctrine of vicarious suffering ... Many Christians who were sincerely shocked by the suffering of the Jews during the Nazi persecution appeased their troubled consciences in the end with the pious sigh that Jews had always had to pay the price of vicarious suffering for being the chosen people.[62]

Though he does not definitively answer it, Maybaum raises a question worth exploring: What is the relationship between the Jewish people and the suffering and sacrifice that have always characterized that people's existence?

In *The Body of Faith: God in the People Israel*, Michael Wyschogrod locates the idea of sacrifice within the fundamental identity of the Jewish people. In fact, for Wyschogrod, the Jewish people themselves are the primary mode of sacrifice, and the temple merely stood as a surrogate for them in this role. He asks,

> Is it not possible that the rabbis understood that the destruction of the Temple and the cessation of sacrifices, rather than signaling the termination of sacrifices as such, restored the people of Israel to its role as the sacrifice whose blood is to be shed in the Diaspora when the holy service in Jerusalem is suspended? If there is no need for sacrament in Judaism, it is because the people of Israel in whose flesh the presence of God makes itself felt in the world becomes the sacrament.[63]

As we saw above, Torrance likewise claims that suffering is inherent in the vocation of the Jewish people, precisely because of their proximity to God.[64] While Wyschogrod portrays temple sacrifices as merely a temporary substitute for the fundamental sacrifice embodied by the Jewish people

---

62. Ibid., 121.

63. Michael Wyschogrod, *The Body of Faith: God in the People Israel* (Northvale, NJ: Jason Aronson, 1996), 25.

64. See Torrance, *Mediation*, 10–12 and "The Divine Vocation and Destiny of Israel in World History," in *The Witness of the Jews to God*, ed. David W. Torrance (Edinburgh: Handsel Press, 1982), 88–90. As Colyer explains, "God subjected the Israelites to intense and often painful interaction with himself so as to adapt Israel's thought, speech, worship, and life into the appropriate human response or creaturely vessel progressively purified and assimilated to God's Word for the communication of that word to all people" (Colyer, *How to Read*, 102).

themselves, Torrance sees temple sacrifices as pointing forward to the once-for-all sacrifice of Christ.[65] Torrance reviews the ancient Yom Kippur (Day of Atonement) liturgy, wherein two types of sacrifices were made on behalf of Israel's sin. One goat "was to be taken inside and slaughtered upon the altar in sacrificial expiation of the sins of the people," and the other "was to be brought forward so that the high priest could lay his hands upon its head and confess over it all the iniquities of Israel and all their acts of rebellion, whereupon it was to be sent away alive into the wilderness, carrying upon itself all the sins of Israel into some waste land."[66] These two sacrifices jointly communicated the dynamics of atonement to the people of Israel, and Torrance shows how both foreshadow the atonement effected through Christ's sacrifice: "Jesus Christ came from God and stands before mankind as the Lamb upon whom all our iniquities and guilt are laid, sacrificed once for all on the altar of the Cross, but cast out of his own people like an unclean thing, bearing the penalty of their guilt."[67]

If we combine Wyschogrod's and Torrance's exegesis of temple sacrifices, we see again the intimate connection between Jesus and the people of Israel. For Wyschogrod, sacrifice is permanently embodied in the Jewish people; for Torrance sacrifice indelibly points to Christ. Could there be a deep and mysterious connection between the suffering of Christ and the suffering of the Jewish people? Is it possible that the repeated usage of the cross of Christ as the only fitting image to express the suffering of the Jewish people in the Holocaust is imbedded with uncanny significance? While these questions cannot be answered definitively, post-Holocaust theology has raised the suggestion that the suffering of the Jewish people somehow

---

65. According to Torrance, the Holocaust—mirroring Christ's crucifixion—paradoxically reveals the power of God. In his words, the Holocaust "must also be understood in relation to the blood of the covenant faithfulness of God sealed in the innermost destiny of Israel, so that Israel comes forth from the Holocaust as a people new-born from the grave. To the unappeasable agony of the question *why*? Christians can only point to the Cross of Christ, which speaks of God himself present in the depth of human violence and abandonment, giving the Cross its unconquerable power, for Jesus remains completely unavoidable even after the world had done its worst upon him. So with Israel: even when the world has done its worst to Israel, Israel remains an unavoidable factor in the heart of world history, in connection with which mankind has to reckon with the God to whom Israel is inseparably bound in covenant mission and purpose" (Thomas F. Torrance, "Christian/Jewish Dialogue," Appendix A(2), in *The Witness of the Jews to God*, 147–48).

66. Torrance, *Mediation*, 35.

67. Ibid.

mirrors or participates in the suffering of Christ. As the flesh-and-blood community of Christ, perhaps this connection is inevitable.

As we saw in the theology of Karl Barth in chapter 1, the election of Israel and the church exists within the election of Christ. It seems that, in the Holocaust, the Jewish people's identification with Christ is remarkably—and dangerously—close. According to Clemens Thoma, "Auschwitz is the most monumental modern sign for the most intimate bonding and unity of Jewish martyrs—representing all Judaism—with the crucified Christ, although this could not have been conscious for the Jews concerned. The Holocaust is for believing Christians, therefore, an important sign of the unbreakable unity, grounded in the crucified Christ, of Judaism and Christianity despite all divisions, individual paths, and misunderstandings."[68]

Seen through the lens of suffering, Christ is no longer the wedge that drives Christians and Jews apart but may instead be the very one who mysteriously unites them. Reconceiving Christology thus necessarily leads to a reconfiguration of ecclesiology vis-à-vis the Jewish people, and it is to this that we now turn.

## ECCLESIOLOGY IN LIGHT OF ISRAEL

As we have seen in the first half of this chapter, the post-Holocaust world has provided a fertile environment for recasting Christology in light of Israel. As Jesus' identity and mission is increasingly considered within the context of God's ongoing election of Israel, the implications of this shift ripple throughout the manifold loci of Christian theology. Accordingly, rethinking Christology inevitably requires a new ecclesiological paradigm.

Christian ecclesiology has long been borne out of the history of strife and rivalry between Judaism and Christianity that reaches back to the first centuries of Christianity's emergence. As two siblings wrestling over their common heritage, the early community of Jesus-followers and the adherents of nascent rabbinic Judaism increasingly came to define themselves in opposition to one another. In this tumultuous environment, belief in the deity of Christ on one hand and Torah observance on the other became the two polar categories of identity demarcation. According to Mark Kinzer,

---

68. Clemens Thoma, *A Christian Theology of Judaism*, trans. Helga B. Croner (New York: Paulist Press, 1980), 159.

The [deity of Jesus/Yeshua] functioned for many centuries of Jews and Christians as a mutually accepted litmus test for distinguishing authentic Judaism from authentic Christianity. It provided a doctrinal correlate to the practical issue of Torah observance, drawing an unambiguous theological line between the two feuding religious communities just as the Jewish imperative and observance (or Christian prohibition and non-observance) of circumcision, Shabbat, holidays, and kashrut [Jewish dietary laws] established a clear boundary on the level of praxis. For the Jewish people, the chief community-defining positive commandment was "You shall observe the Torah" and the chief negative commandment was "You shall not believe that Jesus is the Son of God." For the Christian Church, the chief community-defining positive commandment was "You shall believe that Jesus is the Son of God" and the chief negative commandment was "You shall not observe the Torah."[69]

These mutually exclusive identity markers solidified, and Judaism and Christianity became two completely separate entities with little tolerance for overlap.[70] This stark division endured across the centuries, vacillating between periods of overt hostility and periods of relative harmony between the two religious communities. It is only in recent history that the mutually exclusive paradigm has begun to be called into question.

Barth and Rosenzweig were pioneers in this fundamental reformulation of the relationship between these two religious traditions. The way in which each of them posits an interdependent connection between Judaism and Christianity (Rosenzweig) and Israel and the church (Barth) opens the door for creative new proposals that move past the rivalry. The post-Holocaust theological era has seen a burgeoning of new ecclesiological models that build upon the works of Barth and Rosenzweig. In the three sections that follow, we will explore ways in which post-Holocaust Jewish

---

69. Mark Kinzer, "Finding Our Way Through Nicaea: The Deity of Yeshua, Bilateral Ecclesiology, and Redemptive Encounter with the Living God" in *Searching Her Own Mystery: Nostra Aetate, the Jewish People, and the Identity of the Church* (Eugene, OR: Cascade, 2015), 218.

70. James Parkes provides a sampling of baptismal professions throughout Christian history in which Jews wishing to convert to Christianity were forced to renounce all traces of Jewish practice. See James Parkes, *The Conflict of the Church and the Synagogue: A Study in the Origins of Antisemitism* (London: Macmillan, 1969), 394–400.

and Christian theologians are reconstructing ecclesiology with particular regard to the indelible bond between Israel and the church. These ecclesiological bridges hold great hope for reconciliation and redemptive partnership, and carry us one step closer toward answering Marshall's framing question.

## RENOUNCING SUPERSESSIONISM

Though rooted in Jewish soil, the emerging Jesus movement found far more fertile ground among gentiles and faced increasing opposition from the growing establishment of rabbinic Judaism. In light of this situation, Christian supersessionism became the early Christian community's dominant model for living amid these tensions and understanding its own identity. As Christopher Leighton explains, "Christian supersessionism deflected political and religious criticisms threatening the church from outside" and "blunted doubts and fears about its own integrity that arose within its ranks."[71]

According to a supersessionist paradigm, Christians "saw the failure of Jews to discern the spiritual depths of their own Scriptures as a sign of the 'hard-hearted' and 'carnal' nature of Judaism. In the most fundamental sense, Christians concluded that Jews no longer understood their own Bible and therefore were no longer worthy of being God's covenantal partner."[72] Furthermore, "Christians found confirmation for these interpretations within salient historical events. The destruction of the Second Temple, the defeat of Bar Kochba, and the emergence of the triumphant church were heralded as irrefutable evidence in support of a displacement theology. The early Christians viewed every catastrophe that befell the Jewish community as just punishment for Jewish complicity in the murder of Jesus Christ."[73]

Irving Greenberg explains the devastating consequences of such a stance toward the Jewish people and draws a direct connection between centuries of Christian supersessionism and the Holocaust. In his words, "When one treats others as having less spiritual dignity than oneself, the temptation is to stand by when they are physically in danger as well. Theological contempt cannot be separated from human responsibility. ...

---

71.  Christopher M. Leighton, "Christian Theology after the Shoah," in *Christianity in Jewish Terms*, ed. Tikva Frymer-Kensky, 38.

72.  Ibid., 39.

73.  Ibid.

The tradition of spiritual contempt led many Christians to abandon Jews in the Holocaust."[74] The Holocaust highlighted the problem of Christian supersessionism and has served as a catalyst for theological reformation. As Leighton explains, "The imperative to disarm those dynamics of Christian thought and practice that threaten the Jewish people has in large measure arisen out of the encounter with the Shoah."[75] Accordingly, "the credibility and coherence of the Christian narrative demand a radical recasting of its foundational story."[76]

In his book *The God of Israel and Christian Theology*, R. Kendall Soulen attempts to provide such a recasting of Christianity's framing narrative. Soulen examines the deep-seated legacy of Christian supersessionism throughout history and proposes a paradigmatic shift that overcomes this ingrained and destructive framework. In defining supersessionism, Soulen differentiates between three distinct forms: economic supersessionism, whereby the church replaces Israel not because of Israel's sin but because Israel's role was to prepare the way for spiritual and universal salvation; punitive supersessionism, whereby God abrogates his covenant with Israel on account of Israel's rejection of Christ; and structural supersessionism (which represents the deepest level of supersessionism), according to which Israel (and God's covenant with Israel) is ultimately indecisive in the overarching narrative of salvation history.[77]

In the first part of the book, Soulen surveys Christian theology across the centuries, examining in particular the thoughts of Justin Martyr, Irenaeus, Immanuel Kant, Friedrich Schleiermacher, Karl Barth, and Karl Rahner, noting the common supersessionist themes that underlie them all, albeit in different forms. He concludes his analysis by explaining that Christianity's standard canonical narrative[78] is economically supersessionist, in that it "depicts carnal Israel's role in the economy of redemption as essentially transient by virtue of the spiritualizing and universalizing

---

74. Irving Greenberg, *For the Sake of Heaven and Earth: The New Encounter between Judaism and Christianity* (Philadelphia: Jewish Publication Society, 2004), 174.

75. Leighton, "Christian Theology after the Shoah," 37.

76. Ibid.

77. R. Kendall Soulen, *The God of Israel and Christian Theology* (Minneapolis: Fortress, 1996), 29–33.

78. Soulen defines a canonical narrative as "an interpretative instrument that provides a framework for reading the Christian Bible as a theological and narrative unity" (ibid., 13).

impetus of God's salvific will," and structurally supersessionist, in that it "renders God's identity as the God of Israel largely indecisive for shaping theological conclusions about how God's works as Consummator and as Redeemer engage creation in universal and enduring ways."[79]

In the book's second part, Soulen offers a concrete proposal for renouncing supersessionism by restructuring the Christian canonical narrative. According to Soulen, the standard canonical narrative—which divides God's history with humanity into four episodes (creation, fall, redemption, final consummation) and conceives of God's engagement with creation along two primary lines (God as Consummator and God as Redeemer)— suffers from an incomplete rejection of Gnosticism. While rejecting Gnosticism at the ontological level (and thus resisting the Gnostic tendency to collapse creation into the fall), the standard canonical narrative fails to reject Gnosticism on a covenant-history level and consequently drives a wedge between the gospel and the God of Israel "by collapsing God's covenant with Israel into the economy of redemption in its prefigurative form."[80] Soulen wishes to rebalance the standard narrative by placing "greater emphasis on God's role as the Consummator of creation (that is, the One who sustains and blesses His creation), even if that means somewhat less emphasis on God as the Redeemer from the evil that has come into the world from inevitable ('original') human sin."[81] According to this model, "God's work as Redeemer confirms rather than supplants the centrality of God's work as Consummator,"[82] for the antithesis of sin and redemption fits within the larger narrative context of creation and consummation.[83] Thus, in Soulen's words, "God's history with Israel and the nations is the permanent and enduring medium of God's

---

79. Ibid., 109.

80. Ibid., 110. Italics original.

81. David Novak, "Beyond Supersessionism," First Things 81 (March 1998): 58.

82. Soulen, The God of Israel, 112.

83. According to Randi Rashkover, "Soulen argues that Judaism maintains a creation-consummation model while Christianity has historically attached itself to a sin-redemption model. Soulen argues that Christianity can and ought to recognize its narrative of sin and redemption within the context of the creation-consummation model" (Randi Rashkover, Revelation and Theopolitics: Barth, Rosenzweig and the Politics of Praise [London: T&T Clark, 2005], 164 n. 22). See also Peter Ochs, Another Reformation: Postliberal Christianity and the Jews (Grand Rapids: Baker, 2011), 30.

work as the Consummator of human creation, and therefore it is also the permanent and enduring context of the gospel about Jesus."[84]

Soulen's proposed recasting of the canonical narrative indeed helps to correct Gnostic and supersessionist tendencies. However, it does so by diminishing Christology. Soulen presents Jesus as the one who guarantees God's final victory over the powers that threaten creation and who points forward toward God's eschatological reign. In this volume, Soulen does not address the issue of Christ's divinity,[85] nor does he unambiguously declare Christ's universal applicability and unsurpassibility.[86] John Pawlikowski critiques Soulen on this point, and it is worth quoting him at length:

> In the end Soulen provides us with a "low Christology" which I am afraid will not pass muster with most Christian theologians. Christ appears to be an assured passage to ultimate creational fulfillment but does not alter in any way our basic understanding of the divine-human relationship. For me only a somewhat "higher Christology," in which we Christians do make some claim for a transformation of that understanding, might find a hearing within the church at large. In short, I would not say Soulen has failed in the task he announced—to overcome Christian doctrinal supersessionism while not sacrificing the Christological claims that historically are considered essential to Christianity. But nor do I believe that he has adequately completed that self-assigned task in the Christological reflections he has presented thus far.[87]

---

84. Soulen, *The God of Israel*, 110.

85. It should be noted that Soulen is in the process of writing a two-volume work on the Trinity. The first volume, entitled *The Divine Name(s) and the Holy Trinity: Distinguishing the Voices*, was published by Westminster John Knox in 2011.

86. While Christian missionary efforts to the Jews have admittedly proven problematic, Soulen fails to clarify that Jesus does indeed have definitive relevance for the Jewish people. He speaks of the church's need to be composed of Jews and gentiles, though he chastises gentile-Christian mission to non-Christian Jews. In his words, the primary task of the church of the gentiles is to "live before the Jewish people in such a way that Israel can reasonably infer that here the nations of the world truly worship the God of Israel and in this way manifest the truth of its gospel" (Soulen, *The God of Israel*, 173).

87. John Pawlikowski, "Christology and the Jewish-Christian Dialogue: A Personal Theological Journey," *Irish Theological Quarterly* 72, no. 2 (May 2007): 154.

Similarly, according to Scott Bader-Saye, "The lingering question for Soulen's Christology is this: If Jesus does not inaugurate Israel's redemption but only confirms it, then how is Jesus different from all other faithful Jewish witnesses? ... Soulen's discussion of Christ's life, death, and resurrection does not require that we attribute to Jesus any more than that he was an extremely faithful Jew, trusting in God's promises and living the way of blessing faithfully even unto the cross."[88]

This tension in Soulen's thought highlights again the complexity of affirming both aspects of Marshall's question. In attempting to maintain a high Christology while upholding Israel's ongoing positive vocation in salvation history, it is difficult to avoid falling prey to a zero-sum game. The problems with his Christology notwithstanding, Soulen's contribution to the renunciation of supersessionism is commendable. His work exposes this dark and enduring legacy that stains Christian history and offers a new proposal regarding the relationship between the church and the Jewish people. Rather than viewing the church as replacing Israel as God's covenant people, Soulen challenges us to imagine the church joining Israel in covenantal relationship with Israel's God. This ecclesiological paradigm merits further exploration, and in the next section we will examine ways in which it is being developed.

## CHRISTIANITY AS GOD'S EXPANDED COVENANT WITH ISRAEL

If a non-supersessionist framework rules out replacement theology, how then are we to conceive of the relationship between the church and Israel? A growing number of theologians are appropriating the "grafting in" metaphor of Romans 11 to describe this relationship. Through Christ, the door is opened for gentiles to enter into covenant relationship with Israel's God—without becoming Jewish. This "gentile inclusion" is the fulfillment of Israel's divine mission, which has always been to bring the world into knowledge of God.

According to Will Herberg, Christianity exists to bridge the paradox of a divine-human covenant with a universal scope but a particular referent. In Herberg's words, "All of mankind is to be brought into the covenant and,

---

88. Scott Bader-Saye, *Church and Israel After Christendom: The Politics of Election* (Eugene, OR: Wipf & Stock, 1999), 83–84.

within the covenant, restored to a right relation to God." Yet, "the paradox of Israelite religion was that a covenant of such universal scope and purpose was actualized in a particular folk or ethnic community." As long as the locus of the covenant was the people of Israel, and given the construct of that particular community, covenant relationship with God was categorically not possible for non-Jews. "In this situation, Christianity emerged to break through the paradox and bring the 'nations of the world' to the God of Israel by bringing them under the covenant of Israel in a new form. Through Christianity, God's covenant with Israel was opened to all mankind—without requiring a change of ethnic or 'national' status."[89]

While Israel as a people was called into covenant relationship with God and issued a unique mission by God, Israel's calling was never meant to remain exclusive. In the words of Thomas Torrance:

> The historical partnership between Israel and God took the form of a particular covenant with concrete provisions, in which Israel was given a special priestly status among the nations as God's representative and messenger. By its nature this covenant was not meant to be an end in itself, for through it Israel was steadily and painfully moulded by God into being the instrument of his saving purpose, and made to provide in its very existence among the nations the basis and provisional form of a new covenantal relationship with God which would include all nations.[90]

Through the life, death, and resurrection of Christ, the universal scope of Israel's mission was definitively implemented. Thus, rather than the church replacing Israel as the people of God and the bearer of a unique commission by God, gentile followers of Christ are, in Paul's language, grafted into Israel's mission and redemptive activity. God's election of Israel as a mediator for salvation to the world has not been revoked; rather, it has been expanded. Again, in Torrance's words:

> Gentiles themselves are without hope and without God in the world, for they are aliens from the promises and covenants. Israel alone is

---

89. Herberg, "Judaism and Christianity," 244.

90. Torrance, "Christian/Jewish Dialogue," 140. See David Novak's challenge to this claim, Rosenzweig's Doctrine of the Jewish People (Israel) above.

the people of God, the bearer of divine revelation and the promise of salvation, the one people with Messianic destiny, so that in order to share in the saving purpose of God, Gentiles must be incorporated into the commonwealth of Israel. In no sense does the Church replace Israel and its mission in the divine calling. It is only through *assimilation into Israel* that the Church may share in the divine mission and be engaged in the universalising of that mission to all the world.[91]

Further interpreting Paul's words in a manner that supports this ecclesiological understanding, Torrance writes:

St. Paul insists that it is only as gentiles are incorporated into the covenant people of God and thus made members of God's household, or, as he says elsewhere, are grafted like wild olive branches on to the trunk of Israel, that they may share with them in the revelation of the one true God uniquely mediated to them. They must remember that the branches do not bear the trunk, but the trunk bears the branches. Separated from Israel gentiles have to do only with some unrevealed God who is not God, and are in fact "without hope and without God (*atheoi*) in the world." As our Lord himself said to the woman of Samaria, "You worship what you do not know, we worship what we know, for salvation is of the Jews."[92]

Michael Wyschogrod sees Paul's theology in a similar light. In exploring the significance of the Christ event for Paul, Wyschogrod rightly sees that the death and resurrection of Christ are paramount, for these events alter humanity's standing before God and effect the forgiveness of sins. "Before Christ, the human creature stood guilty before God for not fulfilling the demands of the Law, the obligation God had transmitted to Israel through Moses."[93] However, Wyschogrod does not miss the fact that the law of Moses does not apply equally to Jews and gentiles—a point that Paul was also well aware of. Thus, "central as the Christ event is in the thinking

---

91. Ibid., 142–43. Italics added.

92. Torrance, *Mediation*, 105–06.

93. Michael Wyschogrod, "Paul, Jews, and Gentiles," in *Abraham's Promise*, 188–89.

of Paul, it is incorrect to think of it as having the same effect for Jews and gentiles."[94] For Jews, the Christ event guarantees the final triumph of grace over against justice in the divine economy. "Where previously the aspects of justice and mercy alternated, with Israel sometimes receiving what it deserved and at other times the recipient of God's mercy, with the Christ event and with faith in Christ, God's aspect of mercy becomes the permanent and exclusive mode of his relationship to Israel."[95]

For gentiles, the Christ event essentially serves to create a new type of covenant relationship with God. Wyschogrod explains that, prior to Christ, one was either a full member of the house of Israel or a non-member. "For Paul, the Christ event had made possible a new category: gentiles who were not circumcised and not obedient to the Torah but who were still not excluded from the house of Israel. ... They had become members of the household of Israel, something which prior to Christ could be achieved only by full conversion to Judaism."[96]

As we have noted, to understand Christianity as an expansion of God's covenant with Israel implies an ecclesiological framework whereby supersessionism is excluded. There is a unity between Jews and (gentile) Christians, who collectively constitute the covenant community, but there also remains a distinction between these two groups. Israel as a covenanted people remains intact, and Christians become, in the words of Wyschogrod, "associate members" in the elect people.[97] From Wyschogrod's perspective, "Christianity is part of Greater Judaism. Christianity is not just another faith, as far as Judaism is concerned ... Christianity is, in a sense, the Judaism of the Gentiles."[98]

Will Herberg offers a similar model, and it is significant that for both Herberg and Wyschogrod, viewing Christianity as part of greater Judaism does not nullify or erase the Jewish people's specific covenant responsibilities before God. Rather, Judaism and Christianity retain related but distinct covenantal commissions. Following Rosenzweig, Herberg assigns each community a complementary vocation in the plan and purpose of

---

94. Ibid., 189.
95. Ibid., 197.
96. Ibid., 191.
97. Ibid., 193.
98. Wyschogrod, "A Jewish Perspective," 205.

God. "Judaism and Christianity represent one religious reality, Judaism facing inward to the Jews and Christianity facing outward to the gentiles, who, through it, are brought to the God and under the covenant of Israel, and therefore cease to be gentiles."[99] The Jewish people embody a "static" vocation; their contribution to the coming kingdom of God is to "stay with God" and live a "semi-detached" existence with regard to the world.[100] Accordingly, *halakhah* "is central to normative Jewish faith ... as a holy discipline of life that maintains Israel's existence as covenant-people and therefore enables it to fulfill its vocation."[101] Beginning with circumcision, the Jew "appropriates his covenant existence through the ongoing pattern of *halakhic* observance."[102] Similarly, Jewish liturgy and Judaism's three great pilgrimage festivals (Pesach, Succot, and Shavuot) reenact the "Exodus-Sinai-event," which serves as Judaism's "crucial revelatory redemptive, and community-creating event."[103]

Christians, on the other hand, are tasked with "going out" and making a "religious protest" against the idolatries of the world.[104] Baptism is the genesis of the Christian life, and the Christian "appropriates his covenant existence through the one observance that, in Christian faith, replaces the entire *halakhah*—the Lord's Supper."[105] Because Christ "fulfills the law," "all ritual observances, for the Christian, are performed in the one sacrament of Christ."[106] Likewise, Christian liturgy and holidays "reenact phases of the Christ-event that brought the Church into being."[107] While Herberg refuses the clichéd dichotomy of law vs. gospel by which some have distinguished Judaism and Christianity, he claims that "the characteristic peril of the Jew is legalism" while Christianity's "analogous peril is antinomianism."[108] Herberg's thought here echoes Rosenzweig's description of the

---

99. Herberg, "Judaism and Christianity," 246.
100. Ibid., 248, 250.
101. Ibid., 250.
102. Ibid.
103. Ibid., 248.
104. Ibid., 247-48.
105. Ibid., 250.
106. Ibid.
107. Ibid., 249.
108. Ibid., 251.

dangers that face Judaism and Christianity should they unhitch themselves from one another.[109]

Wyschogrod also closely links the existence of the Jewish people with the observance of Torah. In his words,

> To be a Jew means to labor under the yoke of the commandments. Jews are required by God to live in accordance with the commandments of the Torah while gentiles are required by God to obey the Noachide commandments based on Genesis 9:1-17. ... It therefore follows that a gentile who eats leavened bread during the Passover season (to choose but one example) is in no way displeasing God while a Jew who does so is, from the Jewish point of view, displeasing God because God has forbidden Jews to eat leavened bread during Passover (see Lev. 23:6).[110]

The way in which Herberg and Wyschogrod expressly prescribe *halakhah* to the Jew and not the (gentile) Christian is significant, for it points toward the type of ecclesiological arrangement that Marshall's question tacitly requires. As we will see in the following chapter, Mark Kinzer takes a significant step forward in pioneering this type of variegated (or, to use Kinzer's term, "bilateral") ecclesiology in which Jews and gentiles remain distinct within the one body of Christ.

From a Christian perspective, an ecclesiology that highlights the connection between Israel and the church follows naturally from a Christology that takes seriously Jesus' Jewishness. According to Lutheran and ecumenical theologian Robert Jenson, for whom Barth is a sustained dialogue partner and Israel is consistently in view, "the embodiment of the risen Christ is whole only in the form of the church and *an identifiable community of Abraham and Sarah's descendents*. The church and the synagogue are together and only together the present availability to the world of the

---

109. See Franz Rosenzweig, *The Star of Redemption*, trans. Barbara E. Galli (Madison: University of Wisconsin Press, 2005), 424-30; ch. 2, The Election of Israel in Rosenzweig's Theology.

110. Michael Wyschogrod, "A Letter to Cardinal Lustiger," in *Abraham's Promise*, 206. It is also noteworthy that, according to Wyschogrod, the waters of baptism do not wash away a Jew's obligation to keep Torah. As we will see in the following chapter, this contention is among those that make Wyschogrod a close theological ally for Kinzer.

risen Jesus Christ."[111] Jenson reflects upon the church as the "body of Christ," according to which "the risen Christ is the church and is other than the church."[112] As the body of Christ, the church is that object in the world that "intends Christ"; it is the possibility of relating to Christ in the flesh. But this reality is not yet fully realized, for "the 'whole Christ' of which particularly Augustine among the fathers spoke so much, the one reality of Christ with his own, who will in the End be the second person of God's triune life, exists now only in anticipation."[113]

Along these lines, Jenson asks: "So wherein is the risen Christ other than the church? The suggestion may be surprising, but I commend it to you: in that he is a Jew, in that his proper people is Israel, and in that the continuing community of Israel is an other community than the church. To hold open, as it were, the time of the church, the risen Jew, Jesus the Christ, must not only be embodied as the church, but embodied in the flesh of Israel—until these two are one."[114] The church alone cannot represent Christ in the world, for the church is not a freestanding entity. It is built upon the foundation of Israel's covenant relationship with God, and it is this covenant that through Christ is opened also to gentiles. The implication is clear—to the extent that Christ is separated from Israel, Christology and ecclesiology cannot but be distorted.

Karl Barth's son, New Testament scholar Markus Barth, agrees: "It is not possible to serve God in the name of Jesus Christ and to separate oneself from the Jews."[115] With regard to the twofold people of God, Markus Barth sees an indelible connection between the communal rites of the church and Israel's communal rites. In his words,

> Church and everyday worship can only exist in secret solidarity with the worship in synagogues and Jewish homes. Baptism became

---

111. Robert W. Jenson, "Toward a Christian Theology of Judaism," in *Jews and Christians: People of God*, ed. Carl E. Braaten and Robert W. Jenson (Grand Rapids: Eerdmans, 2003), 13. Italics added.

112. Robert W. Jenson, "Toward a Christian Theology of Israel," *Pro Ecclesia* 9, no. 1 (1999): 55.

113. Jenson, "Toward a Christian Theology of Israel," 54–55.

114. Ibid., 55.

115. Markus Barth, *Jesus the Jew*, trans. Frederick Prussner (Atlanta: John Knox Press, 1978), 40.

the sign of entrance into the church because originally it was a sign of penitence within Israel. The communion meal is the fulfillment of the Passover Meal. Every time that Jews are penitent on the Day of Atonement we too are called on to be penitent. When, during the Passover Meal, they wait for the one who is to come, we wait with them. ... We Gentiles know that we belong to the one people of God only because we are naturalized citizens in Israel (Eph. 2:13-19) and because we wait with the Jews for the *one* shepherd of the *one* flock.[116]

For Torrance, Christology likewise goes hand in hand with ecclesiology. Just as Jesus cannot be properly understood if he is abstracted from his Jewish context, the church cannot understand itself or its relationship to God if it sees itself as somehow separate from the people of Israel. The way in which Judaism and Christianity have consistently built their self-identities in contradistinction from one another represents a distortion that has become deeply imbedded within the one covenant community: "Since there is only one Covenant of grace and only one people of God, the separation of the Christian Church from the Jewish Church represents the deepest schism there could be. So long as that split remains in force Jews and Christians have a distorted understanding of one another. This is nowhere more evident than in regard to who Jesus was and is. When the Gentile Church is cut off from Israel, it is in a measure cut off from Jesus."[117]

According to Torrance, the split between Judaism and Christianity is the most significant, tragic, and distorting split since the coming of Christ.[118] As long as Christians view the church as being separate from Israel, they inevitably hold an inaccurate and incomplete understanding of Christ and the atonement. Because Christ emerges from and exists among the people of Israel, and because the Jewish people continue to mysteriously participate in Christ's atoning work (not least in the form of vicarious suffering, as explored above), ecclesiological formulations must take seriously the deep connection between Israel, Jesus, and the church. If Israel's status

---

116. Ibid., 39–40.

117. Torrance, "Christian/Jewish Dialogue," 143.

118. In Torrance's words, "Schism between Christians and Jews is the deepest schism and the root cause of all other schism in the one People of God" (Torrance, "The Divine Vocation," 87).

before God is viewed as variable, the church's self-understanding will be inevitably unstable. As we will see in the following section, the doctrine of election is only fully comprehensible when God's covenant with Israel provides the historical foundation and informs the theological framework of election.

### RECLAIMING THE DOCTRINE OF ELECTION

As we saw in chapter 1, the doctrine of election stands at the very heart of Barth's doctrine of God. The election of Israel and the church are irrevocable by virtue of their existence within the election of Christ. While Rosenzweig seldom uses the language of election, the specific commissioning of Jews and Christians figures prominently in his theology. God's redemptive purposes are moved forward only by the correlative vocations of Judaism and Christianity, upon whose obedience eschatological consummation hinges. As this trend suggests, the doctrine of election has seen a resurgence in recent scholarship, and it is of paramount importance in the theology of the new Jewish-Christian encounter.

Scott Bader-Saye's book, *Church and Israel After Christendom: The Politics of Election*, has been touted as "one of the best ... recent Christian attempts at a theology of the election of Israel."[119] As we noted in the introduction, Bader-Saye seeks to rethink Christian ecclesiology in light of two seismic twentieth-century events: the demise of Christendom and the Holocaust.[120] Christian theology in today's world cannot proceed as if these two events did not happen, and Bader-Saye explores ways in which "a renewed theology of Israel can provide resources to envision a faithful post-Christendom ecclesiology."[121] In his estimation, reclamation of the doctrine of election is a central component in this task.

According to Bader-Saye, the doctrine of election "has fallen on hard times in modern theological thought, for it bumps up against modern conceptions of freedom and autonomy, it calls into question explanations of the world as a closed system, and its unabashed particularity makes it troubling to the universalist aspirations of the Enlightenment. Election thus has become an embarrassing doctrine to those who wish to commend

---

119. David B. Hart, "Israel and the Nations," *First Things* 105 (August/September 2000): 51.
120. See Bader-Saye, *Church and Israel*, 1.
121. Ibid., 2.

Christianity to modern consciousness."[122] The American church is at a significant crossroads, claims Bader-Saye, and his prescription for a faithful future is a recovery and re-Judaization of the doctrine of election.[123]

To explore election anew from a Christian perspective ought to lead one inevitably to Israel, for it is Israel's election into which the church is grafted.[124] In order for the church to rediscover its true identity before God and the world, it must understand the "politics" of Israel's election as somehow also characterizing its own existence. However, the church has historically appropriated a supersessionist understanding of its own election, one in which the church replaces Israel as the people of God:[125]

> In the West, election slowly ceased to be imagined in terms of God shaping for Himself a particular people with a particular vocation, and came to be mistaken for a doctrine concerning the eternal predestination of souls. It was this forgetfulness of Israel's irrevocable "carnal election" that—so Bader-Saye claims—opened up a sociopolitical vacuum, ultimately to be filled by 'Constantinianism' and by various myths of national "election" that have long estranged the Church from its true calling.[126]

The church's preoccupation with individual salvation is part and parcel of its supersessionist theology, for it views its own election as an alternative to Israel's. According to Bader-Saye, to the extent that the church has misunderstood the true foundation of its election, it has replaced the "politics of election" with the politics of power: "Had Christians remembered all along that only Israel is the elect nation of God, so the argument goes, and its election the concrete earnest of cosmic peace, they would not have yielded their

---

122. Ibid., 3.

123. Ibid., 27.

124. While Bader-Saye acknowledges and lauds the way in which Barth "shook the foundations of the classical doctrine of election," he ultimately critiques Barth on two fronts. First, similar to the critiques of Sonderegger and Wyschogrod, Bader-Saye claims that "Barth is unable to affirm any ongoing positive witness of Israel." Second, Bader-Saye critiques the way in which the election of the community ends up bowing to the election of the individual, which finally trumps in Barth's dialectic between collectivism and individualism. See ibid., 73–77.

125. Ibid., ch. 3.

126. Hart, "Israel and the Nations," 52–53.

political soul to the prudential violence of the powers, or mistaken national destinies for some part of the economy of salvation."[127]

More recently, a number of post-Holocaust theologians have swung to the opposite extreme, often sacrificing orthodox Christology or jettisoning the universal applicability of Christ in order to avoid treading on the hallowed ground of Israel's covenant with God. In an attempt to overcome anti-Judaism, Christian theology falls prey to sacrificing that which makes it distinctively Christian.[128] According to this theological framework, the church's self-understanding is even more disconnected from Israel, as evidenced by the "dual-covenant" constructions that often result. As Bader-Saye explains, both of these alternatives—the supersessionist option and the "post-Holocaust" option—lead to a fatal distortion of the church's identity.

In order to understand the true nature of the church's election, one must first understand Israel's election and how, through Christ, the nations are invited to participate in Israel's covenant with God. It is in the particulars of Israel's election that we see the ultimate purposes of God at work. Bader-Saye notes the fact that Israel's election precedes its having a homeland, a constant reminder that the domain of Israel's redemptive mission far transcends territorial boundaries.[129] Ultimately, Israel's election is not about violently defending a scarce resource but rather about being the instrument of the cosmic and tangible redemption of creation. The Torah as the blueprint for Israel's faithful living demonstrates the all-encompassing nature of covenant life, and beneath what Christians have attacked as "legalism" lies the true path to human freedom—for "true freedom is not boundless arbitrary choice but liberation from sin."[130] By virtue of being an elect community, we see that the individual can only be understood in the context of the larger commissioned body to which they belong, and that election, while calling for human response, is grounded in God's faithfulness, not humanity's.

God's promise to create a "new covenant" (as we see in Jeremiah) was never to the exclusion or contradiction of his original covenant with Israel. Rather than coming to cast off Israel and create a new people and a new

---

127. Ibid., 53.

128. Bader-Saye, *Church and Israel*, ch. 4.

129. Michael Wyschogrod makes a similar point in his essay, "Judaism and the Land," in *Abraham's Promise*, 91–103.

130. Hart, "Israel and the Nations," 53.

basis of election, Jesus came as the visible *telos* of Israel's covenant relationship with God. "Jesus' work of healing, forgiving sins, seeking out the lost, eating with the outcast, proclaiming the reign of God, and calling Israel to obedience is the visibility of redemption."[131] Through the Spirit, the church becomes a community of co-ambassadors with Israel of the one covenant whose universal scope has now been gloriously unveiled. In Bader-Saye's assessment, gaining a non-supersessionist self-understanding is the church's only hope for recovering a biblical understanding of its election. Participation in Israel's election both lends the church its true identity and unmasks the ways in which it has become co-opted with the secular powers and bound to the myths of the surrounding empires. In order for the church to properly understand itself and walk faithfully before God, it must find itself underneath the umbrella of Israel's election. It must join Israel in the work of bringing about *shalom*—cosmic wholeness—by choosing radical community over opportunistic individualism, by embodying messianic peace instead of violent power, and by living out the all-encompassing cruciform discipleship that characterizes life in the kingdom.

George Lindbeck, whose theological interaction with Barth is a constant throughout his work and whose theology has resonances with Rosenzweig's thought,[132] comes to a similar conclusion. In his essay "The Church as Israel: Ecclesiology and Ecumenism," Lindbeck traces the history of Christianity's use of Israelhood in its self-definition, with the ultimate goal of recommending a non-supersessionist ecclesiological appropriation of this concept. Lindbeck dares to challenge the prevailing winds of the past half-century in which the idea of the church as Israel has come to be seen as the dangerous road that led directly to the Holocaust. According to many modern theologians, (supersessionist) understandings of the church as Israel "must be counted among the historical sources of the anti-Semitism that made Auschwitz and comparable crimes possible."[133]

---

131. Bader-Saye, *Church and Israel*, 106.

132. See especially Peter Ochs, "A Rabbinic Pragmatism," in *Theology and Dialogue: Essays in Conversation with George Lindbeck*, ed. Bruce D. Marshall (Notre Dame: University of Notre Dame Press, 1990), 213–48; Leora Batnitzky, *Idolatry and Representation: The Philosophy of Franz Rosenzweig Reconsidered* (Princeton: Princeton University Press, 2000), 207–25.

133. George Lindbeck, "The Church as Israel: Ecclesiology and Ecumenism," in *Jews and Christians*, 79.

According to Lindbeck, the New Testament paved the way for gentile Christians to understand themselves through the lens of the Old Testament, as those who now existed within the commonwealth of Israel. In other words, the early church came to understand itself "in the mirror of Old Testament Israel in the light of Jesus Christ."[134] Thus, the Old Testament functioned as the "ecclesiological textbook" for the church's self-definition. However, the destruction of the Jerusalem temple provided the first major upset to this expansive ecclesiology. In the aftermath of this event and the consequent "distancing of gentile from Jewish Christians and the alienation of both from the synagogue,"[135] the self-understanding of these two groups became wildly dissimilar. Eventually, as a result of these divergent self-conceptions, Torah observance among Jewish believers became less tolerated and eventually "the few Jews within the church were canonically compelled to be non-practicing, that is, assimilated and in effect deprived of their Jewish identity."[136]

Eventually, as the church both spread out geographically and became increasingly diverse liturgically, the peoplehood of Israel became a key metaphor for maintaining a sense of broader unity within Christianity. In a similar way, those same Jewish scriptures that shaped the church's identity also molded the developing self-understanding and unity of nascent rabbinic Judaism: "What the rabbis did to make the Jews in diaspora an interconnected people, the catholics did for the gentile Christians. Both went far beyond their common scripture, and they did so in different directions, one by means of the oral Torah, and the other through the New Testament. Yet each group lived in the world of Israel's story and of Israel's God and claimed to be his chosen people."[137]

However, following Constantine's victory in 312 CE and the drastic changes this event brought about for Christianity, the church's self-understanding no longer cohered with the contours of Israel's Old Testament sojourn. The Roman emperors who had previously been cast as Pharaohs in the story now came to be cast as Moses or David: "Power relations had been reversed, and what had been cries of anguish in the mouths of the helpless became incitements to violence against the newly

---

134. Lindbeck, "The Church as Israel," 81.
135. Ibid., 83.
136. Ibid.
137. Ibid., 87.

defenseless when repeated from positions of strength."[138] The church slowly ceased to understand itself in terms of Israel, and by the time Thomas Aquinas wrote in the thirteenth century, this concept can scarcely be found. This trend intensified, such that:

> Under the influence of Enlightenment rationalism, itself a reaction against the wars of religion, everything within Christianity that was deemed to be specifically Jewish came increasingly under attack. ... Old Testament (i.e., Jewish) religion was rejected root and branch as primitive, legalistic, and intolerant. Whatever was good about it, such as the moral duties inculcated in the Ten Commandments, was simply part of the natural law or general revelation available to all human beings. There was nothing specific to Israelite religion that enlightened Christians wanted to appropriate or expropriate. In a move somewhat like Marcion's, they displaced a supersessionist by a rejectionist understanding of the relation of Christianity to Judaism. ... Thus anti-Judaism, in the sense of contempt for the religion of the Jews, became more virulent under Enlightenment influence even while Jews as individuals became more acceptable.[139]

In today's post-Enlightenment climate of hostility and division, Lindbeck sees it as essential that the church once again adopt a non-supersessionist understanding of Israelhood in its self-definition. Rather than merely re-appropriating the "favorable prefigurations" of God's chosen people in the Old Testament, Lindbeck declares that the church must also see itself in light of the warnings and punishments for disobedience to which Israel was constantly subject. The church must come to see itself as a referent for "all the Old Testament denunciations of Israel's wickedness, prophetic threats of destruction and exile, and lamentations over Israel's God-forsakenness"[140] and not merely the praises and blessings which also belonged exclusively to Israel. In order for the church to overcome the deep schisms that characterize its existence—not to mention the deep schism between the church and the Jewish people—it must

---

138. Ibid., 88.
139. Ibid., 90.
140. Ibid., 91.

become "as communally self-critical and penitent as Old Testament Israel (and much contemporary Judaism)."[141]

If the church comes to see itself in this light, a new understanding of the Jewish people will inevitably follow. The widely held tenet of replacement theology whereby, as a result of the Jewish people's rejection of Jesus, God annulled his promises to them and transferred them to the church, is no longer sustainable if the church sees its covenant with God as reflecting the same conditions as Israel's covenant with God: "Unless election is irrevocable for Israel, Christians cannot see their communities as the prophets saw Israel, as the adulterous spouse whom the Lord God has cast off for a time but has irreversibly promised never to cease loving, never to divorce."[142] Along with rebuking any traces of self-righteousness within the church, this stance will also bolster ecumenism as certain branches of the church come to see the church universal as existing within these covenantal promises.

While a non-supersessionist understanding of the church as Israel can, as stated above, offer the church a renewed perspective on the Jewish people and contribute to ecumenical reconciliation, Lindbeck points out three additional consequences of this understanding. First, adopting this self-definition hedges against individualism, for membership in Israel was never about personal salvation but always had in its scope the ultimate redemption of the world. Second, the unity that characterizes the one people of Israel cannot but serve to correct the church's "intramural and extramural divisiveness and lovelessness" in which competitiveness runs rampant and somehow the failure of another Christian movement bolsters the self-confidence of one's own Christian movement. Third, Israel's history of suffering and rejoicing together can serve to correct today's church environment whereby "church membership is increasingly, even for Roman Catholics, a matter of changeable personal preference rather than lifelong communal loyalty."[143] Israel's prophets never abandoned Israel in search of a more pure people of God, for it was understood that it was this people that God promised to both bless and chasten.

The trend we have been tracing of Christian theologians rediscovering the election of Israel as the guiding concept for understanding the church

---

141. Ibid., 92.

142. Ibid.

143. Ibid., 93.

finds significant parallels in the Jewish world. While the Jewish thinkers espousing this renewal of the doctrine of election are not doing so primarily for the sake of the church's self-understanding, they do nevertheless see this as an ancillary benefit of a proper understanding of Israel's election.

In *The Election of Israel: The Idea of a Chosen People*, David Novak (whose work reveals a deep appreciation for and critique of both Barth and Rosenzweig[144]) endeavors to "retrieve" the doctrine of Israel's election, which he argues has been under a philosophical attack initiated by Baruch Spinoza. Novak begins with the complex question of "who is a Jew?" and writes the following: "The ultimate answer to any question of Jewish identity is theological, the one that points to the factors of election and covenant, the one that points to God's relationship with his people. More specific answers, legal or otherwise, will have to be consistent with this ultimate answer in order to be truly cogent."[145] For Novak, any attempt to answer this fundamental question is inadequate if it does not consider Israel's chosenness.

For Novak, Israel's election is inseparable from Israel's unique mission in the world. In this regard, Novak explores the connection between election and commandment. God chooses Israel for a purpose, and Israel fulfills that purpose by living out its divine calling: "The ultimate consequent of the election of Israel is the final redemption itself (*ge'ulah*)."[146] God's redemptive purposes are cosmic in scope, and his means for bringing about cosmic redemption are localized in the people of Israel.

Novak's reclamation of the doctrine of election for the Jewish people has direct implications for the church. It is precisely God's faithfulness to Israel—safeguarded within the doctrine of election—that guarantees God's faithfulness to the church. Thus, any attempt to attribute elect status to the church must be based on the prior election of Israel, and the ongoing validity of that election. This is the point to which supersessionism is profoundly blind: "If God broke his original promise to Israel, which is precisely the hidden premise of supersessionism, then how could the

---

144. See David Novak, *The Election of Israel: The Idea of the Chosen People* (Cambridge: Cambridge University Press, 1995); Novak, *Jewish-Christian Dialogue: A Jewish Justification* (New York: Oxford University Press, 1989); Novak, "Karl Barth and Divine Command: A Jewish Response," in *Talking with Christians: Musings of a Jewish Theologian* (Grand Rapids: Eerdmans, 2005), 127–45.

145. Novak, *The Election of Israel*, 5.

146. Ibid., 252.

Church—as the branch grafted onto the tree—possibly believe God's ultimate promise to her?"[147] Bader-Saye agrees: "The problem with becoming a replacement people is that one has no assurance one will not meet the same fate as those who went before."[148] Hence, a proper understanding of Israel's election is essential to a coherent understanding of the church's election.

Michael Wyschogrod has likewise placed significant emphasis on the election of Israel. Wyschogrod distinguishes between election as it has traditionally been conceived in Christianity and the "carnal" election of Israel. According to a Jewish doctrine of election: "God did not formulate a teaching around which he rallied humanity. God declared a particular people the people of God. He could have brought into being another kind of people of God, membership in which would have been a function of the individual's faith and/or virtue. This is how the Church came to understand its election."[149] To many, Wyschogrod admits, the election of carnal Israel is a scandal. Our modern mindset would much prefer an election based upon some sort of merit or worth. Nevertheless, the election of Abraham and his physical descendants clearly demonstrates that a Jew "is a Jew irrespective of what he believes or how virtuous he is."[150] In fact, Wyschogrod attributes great significance to election's disregard for merit; election is the sovereign decision of God, with no correlation to the attributes of the elect: "The implication is that God chooses whom he wishes and that he owes no accounting to anyone for his choices."[151]

In electing Israel, God made this people his dwelling place in the world. The Jewish people are therefore the "visible presence of God in

---

147. David Novak, "From Supersessionism to Parallelism in Jewish-Christian Dialogue," in *Talking with Christians*, 12.

148. Bader-Saye, *Church and Israel*, 96.

149. Wyschogrod, *Body of Faith*, 175.

150. Ibid., 176. Novak and Wyschogrod differ in their understanding of the relationship between election and revelation (that is, between Israel and Torah). In response to Wyschogrod's assertion that a Jew's membership in the covenant is not contingent upon their beliefs or obedience to the Torah, Novak claims that "the covenant requires that the people of Israel merit it by keeping God's commandments in the Torah. ... Wyschogrod's Biblicism and his effective subordination of the Torah to the Jewish people are not adequate to the genuine dialectic between grace and merit, between election and obligation, within classical Jewish teaching" (Novak, *The Election of Israel*, 246).

151. Wyschogrod, *Body of Faith*, 176.

the universe," the people with whom God has chosen to hyphenate his own name.[152] Wyschogrod demonstrates that, by virtue of being the people of the covenant, Israel is the means by which humanity gains knowledge of and access to God: "Although God is both the creator and ruler of the universe, he reveals himself to humankind, not as the conclusion of the cosmological or teleological proofs, but as the God of Abraham who took the people of Israel out of the land of Egypt and whose people this nation remains to the end of time. He thus remains inaccessible to all those who wish to reach him and, at the same time, circumvent this people."[153] Israel's election makes the true God known by continually unmasking the idols of the world: "Minute by minute, the existence of Israel mocks the pagan gods, the divine beings who rise out of the consciousness of all peoples but which are gentile gods because they are deifications of humanity and the forces of nature rather than the true, living God of Abraham."[154]

Wyschogrod describes how the nations often rebel against Israel's chosenness, and this is at least part of the explanation of the repeated hostilities carried out against Israel over the centuries: "Instead of accepting Israel's election with humility, [the nations] rail against it, mocking the God of the Jews, gleefully pointing out the shortcomings of the people he chose, and crucifying it whenever the opportunity presents itself."[155] However, Wyschogrod sees a notable exception when it comes to Christianity. The church, for Wyschogrod, is a sign that Israel's universal mission of making God known in the world is beginning to be fulfilled. The church uses the vocabulary of Israel and hears in Israel's scriptures the word of God. For Wyschogrod, this is cause for great rejoicing.[156]

However, Wyschogrod laments the replacement ideology that often accompanies Christians' claims to be followers of Israel's God. Commenting on the idea of the church as the "new Israel" or "new people of God" (reflected not least in the Vatican II documents *Lumen Gentium* and *Nostra Aetate*), Wyschogrod claims that any such understanding relegates Christianity back into the ranks of the rebellious nations who covet and

---

152. Ibid., 10–11.
153. Wyschogrod, "Israel, the Church, and Election," 180.
154. Ibid., 182.
155. Ibid.
156. See ibid., 183.

therefore seek to destroy Israel's divine election. Wyschogrod recommends an interesting test whereby Christianity's commitment to seeing itself as a partaker in rather than a replacer of Israel's covenant with God can be assessed: "Had the Church believed that it was God's will that the seed of Abraham not disappear from the world, she would have insisted on Jews retaining their separateness, even in the Church."[157] In other words, if the church truly believes in and affirms the ongoing election of Israel, it will support the Jewish people in their faithful adherence to Torah—even those Jews who are part of the church. We will examine this idea at great length in the following chapter.

## CONCLUSION

The post-Holocaust theologians surveyed above embody the heart of the new Jewish-Christian encounter, and their theological constructs challenge existing models and hasten toward a thoroughly reconceived understanding of the relationship between Judaism and Christianity. In significant ways, the christological and ecclesiological distinctives we have just reviewed augment and extend the frameworks offered by Barth and Rosenzweig, whose thoughts are deeply imprinted upon each of these post-Holocaust theologians. Having reviewed these six theological developments, we are now prepared to assess the ways in which the novel contributions of this group of thinkers aid us in our efforts to answer Marshall's framing question. Specifically, to what extent do these theologians affirm the ongoing election of the people of Israel while not sacrificing the universal applicability and unsurpassability of Christ? How do they connect the ongoing election of Israel with the ongoing practice of Judaism?

As we have seen, approaching Christology through the lens of Israel issues a reminder that Jesus' context matters. He cannot be abstracted from the Jewish people, and his salvific work cannot be unhitched from Israel's mission. While the gospel message can and should be endlessly translated and appropriated into diverse historical and geographical contexts, we cannot allow the significance of Jesus' concrete particularities to be obscured. It is not a matter of indifference that the Jewish Jesus came as Israel's messiah, and we cannot properly construe Christology if we

---

157. Ibid., 183.

lose sight of this framework. The christological strides taken by the post-Holocaust theologians reviewed above take a significant step forward in terms of elucidating and emphasizing the connection between Jesus and Israel.

However, two dangers become apparent as we assess the christological developments highlighted in this chapter. The first danger is that of summing up Israel's vocation in Christ to such an extent that the Jewish people do not retain any positive vocation of their own. It is to essentially collapse Israel into Christ. This dynamic is at work in Barth's theology and is likewise visible in aspects of Torrance's thought. As we saw above, Torrance depicts Christ as the climax of the conflict that is played out in Israel between divine revelation and human resistance. Christ's person and work is thus only intelligible within the context of Israel's story, and Israel continues to witness to the perpetual reverberations of God's final victory in Christ. Israel's suffering constitutes its participation in Christ's reconciling work, thus reinforcing the deep mutual indwelling of Christ and Israel. Here Torrance closely follows Barth, and ultimately falls prey to the same weakness. To define Israel's continued mission in the world in terms of its participation in Christ's atoning suffering/sacrifice is to cast Israel's witness in the purely negative terms that Wyschogrod warns against.[158] Israel remains bound to the crucifixion, perpetually inhabiting the dark theological shadow that human disobedience casts over salvation history.

Furthermore, for Israel to represent the "atonement prolonged into history" does not imply that Israel must live in any special way to carry out this vocation. In other words, it posits no necessary connection between the Jewish people and Jewish practice. According to this construct, a visible and distinct community of Israel is presupposed rather than prescribed.

---

158. See chapter 1, The Election of Israel in Barth's Theology, above. According to Wyschogrod: "Along with the unfaithfulness, there is also Israel's faithfulness, its obedience and trust in God, its clinging to its election, identity and mission against all the odds. True, all of Israel's obedience is tinged with its disobedience but all of its disobedience is also tinged with its obedience. It is true that Israel does not deserve its election but it is also true that its election is not in vain, that this people, with its sin, has never ceased to love its God and that it has responded to God's wrath ... by shouldering its mission again, again searing circumcision into its flesh and, while hoping for the best, prepared for what it knows can happen again" (Wyschogrod, "Why Was and Is the Theology of Karl Barth of Interest to a Jewish Theologian?" in *Abraham's Promise*, 223–24).

The conditions that must be in place to make the ongoing presence of the Jewish people a tangible reality (i.e., Torah observance) are glossed over completely.[159]

Torrance does move beyond Barth in his description of what the church must continually learn from Israel, and the ways in which Christian theology will be led astray without an ongoing Jewish corrective. For Torrance, Jewish monotheism prevents Christian Trinitarianism from lapsing into tritheism, Jewish Christology guards against Christian docetism and dualism, and Jewish iconoclasm corrects Christian anthropomorphism.[160] In a manner reminiscent of Rosenzweig, Torrance casts Jewish thought as a necessary protective measure against Christian heresy. Hence for Torrance, Judaism is more than Barth's "Synagogue of the time after Christ," depicted as "the more than tragic, uncannily pitiful figure with bandaged eyes and broken lance."[161] Nonetheless, even these positive functions of Jewish thought are not explicitly connected to Jewish practice. Though Torrance begins to correct Barth's unequivocally negative construal of Judaism's witness, the actual life of the Jewish people is still not given an adequate reckoning. Ultimately, while Torrance's thought posits a tight correspondence between Jesus and Israel, he does not address the necessary—and ongoing—connection between Israel and Torah.

If part of Torrance's shortcoming (mirroring Barth's) is collapsing Israel into Christ, the opposite extreme is also problematic. As we saw in Soulen's Christology, one way to preserve Israel's ongoing positive vocation is to diminish Christ, such that he becomes merely an exemplary model of Israel's faithful obedience. It seems that for Soulen, preserving Israel's election entails downplaying the unprecedented significance of the Christ event. We are left wondering if God's plan of cosmic redemption through the election of Israel might have been carried out just the same if Christ had never come. As we will see below, an even more pronounced version of this danger can be seen in the dual-covenant model, whereby Christ's significance never even makes contact with the people of Israel. These two extremes make it seem as though we must choose one or the other—either

---

159. Wyschogrod picks up on this necessity clearly, as we will explore in great detail in the following chapter.

160. See Torrance, *Mediation*, 19–20; 106–7.

161. Barth, *Church Dogmatics* I/2, 101.

Christ sums up Israel's destiny and Israel loses its significance, or Israel retains its vocation and a full-orbed Christology is blurred beyond recognition. The challenge of upholding a high Christology while simultaneously affirming Israel's unique vocation in the world—both before and after the coming of Christ—remains.

With regard to the topic of suffering, the theologians surveyed in this chapter move toward a model in which Israel's suffering and Christ's suffering coinhere. By reclaiming the cross as a symbol of Jewish suffering rather than Christian triumph, Maybaum jarringly alerts us to the ways in which Christ's crucifixion absorbs and embodies the repeated suffering and persecution of the Jewish people. Ultimately, however, Maybaum's intense critique of Christianity's appropriation of the cross serves to obscure the deep connection between Christ's suffering and Israel's suffering. Likewise, attributing atoning significance to Jewish suffering in the Holocaust without regard to Christ treads upon and transgresses Christian atonement theology. In the end, Maybaum constructs an either/or framework whereby the connection between the Jewish people and Jesus is eclipsed.

Wyschogrod's language of the Jewish people as a "sacrifice" and "sacrament" comes closer to elucidating their unyielding bond to Christ, though his thought does not make this relationship explicit. Torrance clearly exposits this link, though his understanding of Israel's participation in Christ's suffering looms so large that any ongoing vocation of the Jewish people separate from this participatory affliction is largely neglected. Once again, it seems to be Jewish theology rather than the Jewish people themselves that serves as a necessary check on Christian doctrine. While these theologians point toward the fundamental link between the crucifixion and Jewish suffering, the particulars of this connection are left unassembled. As we will see in the following chapter, Mark Kinzer takes up these pieces and configures them in a powerfully integrative way. Israel's participation in Christ's redemptive suffering serves as a key hermeneutical principle in Kinzer's theology.

As this chapter has made clear, rethinking Christology in light of Israel has embedded ecclesiological implications. To place Jesus within his Jewish context is to necessarily draw a connection between Israel and the church. Construing Christianity as "Judaism for the Gentiles" and Christ as the means by which the nations enter into covenant with God successfully hedges against supersessionism and posits an integral connection between Judaism and Christianity. However, it leaves open the possibility (and oftentimes the actuality) of obscuring Christ's relevance for the Jewish people. This perspective on Christianity often espouses some form of dual-covenant theology (as we saw in Herberg), thus functionally denying the universality of Christ's mission. If Jesus is the means by which gentiles enter into covenant relationship with the God of Israel, what significance does Jesus hold for those who already exist in covenant relationship with God? Dual-covenant theology rightfully assigns the Jewish people a continuing role in salvation history, but it fails to apply Christ's significance to their corporate life and vocation in any meaningful way. According to this model, Christ's unsurpassibility is in effect sacrificed at the expense of Israel's ongoing positive vocation in the world. From the lens of Marshall's question, this gap between Christ and Israel constitutes another version of the selective scope of Rosenzweig's Christology.

In its extreme form, granting Israel and the church separate covenantal particulars leads to a thoroughgoing separation between the two covenant communities. As Soulen rightly points out, the distinction between Jew and gentile is one that endures permanently according to the plan and purpose of God. This claim goes hand in hand with the affirmation of Israel's continued positive vocation in the world—in order for Israel to have a unique commission, it must be a unique people. However, this reality cannot obscure the way in which Jews and Christians together constitute the one people of God. We cannot allow Israel's uniqueness to overshadow its close redemptive and consummative connection with the Christian church. Christologically speaking, Christ cannot solely be the possession of the church. He must be the bridge between these two communities lest they remain comfortably and categorically separate.

It is an enduring struggle to elucidate the election of Israel and the church under the same umbrella while still preserving the distinctiveness of these two halves of the one people of God. Barth successfully connects Israel and the church (who collectively constitute the community of God) by positing that the election of both exists in Christ, but ends up portraying Israel's vocation in purely negative terms. For Rosenzweig, both communities have a positive and complementary vocation, but they exist in almost total freedom from one another. While Judaism and Christianity correct each other's respective dangers, their separate redemptive trajectories only come together eschatologically. The ecclesiological frameworks of Barth and Rosenzweig stem at least in part from their respective christological scaffolding. Whereas for Barth, Christ serves as the link between the two covenant communities, Rosenzweig's Christology has little direct bearing upon the Jewish people.

The post-Holocaust theologians partially bridge this gap between Barth and Rosenzweig by further fleshing out the christologically grounded twofold nature of the one elect community. Following Barth, Jenson refuses to define ecclesiology in unilateral terms and contends that the body of Christ is ultimately comprised of the church and the people of Israel. Bader-Saye and Lindbeck make a similar claim with regard to election, arguing that the church's election is utterly incomprehensible when not viewed as derivative of and participatory in Israel's election. Novak's reclamation of the doctrine of Israel's election ultimately serves to reinforce this claim.

As we have said, Marshall's question requires that while Israel and the church share in a common election, the two communities must also somehow remain distinct. According to Marshall, Israel "has special responsibilities toward God, namely to observe Torah, which is incumbent upon them alone."[162] Herberg points toward the kind of ecclesiological variegation that must accompany a twofold understanding of the people of God, though he fails to connect Christ to Israel. Perhaps more strikingly, Wyschogrod not only emphasizes the connection between Israel and Torah, but explicitly claims that a Jew's obligation to follow Torah is not washed away by the waters of baptism. However, Wyschogrod stops shy of claiming that Christ has any particular relevance for the Jewish people.

As helpful as the thinkers and ecclesiological models we have explored have been, we do not yet have a clear picture of how Israel's unique mission can be preserved while simultaneously upholding the connection forged through Christ between Israel and the church. In the final chapter, we will explore the way in which Mark Kinzer's Messianic Jewish theology builds upon the thoughts of Barth, Rosenzweig, and the post-Holocaust theologians. As we will see, Kinzer leads us yet another step in the direction of a providing an answer to Marshall's framing question.

---

162. Marshall, "Christ and the Cultures," 83.

**4**

—

# HASTENING TOWARD THE "DAY THAT IS ENTIRELY SHABBAT": MARK KINZER'S MESSIANIC JEWISH THEOLOGY

## INTRODUCTION

In chapter 3, we surveyed a number of key post-Holocaust Jewish and Christian theologians who are contributing to the widespread reconception of Christology and ecclesiology in light of Israel. Extending the trajectory begun by Barth and Rosenzweig, these theologians challenge a static and mutually exclusive construal of the relationship between Judaism and Christianity. Accordingly, they are among the key theological architects of the new Jewish-Christian encounter. However, in our assessment, we saw clearly the way in which upholding Israel's election and ongoing positive vocation is often competitive with a robust Christology. The two dangers we saw in chapter 3 were elevating Christology with the effect of essentially eclipsing Israel, or maintaining Israel's central role by compromising orthodox Christology (not least by denying Christ's relevance for Israel). Their significant strides notwithstanding, the post-Holocaust theologians we surveyed still fell short of providing an adequate answer to Marshall's framing doctrinal question.[1] The goal of maintaining a high Christology and a doctrine of Israel that takes seriously both Israel's election and Israel's covenantal obligations has remained elusive.

---

1. Once again, we will recall that Marshall seeks an affirmation of both the universal, ecclesially mediated saving mission of Christ *and* the irrevocable election of Israel, which necessarily includes the ongoing practice of Judaism. For the specifics of Marshall's theological framework, see Introduction: Marshall's Challenge, above.

In the final chapter of this study, we will explore and assess the thought of Messianic Jewish theologian Mark Kinzer. The novelty of Kinzer's theology offers a unique perspective on Jewish and Christian doctrinal claims, and Kinzer's contribution to the new Jewish-Christian encounter has yet to be fully appreciated. His work is done in intentional dialogue with the thinkers reviewed in chapter 3,[2] and his theological paradigm clearly bears the marks of Barth's and Rosenzweig's influence. By building upon the trajectory we have been tracking, Kinzer's thought enables us to take one step closer to answering Marshall's question. As we will see, a Messianic Jewish perspective on Judaism and Christianity opens vistas that thus far have remained obscured, particularly with regard to Christology and ecclesiology.

Before expounding Kinzer's thought, it is important that we say a word about Messianic Judaism more broadly. Since its emergence in the 1970s, Messianic Judaism has proven controversial in the larger landscape of Jewish-Christian relations. The Messianic Jewish voice has historically been muted in many spheres of Jewish-Christian dialogue, and oftentimes Messianic Judaism's contributions have indeed proven problematic.[3] While Messianic Jewish theology is not monolithic, the Messianic Jewish movement has consistently imbibed key characteristics of conservative evangelical Christianity and has oftentimes paradoxically aimed its message at Jews but against Judaism.[4] It has not always been clear what made Messianic

---

2. Rich Robinson has observed that, with regard to the "theological sphere" in which Kinzer moves, "almost all of Kinzer's interactions are with what are now termed 'postliberal' authors, both Jewish (post-Holocaust theologians) and non-Jewish" (Rich Robinson, "Postmissionary Messianic Judaism: A Review Essay," *Mishkan* 48 [2006]: 10).

3. For David Novak's critique of Messianic Judaism, see David Novak, "When Jews Are Christians," in *Talking with Christians: Musings of a Jewish Theologian* (Grand Rapids: Eerdmans, 2005), 218–28; Novak, *Jewish-Christian Dialogue: A Jewish Justification* (New York: Oxford University Press, 1989), 21–23; Novak, *The Election of Israel: The Idea of the Chosen People* (Cambridge: Cambridge University Press, 1995), 197–99. In chapter 8 of *Postmissionary Messianic Judaism*, Kinzer reviews the history of the Messianic Jewish movement, pointing to some of the same weaknesses and problems Novak highlights (see Mark Kinzer, *Postmissionary Messianic Judaism* [Grand Rapids: Brazos Press, 2005], 263–302).

4. For example, in the words of Messianic Jewish leader Daniel Juster, "I have become convinced that Rabbinic Judaism is a more severe departure from Biblical faith than I had ever realized in my early days of Jewish recovery. Although there are good things to be found in Rabbinic Judaism, and true wisdom from the Rabbis need not be rejected, I believe that the heart essence of Rabbinic Judaism is the rejection of the prophetic Spirit that forms the essence of the Hebrew Scriptures and the New Covenant Scriptures. The atmosphere of the New Testament carried on the Spirit of the Hebrew Scriptures pervasively and profoundly.

Judaism particularly Jewish, and its existence in the boundary space between Judaism and Christianity has made mapping Messianic Jewish theology a complex endeavor. Kinzer is in effect forging a new stream of Messianic Judaism, and his endorsement of rabbinic Judaism and traditional Jewish *halakhah*[5] is unique amid the landscape of Messianic Jewish theology. The lucid and constructive nature of Kinzer's thought merits consideration, as it offers considerable resources to answering Marshall's framing question.

In the pages that follow, we will explore the ways in which Kinzer's high Christology coinheres with his robust doctrine of Israel's election and unique vocation. For Kinzer, these doctrines are mutually reinforcing rather than competitive; Messianic Jewish theology contends that Israel and Jesus can only be understood with reference to one another. In this chapter, we will provide an overview of the method and contours of Kinzer's theology before moving on to explicate his doctrines of Israel, Jesus, and the church. While in the previous chapters we have treated Christology first, in this chapter, we will explicate Kinzer's doctrine of Israel first, as it is only in light of Israel that his Christology can be understood. From there, we will go on to explore the ecclesiological implications of Kinzer's Christology in light of Israel and assess his thought with regard to Marshall's question.

## THE SHAPE OF MESSIANIC JEWISH THEOLOGY

### THE CONNECTION BETWEEN ISRAEL AND JESUS

The mainstay of Kinzer's Messianic Jewish theology is the connection between Israel and Jesus.[6] From a Messianic Jewish perspective, every theological topic "must be considered in connection with Israel, and in

---

The essence of Rabbinism is a severe departure, replacing revelation with human reason. The rationalistic decisions of a majority of the rabbis using even hellenistic models of reasoning becomes authority in the Jewish community" (Daniel C. Juster, *Jewish Roots: A Foundation of Biblical Theology* [Shippensburg, PA: Destiny Image, 1995], xi).

   5. For a definition of *halakhah*, see Introductino, note 45 above.

   6. Since the original publication of this book, Kinzer has written a number of books and articles that elucidate his thought more fully. The most significant among these, for our purposes, is *Jerusalem Crucified, Jerusalem Risen: The Resurrected Messiah, the Jewish People, and the Land of Promise* (Eugene, OR: Cascade, 2018), in which Kinzer demonstrates the way in

connection with Yeshua, and Israel and Yeshua must always be considered in relation to one another."[7] This interrelationship is the fundamental starting point of Messianic Jewish theology, which Kinzer defines as "disciplined reflection about God's character, will, and works, and about God's relationship to Israel, the nations, and all creation in the light of God's irrevocable election of Israel to be a kingdom of priests and a holy nation, and God's creative, revelatory, and redemptive work in Messiah Yeshua."[8]

While Jewish theology traditionally places God's covenant with Israel at the center, and Christian theology is traditionally built around Christology, Messianic Jewish theology holds these twin convictions together. As Kinzer explains, "Israel's enduring covenantal vocation and Yeshua's pivotal role in the divine plan are central presuppositions of Messianic Jewish theology, not the products of its reflective process. Thus, these are beliefs that provide the basic shape of Messianic Jewish theology. If these twin convictions lose their centrality and cease to function as presuppositions and criteria of truth-value, the theology in question is no longer Messianic Jewish theology."[9]

---

which the gospel of Jesus is integrally tied not only to the ongoing story of God's covenant with Israel, but also the land that stands at the heart of that covenant.

7. Mark Kinzer, "The Shape of Messianic Jewish Theology," Lecture 8: Oral Torah, 4. Lectures and syllabi sent via personal correspondence.

Referring to Jesus by his Hebrew name, Yeshua, issues a reminder that Jesus was (and is) a Jew and that this fact carries with it certain implications that are all too often overlooked by the church. Kinzer feels strongly about this and related terminological specifications, for they serve to linguistically reinforce his theological position. In *Postmissionary Messianic Judaism*, Kinzer includes the following explanation of terms: "The one known in the church as Jesus Christ will here be referred to as *Yeshua the Messiah*. As a matter of historical record, all scholars today recognize that the first-century figure Yeshua of Nazareth was a Jew. However, very few of those who believe that he was raised from the dead acknowledge that he remains a Jew today and will do so forever, or consider the implications of this fact. By using an alien, Jewish-sounding name to refer to the one who is so familiar to the church, I hope to suggest that Yeshua is still at home with those who are literally his family, and that the church must reckon with the subtle ways it has lost touch with its own identity as a messianic, multinational extension of the Jewish people" (Kinzer, *Postmissionary Messianic Judaism*, 22).

8. Kinzer, "The Shape of Messianic Jewish Theology," Lecture 1: The What, How, and Why of Messianic Jewish Theology, 2. Notice that the breakdown of Kinzer's Christology follows the pattern of Rosenzweig's thought—creation, revelation, and redemption.

9. Ibid., 3.

## MESSIANIC JUDAISM AS A BRANCH OF JUDAISM

Though Messianic Judaism's doctrinal commitments place the Messianic Jewish movement somewhere between Judaism and Christianity, Kinzer clearly argues that the Messianic Judaism he envisions is properly a branch of Judaism, not a Christian denomination. While Kinzer readily admits that such a Messianic Judaism is scarcely a reality, he continues to dedicate his life and work to building its theological scaffolding and bringing it into existence. Commenting on the terminological shift that took place in the 1970s, whereby Hebrew Christianity came to be known as Messianic Judaism, Kinzer asserts that the "relationship to the Jewish people and Jewish religious tradition was given new emphasis."[10] Because Judaism refers primarily to the Jewish people and secondarily to the unique set of practices historically embodied by that people, "when we call our movement a type of Judaism, we are affirming our relationship to the Jewish people as a whole, as well as our connection to the religious faith and way of life that that people has lived throughout its historical sojourn."[11]

Claiming Messianic Judaism as a branch of Judaism has both practical and theological implications. Practically, Messianic Judaism thus defined "implies that our movement is fundamentally among Jews and for Jews. It may include non-Jews, but it is oriented toward the Jewish people, and those non-Jews within it have a supportive role."[12] Further, that Israel and Torah are inseparable for Kinzer means that Messianic Judaism fundamentally endorses and seeks to uphold rabbinic Judaism. We will discuss this facet of Kinzer's theology in more detail below. Theologically, "Messianic Jewish theology should draw its overall structure and substance from the Jewish theological tradition, while continually reinterpreting its content in light of God's self-revelation in Messiah Yeshua."[13] While, according to Kinzer, Messianic Judaism's primary identity is with the Jewish people and Jewish tradition, its understanding of Judaism is thoroughly interpreted through a christological lens. In Kinzer's words,

---

10. Mark Kinzer, "Toward a Theology of 'Messianic Judaism,'" in *Israel's Messiah and the People of God: A Vision for Messianic Jewish Covenant Fidelity*, ed. Jennifer M. Rosner (Eugene, OR: Cascade, 2011), 16.

11. Ibid., 17.

12. Ibid., 18.

13. Kinzer, "The Shape of Messianic Jewish Theology," Course Syllabus (online), 1.

Messianic Judaism involves more than the subtle tweaking of an existing form of Jewish life and thought—adding a few elements required by faith in Yeshua and subtracting a few elements incompatible with that faith. Instead, the Judaism we have inherited—and continue to practice—is entirely bathed in the bright light of Yeshua's revelation. In a circular and dynamic interaction, our Judaism provides us with the framework required to interpret Yeshua's revelation even as it is reconfigured by that revelation. In this way our Judaism and our Yeshua-faith are organically and holistically "integrated."[14]

Even as Messianic Jewish theology is a distinctively Jewish endeavor, it seeks to reveal the consonance between Judaism's core theological tenets and Christianity's central doctrinal claims.[15] In agreement with the post-Holocaust theologians we assessed in the last chapter, Kinzer challenges the way in which Judaism and Christianity[16] have, since the proverbial "parting of the ways," been construed in mutually exclusive terms. According to this traditional schema, Jesus becomes the dividing line between these two religious traditions that define themselves in contradistinction from one another. Against this ingrained paradigm,

---

14. Mark Kinzer, "Prayer in Yeshua, Prayer in Israel: The Shema in Messianic Perspective," in *Israel's Messiah and the People of God*, 63.

15. In Kinzer's words, "As a form of Judaism, our theology is rooted in the fundamental and essential Jewish teaching of covenantal monotheism: that the one who established a covenant with the patriarchs and matriarchs, redeemed their descendants from bondage in Egypt and gave them the Torah at Sinai, is the one and only God of the universe. But as *Messianic* Judaism, we also find Israel's God revealing himself in a unique and definitive manner in the person and work of Yeshua. Our theological task, then, is to clarify the meaning of these two convictions and to formulate them in such a way that they are recognized as mutually reinforcing rather than contradictory" (Kinzer, "The Shape of Messianic Jewish Theology," Lecture 2: The God of Israel, 1).

16. Kinzer understands the term "Christianity" to refer to the religious tradition of the gentile wing of the body of Messiah that developed to a large extent in distinction from and opposition to Judaism. In *Postmissionary Messianic Judaism*, Kinzer writes: "Because the terms themselves imply mutual exclusivity, in this book I will not use the words *Christianity*, *Christians*, and *church* in a conventional manner. I will employ them only to refer to the developed institutional reality that became overwhelmingly Gentile in composition and character. In speaking of realities that should be conceived of as integrally bound to Judaism and the Jewish people, or even as situated within those spheres, I will speak of Yeshua-*faith* (rather than Christianity), Yeshua-*believers* (rather than Christians), and the ekklesia (rather than the church)" (Kinzer, *Postmissionary Messianic Judaism*, 22).

Kinzer proposes a Christology in which Jesus is the essential link between Judaism and Christianity rather than their fundamental distinguishing factor. According to Kinzer's Christology, Jesus as the thoroughly Jewish Messiah of Israel is also the Lord of all creation. Accordingly, Jesus' call to discipleship goes out to all of humanity universally, though a response to that call looks different for Jews than it does for non-Jews. Again, we will explore these claims in detail in what follows.

Kinzer's refusal to accept Judaism and Christianity as two completely separate phenomena is based primarily on his reading of the New Testament. Kinzer dedicates two full chapters of his first book, *Postmissionary Messianic Judaism*, to expounding a New Testament theology of both the Jewish people and Jewish practice.[17] The conclusions that he draws undergird his entire theological program, according to which these two religious traditions are fundamentally linked and inextricably bound together—to each other and to God's redemptive purposes for all of creation. Of course, this argument cannot undo or deny the historical development by which the two have empirically become separate, distinct, and in many ways averse to one another. Like Rosenzweig, Kinzer claims that each tradition holds a unique component of creation's unfolding redemption, and the truth is only revealed when these two pieces are united. As we will see in more detail below, in Kinzer's paradigm, Messianic Judaism and Messianic Jews provide the link that binds these two realities together. Thus, Kinzer's ideas have relevance that reaches far beyond Messianic Judaism alone—his claims, if true, inform the identity of both the church and the people of Israel.

The radical nature of Kinzer's proposal has produced a host of critics,[18] yet the connection that Kinzer builds between Israel, Jesus, and the church creates a rich and nuanced interpretation of salvation history and God's redemptive work in the world. In what follows, we will explicate each of these facets of Kinzer's theology in turn, followed by an assessment of Kinzer's theology in light of Marshall's question.

---

17. See ibid., chs. 2 and 3.

18. See Mark Kinzer, "*Postmissionary Messianic Judaism*, Three Years Later: Reflections on a Conversation Just Begun," in *Israel's Messiah and the People of God*, 175–95, 202–04.

## THE ELECTION OF ISRAEL
## IN KINZER'S THEOLOGY

According to R. Kendall Soulen, the traditional Christian canonical narrative is driven forward by the tension and resolution of human sin and divine salvation. This "sin-redemption" paradigm highlights God's role as redeemer and portrays Christ as the definitive divine triumph over the destructive forces of sin and death. In contrast, the traditional Jewish canonical narrative emphasizes creation's movement toward final consummation, a process that is carried out through divine-human covenantal partnership. This "creation-consummation" paradigm highlights God's role as consummator and portrays Israel as God's chosen agent in creation's ongoing movement toward its intended *telos*. Like Soulen, Kinzer situates the dramatic tension of sin and redemption within the larger framing narrative of creation and consummation. We will explicate each of these strands of the narrative in turn, as Kinzer reads them.

### "CREATION-CONSUMMATION"

Kinzer points out that in the Genesis creation narrative, we are told six times that God beholds what he has made and calls it good, and finds the whole of his creation very good.[19] However, the climax of the narrative comes not on the sixth day (that is, creation's completion), but on the seventh (that is, the blessing and sanctification of the Sabbath). While creation is repeatedly called good, the word holy only appears with reference to the Sabbath. As Kinzer explains, "The world, untarnished by any evil, was very good. But it was not yet holy. It was *chol*—profane, secular."[20] In Genesis 2, the Sabbath is "not an institution but a hope,"[21] a sign that points toward creation's eschatological *telos*—holiness (*kedushah*). Before human sin and death even enter the narrative, the good/holy construct is already in place. The Genesis creation account sets the narrative in motion, pointing the way toward the intended sanctification of God's good creation.

As we follow the narrative forward, we see in Exodus that the redeemed and delivered people of Israel are commissioned to be a "kingdom of priests

---

19. Mark Kinzer, "Beginning with the End: The Place of Eschatology in the Messianic Jewish Canonical Narrative," in *Israel's Messiah and the People of God*, 95.

20. Ibid.

21. Ibid.

and a holy nation."[22] The holiness associated with the Sabbath gains fuller clarity through the calling and shaping of the people of Israel. According to Kinzer, "Only with the establishment of Israel as a holy people ... does *kedushah*, that eschatological destiny of consummated creation, descend to earth and become a signpost pointing the way to the world's ultimate fulfillment."[23] The holy people are fittingly commanded to observe the Sabbath, the holy day.[24] Likewise, as the nation commissioned to usher the divine presence into creation, Israel is tasked with building God's earthly abode— that is, the tabernacle and later the temple. The Sabbath as sanctified time and the tabernacle/temple as sanctified space are closely correlated; effectually, the Sabbath is a "temple in time" just as the temple is a "Sabbath in space."[25] The biblical narrative concretizes this connection by patterning the building of the tabernacle/temple after the six days of creation, with the tabernacle/temple as the *telos* of Israel's work mirroring the Sabbath as the *telos* of God's work.[26]

As Kinzer explains, "Both the holy day and the holy place are signs of the covenant between Hashem [God] and Israel. ... Both are also eschatological signposts. They show that the world has not yet attained its appointed goal of unrestricted *kedushah*, for only one day, one place, and one people are set apart as holy. Yet, they also show that holiness has pitched its tent in this world."[27] God's holiness in the midst of Israel, the Sabbath, and the tabernacle/temple points forward to the final consummation of creation—God's unrestricted presence and the final removal of the secular/

---

22. Exodus 19:6. According to Kinzer, "It is surely significant that the various forms of the Hebrew root *koph-dalet-shin* appear nowhere else in the book of Genesis. They are not seen again until Hashem's revelation to Moses at the burning bush (Exodus 3:5), and then with the first commandments given to Israel—in Egypt (Exodus 12:16; 13:2) and at Sinai (Exodus 19:6, 10, 14, 23)" (Kinzer, "Beginning with the End," 96 n. 8).

23. Kinzer, "Beginning with the End," 96.

24. Exodus 20:8. As Kinzer explains, "Shabbat only becomes a human institution after the exodus and in connection with Sinai and Israel's national constitution (coinciding with Israel's call to be a holy people and to construct a holy place); it is the preeminent sign of the covenant between God and Israel (Exodus 31:16-17)" (Kinzer, "The Shape of Messianic Jewish Theology," Lecture 3: Creation, Covenant and Consummation, 4).

25. Kinzer, "Beginning with the End," 96. See Abraham Joshua Heschel, *The Sabbath* (New York: Farrar, Straus & Giroux, 1951), 8, 21.

26. See Jon D. Levenson, *Sinai and Zion: An Entry into the Jewish Bible* (New York: HarperOne, 1985), 142-45.

27. Kinzer, "Beginning with the End," 96.

holy barrier. Jewish tradition describes the world to come as "a day that will be entirely Shabbat,"[28] and Scripture (perhaps most notably Zechariah 14 and Revelation 21) offers an eschatological vision in which God's holiness ultimately blankets all of space and time.

While Israel's holiness (which points forward toward this eschatological holiness) is expressed through its connection to the Sabbath and the tabernacle/temple, it is not ultimately contingent upon these things. According to Kinzer:

> The destruction of the *Bet Mikdash* [temple] in 70 A.D. and the subsequent exile from Jerusalem raised serious questions for the rabbinic tradition. Had Israel lost its *kedushah*? With no temple, no high priest, and no sacrifices, and with a life lived in the impure lands of the *goyim* (nations), how could Israel maintain its holiness? The answer of the rabbis is striking. They did not merely claim that Israel maintains its holiness, despite its loss of the temple system and the land. They went further and asserted that Israel's holiness was never entirely dependent on these factors.[29]

As Jacob Neusner explains, "The Mishnah may speak of the holiness of the Temple, but the premise is that the *people*—that kingdom of priests and holy people of Leviticus—constitute the center and the locus of the sacred."[30] As we saw in chapter 3, Michael Wyschogrod likewise argues that along with the temple in Jerusalem, the Jewish people are God's actual dwelling place in the world. According to Wyschogrod, "This is the utter seriousness of the election of Israel. God has decided to tie to himself a people, a people defined by a body, by the seed of Abraham and Sarah, Isaac and Jacob, and this people, who constitute a physical presence in the world, are at the same time the dwelling place for God in the world."[31] For Kinzer, Israel's existence as God's dwelling place is made manifest through

---

28. See M. Tamid 7:4; Genesis Rabbah 17:5; *The Koren Siddur*, 990.

29. Kinzer, "Beginning with the End," 100.

30. Jacob Neusner, *A Short History of Judaism: Three Meals, Three Epochs* (Minneapolis: Fortress, 1992), 47, quoted in Kinzer, "Beginning with the End," 100–1. Italics added.

31. Michael Wyschogrod, "A Jewish Perspective on Incarnation," 212–13. Note the connection to the Jewish people as sacrifice in chapter 3, Theology of Suffering, above; Wyschogrod, *The Body of Faith*, 25.

its distinctive covenantal responsibilities and practices. Kinzer describes the way in which every facet of Jewish life expresses the holiness allotted to Israel and hastens toward the sanctification and consummation of all of creation. For example, "just as *Shabbat* provides a weekly taste of the coming age, so every morning the observant Jew enters in a preliminary and preparatory way into the ecstatic praise offered on that day that will be completely *Shabbat*."[32] The people of Israel—with or without the temple, whether in the land or in exile—participate proleptically in the unbounded holiness that will characterize eschatological consummation. Their collective life and practices are postured toward ushering creation from being good to being holy: "*Kedushah* is an eschatological reality, and Israel shares in that reality in anticipation and also extends that reality as part of the process of preparing for the final redemption."[33] For Kinzer, as for Rosenzweig, Israel already lives in the intimate covenantal fellowship with God for which all creation is destined.

According to Kinzer's theology, creation's movement toward consummation provides the canonical narrative's overarching frame. It is within this primary narrative that the secondary narrative of sin and redemption unfolds, and it is to this sub-narrative that we now turn.

### "SIN-REDEMPTION"

Kinzer explains that the Genesis creation account is also about God restraining the forces of chaos that threaten to unravel creation's order and promulgate death and destruction: "The act of creation in ancient Near East religion is often pictured as a divine victory in combat over the powers of Chaos, which are symbolized by the raging sea, described as a serpent or dragon. The Psalms draw upon these traditions to emphasize the power of Hashem over all the forces of chaos that rage in the world. Chaos is not simply disorder; most fundamentally, it is the rejection of limits, a rebellion against finitude."[34] Creation as a series of divine separations reveals God as the one who restricts chaos by drawing boundaries and setting limits. The result of these boundaries is that the formless, empty, and dark void

---

32. Kinzer, "Beginning with the End," 100.

33. Ibid., 102.

34. Kinzer, "The Shape of Messianic Jewish Theology," Lecture 6: Evil and Its Conquest, 1. See, for example, Psalms 74:13–17, 89:9–11.

described in Genesis 1:2 is transformed into a vibrant and interconnected system of life, teeming with fullness and vitality.

The story of the flood in Genesis 6–8 demonstrates the interconnect-edness between the primordial powers of chaos and human conduct. As human beings give themselves over to deceit and violence (Adam and Eve's disobedience in Gen 3, Cain's murder of Abel in Genesis 4, the transgression of sexual boundaries in Gen 6), the perilous forces of chaos gain momen-tum and rise up. Genesis 7:11 reports that the "floodgates of the heavens were opened," and Kinzer explains that the torrents of rain represent "a breakdown in the firm boundaries established in Genesis 1 and a return to primeval chaos."[35]

The forces of chaos that reign in the flood narrative continue to plague creation, though their form morphs and intensifies: "As the biblical nar-rative advances, these powers of Chaos rise again to threaten the good creation, but now they are embodied in historical rather than natural forms—in the bloodthirsty, power-hungry empires of the ancient world. Through association with these empires, the character of Chaos is given a human face: arrogance, self-deification, savage cruelty and rejection of moral restraint. In taking a national form, Chaos is seen to express itself within the communal structures of human existence."[36] The defeat of these empires is repeatedly depicted using the same imagery seen in the Psalms to describe the subduing of the chaotic forces in the creation narrative.[37]

Just as chaos takes corporate human form in the oppressive and tyran-nical empires of the world, so the harmonious and differentiated order of creation takes on a communal form in the people of Israel, a kingdom of priests and a holy nation (Exod 19:6). Israel thus becomes God's agent of redemption, combating the chaotic forces of human sin and self-exaltation

---

35.  Kinzer, "The Shape of Messianic Jewish Theology," Lecture 6, 2. According to Jonathan Sacks, "Each element of creation has its proper place. The Hebrew word *averah*, like its English equivalent 'transgression,' signifies that sin involves crossing a boundary, entering forbidden territory, failing to respect the separation between different spaces and times. Adam and Eve transgress the boundary between permitted and forbidden foods; Cain transgresses the boundary of human life itself" (Jonathan Sacks, *To Heal a Fractured World: The Ethics of Responsibility* [New York: Schocken Books, 2005], 76.)

36.  Kinzer, "The Shape of Messianic Jewish Theology," Lecture 6, 2.

37.  For example, see Exodus 15:4–5, 8, 10; Psalm 77:16–20; Isaiah 27:1, 51:9–11; Daniel 7:2–3.

that threaten human life and God's good creation. The narrative plot continually centers on the struggle between Israel and the adversarial empires of the ancient world. Through its sacrifice and submission to God, Israel has the power to defeat chaos and restore creation's proper order.

Already in Genesis, the narrative hastens toward Israel's vocation on behalf of all of creation. Noah's postdiluvial sacrifice to God in Genesis 8:20 points forward toward Israel as God's partner in restraining the forces of chaos that threaten creation. As we have already noted, the building of the tabernacle and temple mirror the Genesis creation narrative, and the Akedah (the binding of Isaac in Gen 22) becomes the archetype for temple sacrifices. As Kinzer explains:

> Abraham and Isaac's response to God in the Akedah is the polar opposite of the characteristics seen in the human face of Chaos: instead of arrogance and self-deification, there is wholehearted surrender and obedience to God; instead of cruelty to others, there is the willingness to endure cruelty oneself. The Akedah, however, is more than an isolated incident in the life of Abraham. The identification of the site where it occurs as Moriah (the future Temple Mount) and the allusion to future temple worship found in Genesis 22:14 make it clear that Abraham's willingness to offer Isaac as a sacrifice underlies the efficacy of the temple sacrifices that will be offered in the coming generations. This connection between the Akedah and the temple sacrifices points to the true meaning of sacrifice: it is not just an act of ritual, but an offering of one's life and of what is most precious in one's life to God in faith, obedience, and love. It is giving the gift of oneself.[38]

While the Akedah provides the theological framework for temple sacrifices, we will recall that, according to Wyschogrod, the temple merely stood as a surrogate for Israel's primary mode of sacrifice—the Jewish people themselves. According to Kinzer, "In Rabbinic tradition, though Isaac was not actually slain, the Akedah is seen as the first and greatest act of Kiddush Hashem (martyrdom), so that when the Akedah is remembered before God one is also remembering all the faithful children of Israel who

---

38. Kinzer, "The Shape of Messianic Jewish Theology," Lecture 6, 3.

have given their lives throughout the generations to sanctify the Divine Name. Martyrdom is thus linked to the temple sacrifices, and is seen as having its own atoning power."[39]

As we will see below, Kinzer's Christology derives from Israel's divinely assigned vocation to be both a sanctifying agent that leads creation toward consummation and a corporate sacrifice that combats the self-exalting forces of chaos. However, before we move on to Christology, it is important that we note the necessary connection Kinzer draws between Israel's election and Israel's corporate life—that is, between Israel and Torah. We will recall that this connection is central in Marshall's description of what the election of Israel entails and in his question that frames our study.

## ISRAEL AND TORAH

In his exposition of Israel as God's agent of both consummation and redemption, Kinzer presupposes an intimate connection between Israel and Torah. While God's holiness dwells amid the people of Israel, it is in their collective life that that holiness is embodied and made manifest. Likewise, it is in the temple sacrifices (and the religious acts that replace temple sacrifices post-70 CE[40]) that Israel lives out its sacrificial vocation. Here Kinzer follows thinkers like Rosenzweig and Wyschogrod who posit the necessity of Torah observance for Israel to live out its covenantal commission. The connection between obedience and blessing (and disobedience and curses) is evident throughout the winding story of ancient Israel, and Jewish prayer and theology continue to reflect this connection. According to Hayim Halevy Donin, an essential element of Jewish belief is "the principle of reward and punishment. God promises to send blessings if His commandments are kept, and to withhold His blessing ... if they are ignored. The promise of reward and the threat of punishment ... are of a communal nature, directed to the collective body of Israel."[41]

Kinzer reminds us that the connection between Israel and Torah was not challenged until the modern era, in which Judaism was forced to

---

39.  Ibid. Compare with Wyschogrod and Maybaum on Israel's suffering as atonement, chapter 3, Theology of Suffering, above.

40.  Namely, Torah study, prayer, and acts of loving-kindness (see Pirkei Avot 1:2).

41.  Hayim Halevy Donin, *To Pray as a Jew: A Guide to the Prayer Book and the Synagogue Service* (New York: Basic Books, 1980), 153. See Kinzer, "Prayer in Yeshua, Prayer in Israel," 71–74.

define itself in post-Enlightenment terms.[42] As Kinzer explains, "In pre-modern Judaism authority was localized in three core realities, each of which was ordered in relation to the other: God, Torah, Israel."[43] God's election of and love for Israel as expressed through the gift of the Torah (which enables Israel to fulfill its vocation in the world) formed the cornerstones of Judaism's self-understanding.

Pre-modern Judaism's threefold understanding of authority was dealt a powerful ideological and sociological challenge by the Enlightenment. Judaism was not exempt from the sweeping forces of modernity, and it too had to navigate "the rise of the nation-state and its required individualization of society and the transformation of traditional communities into voluntary associations."[44] In the aftermath of the *Haskalah* (Jewish Enlightenment) and Jewish emancipation in Europe, individual Jews were now forced to define Judaism for themselves and choose with which Jewish community to affiliate. As a result of this challenge, rates of Jewish assimilation and conversion increased sharply and Judaism splintered into various streams, each of which offered a different response to modernity's challenge.

Kinzer maintains that these modern developments notwithstanding, Israel remains God's elect nation, commissioned with a unique vocation in the world that is ultimately for the sake of the world: "Hashem calls Israel to fulfill on earth a priestly role, living as a holy people set apart for the worship of God and for bearing witness to the holiness of the divine Name. ... Observance of the Torah ... [provides] the shape of the community's priestly service."[45] It is from this angle that Israel's ongoing corporate life is to be understood.

Likewise, it is in this light that the history of Christian anti-Judaism is to be assessed. While Christian supersessionism claims that Israel's widespread rejection of Jesus renders its continued election and service to God

---

42. For a more detailed account of the history of modern Judaism, see Introduction, the Emergence of Modern Judaism, above.

43. Mark Kinzer, "Modern Judaism," Lecture 5: Authority in Modern Judaism, 1–2.

44. Ibid., 2.

45. Mark Kinzer, "Messianic Jewish Community: Standing and Serving as a Priestly Remnant," Kesher 28 (2014), 79–101.

null and void, Kinzer maintains a high regard for Israel's ongoing role in salvation history. Kinzer argues that not only is Israel's vocation still in effect despite its rejection of Christ, but that its vocation actually in some sense required this rejection. While Kinzer is not unaware of God's judgment upon Israel throughout its history, he maintains that Israel's redemptive vocation is not nullified or obstructed by its repeated experience of divine chastisement.[46]

In agreement with Soulen and Wyschogrod, Kinzer explains how "the Gentile ekklesia's no to Israel was expressed and embodied in its no to Jewish practice."[47] Kinzer outlines the contours of the so-called "parting of the ways" and the growing tradition of Christian anti-Judaism, explaining that "the most influential Christian writers of the second century agree in teaching that the Jewish people no longer enjoy the privileges of the covenant and that Jewish practice (that is, circumcision, Sabbath observance, dietary laws) is an invalid expression of the life of the covenant."[48] The gospel message preached to the Jewish people beginning in the second century "spoke of how Israel's covenant and way of life had been annulled in the Messiah, and it claimed that Jewish identity and practice were of no value or even prohibited."[49]

To the extent that the Christian gospel is preached to Jews as a mandate to abrogate Jewish practice and covenantal life, Kinzer questions whether we can speak of a "Jewish rejection of Jesus" simpliciter. According to Kinzer's line of argumentation, to preach Jesus as being against Jewish practice is to proclaim an aberrant gospel, and thus the Jewish rejection of such a message cannot be straightforwardly condemned as unfaithfulness: "Any Jew who was loyal to the covenant would conclude that such a message could not possibly come from the God of Israel."[50] In fact, according

---

46. In this regard, Kinzer follows both Barth (in claiming that "Israel's history is an exposé of human nature in both its noble and ignoble aspects") and Torrance (in maintaining that Israel's suffering is on account of its unique nearness to God). Kinzer reminds us that "the real biblical theme is not so much Israel's infidelity as Hashem's unswerving fidelity in the face of Israel's infidelity." See Kinzer, "The Shape of Messianic Jewish Theology," Lecture 4: The People of Israel and the Nations, 2.

47. Kinzer, *Postmissionary Messianic Judaism*, 183.

48. Ibid., 187.

49. Ibid., 224.

50. Ibid.

to Kinzer, "To reject such a purported Messiah would be an act of fidelity to God rather than infidelity!"[51] Kinzer quotes Paul van Buren's explanation of this point:

> The Gospel met Gentiles as a demand to abandon their pagan ways and service of gods that are not God. The Gospel met Jews, as the church after Paul's time preached it, as the demand to abandon the express commands and covenant of the very God whom the church proclaimed! Here is a profound incoherence that has arisen because of the lack of a proper Christian theology of Israel. The theological reality which such a theology must address, then, is that Israel said No to Jesus Christ out of faithfulness to his Father, the God of Israel.[52]

If God's covenant with Israel is irrevocable, and Israel is called to express this covenant through Torah observance, then any gospel that challenges the connection between God and Israel or Israel and Torah in effect denies God's faithfulness as well as God's central promises and works throughout history. In this way, continued Jewish faithfulness to God (which, as we have just explained, has historically necessitated a rejection of the gospel as it has been preached to the Jewish people) issues a stark reminder to the church that its theology must take into account not only Israel, but also Torah.

Here Kinzer's theology diverges from Barth's and resonates with Rosenzweig's. Whereas for Barth, confession of Christ is tantamount to faithfulness and rejection of Christ is by definition unfaithfulness, Kinzer (like Rosenzweig) construes the church and the Jewish people as providentially preventing one another from falling into heresy. While the church is tasked with holding the Jewish Messiah before the eyes of the Jewish people, the Jewish people are tasked with reminding the church just what that Messiah's Jewish identity entails. In other words, part of the Jewish people's ongoing vocation is to continually call to the church's attention the God of Israel's indelible covenant with the people of Israel.

---

51. Ibid.

52. Paul M. van Buren, *A Christian Theology of the People of Israel*, vol. 2 of *A Theology of the Jewish-Christian Reality*, 3 vols. (San Francisco: Harper & Row, 1983), 34, quoted in Kinzer, *Postmissionary Messianic Judaism*, 224.

While Kinzer applauds the recent steps taken by the Catholic Church and other Christian organizations and individuals to renounce supersessionism, he laments that these efforts have not gone far enough: "While most Christian churches and theologians now recognize the irrevocable nature of the covenant between God and Israel, few have considered the implications of this recognition for the validity and importance of Jewish practice for all Jews (including those who believe in Yeshua), and even fewer have considered the implications for ecclesiology and the church's own self-definition."[53]

As we will see in the sections that follow, Kinzer's Christology and ecclesiology are intimately tied to his conception of Israel, which serves as a fundamental lens for his entire theological system. Likewise, the connection between Israel and Torah significantly undergirds his ecclesiological proposal. Let us address these theological loci in turn.

## THE MISSION OF CHRIST IN KINZER'S THEOLOGY

As we have already noted, Kinzer's Christology highlights the continuity between God's work in Israel and the mission and identity of Israel's Messiah. Kinzer's Christ exists squarely within the narrative framework of Israel and comes as the perfect fulfillment of Israel's destiny. Likewise, following Barth, Kinzer asserts that Israel's election is ultimately grounded in Christ's election.[54] Christ definitively carries out Israel's twofold mission of ushering creation into consummation and defeating the forces of chaos that threaten creation. We will assess the way in which Kinzer establishes these links between Israel and Jesus by focusing on three interrelated christological themes: the incarnation and life of Christ, the crucifixion and death of Christ, and the resurrection and victory of Christ.

### THE INCARNATION AND LIFE OF CHRIST

For Kinzer, God's incarnation in Christ is understood in consonance with God's incarnation in the Jewish people. While Israel is the primary locus of God's holiness in creation (expressed not least through Israel's

---

53. Kinzer, *Postmissionary Messianic Judaism*, 182.

54. See Kinzer, "Messianic Jewish Community: Standing and Serving as a Priestly Remnant," 11.

observance of the Sabbath and worship in the temple/tabernacle), God's incarnation in Christ commences a new phase in creation's movement toward consummation. Kinzer explains that "while the enfleshment of the Memra (Word) is a new and unique event, it should nonetheless be viewed in continuity with what precedes it—as a concentrated and intensified form of the divine presence that accompanies Israel throughout its historical journey. Thus, contrary to the common Christian canonical narrative, the divinity of Yeshua can be seen not as a radical rupture and disjunction in the story but as a continuation and elevation of a process initiated long before."[55]

This aspect of Kinzer's incarnational theology resonates with Wyschogrod's thought. We will recall that, while Wyschogrod does not accept the idea of God's incarnation in the person of Jesus, he sees this claim as a variation of a Jewish idea rather than something entirely novel.[56] For Wyschogrod, the Christian doctrine of incarnation merely nuances the Jewish understanding of incarnation by claiming that God dwells in one Jew rather than in the Jewish people corporately. Wyschogrod's description of Christian incarnational theology aptly characterizes Kinzer's Christology. In fact, following Herberg, Kinzer posits that Yeshua is the "one-man Israel."[57]

As Kinzer explains, "The New Testament employs many biblical images in its attempt to explore the meaning and significance of Yeshua. One of those images has special relevance to our topic of study: Yeshua as representative and individual embodiment of the entire people of Israel."[58] The incarnation both sums up the story of Israel and points forward toward the prophetic fulfillment of Israel's ultimate destiny as a light to the nations and the sanctifying agent for the whole world. Israel's anticipatory experience of holiness is brought to a new height as the divine word becomes flesh in the person of Christ. In the incarnation, God's role as consummator is further revealed and God's good creation moves one significant step closer toward sanctification.

---

55. Kinzer, "Beginning with the End," 104.

56. See chapter 3, God's Incarnation in the Jewish People, above.

57. See Kinzer, "Beginning with the End," 109.

58. Kinzer, Postmissionary Messianic Judaism, 217.

Jesus' embodiment of "a concentrated and intensified form of the divine presence" can be seen through the invasive quality of his holiness: "Yeshua's enfleshed *kedushah* stands in continuity with the holiness of the *Mishkan* [tabernacle] and the *Bet Mikdash* [temple]—but there is also something new about his *kedushah*. The character of his life and mission displays a dynamic, outgoing, prophetic *kedushah* that will eventually lead to the sanctification of the entire created order (as envisioned in Zechariah 14 and Revelation 21)."[59]

While Israel was commanded to refrain from contact with ritually unclean objects and persons, lest Israel's holiness be defiled,[60] Jesus' holiness flows outward into the impure world. Through Jesus, the holiness embodied by Israel begins to ripple throughout creation, as it was always intended to do: "Yeshua's contact with the impure does not defile him, but instead transmits purity, holiness, and life to the impure ones around him. Yeshua's life and mission thus display a new type of *kedushah*, a prophetic, invasive holiness that needs no protection, but reaches out to sanctify the profane."[61] Kinzer points to Jacob Milgrom's list of the three sources of impurity according to the Torah—that is, corpses/carcasses, scale disease, and genital discharges.[62] According to the Gospels, Jesus comes into contact with all three.[63] In these instances, Jesus does not become defiled or ritually impure; rather, the sources of impurity become sanctified. In Christ, "the Holy One marches forth to make war on the kingdom of impurity."[64]

Here we see Yeshua enacting the fulfillment of Israel's destiny, as Israel's holiness was always intended to expand outward and sanctify the world. When Abraham is called by God in Genesis 12, this element

---

59. Kinzer, "Beginning with the End," 104.

60. As Kinzer explains, "The holiness of Sinai, the *Mishkan*, and the Jerusalem temple required fences, boundaries, and guards, so that the holy might not be defiled by contact with the impure or insufficiently holy" (Kinzer, "Beginning with the End," 104–5).

61. Ibid., 107.

62. Jacob Milgrom, *Leviticus 1–16*, Anchor Bible (New York: Doubleday, 1991), 46; see Kinzer, "Beginning with the End," 105.

63. See Matthew 8:1–4, 9:18–26; Mark 1:40–45, 5:21–43; Luke 5:12–14, 7:11–17. Kinzer also describes the "communal meal" as another " 'new channel' through which Yeshua mediates the sacred" (Kinzer, "Beginning with the End," 107).

64. Kinzer, "Beginning with the End," 106.

of outward expansion is already present—"I will bless those who bless you, and whoever curses you I will curse; and all peoples on earth will be blessed through you"(12:3). The prophet Isaiah repeats this idea: "It is too small a thing for you to be my servant to restore the tribes of Jacob and bring back those of Israel I have kept. I will also make you a light for the Gentiles, that you may bring my salvation to the ends of the earth"(49:6). In this way, God's holiness amid Israel is transmitted to the world through Christ. In Kinzer's words, "Yeshua mediates the divine presence as the fleshly *Mishkan*, but he is not surrounded by a series of concentric barriers designed to restrict access to a privileged few. Instead, he anticipates and prepares the way for the sanctuary of the new Jerusalem, in which the city and the holy of holies are one and the same."[65]

## THE CRUCIFIXION AND DEATH OF CHRIST

Just as Kinzer understands the incarnation to be an intensification of God's presence in Israel, he views Christ's death in terms of Israel's vocation and destiny: "As the true Israelite, blameless and holy, Yeshua sums up all that Israel was intended to be. He becomes the perfect temple, priest, and sacrifice, offering himself to God on behalf of Israel, the nations, and the entire creation. Yeshua dies not only as a sacrifice but also as Israel's perfect martyr, who, like Isaac in the *Akedah*, embodies all of Israel's martyrs in himself, and whose blood is shed both to atone for sins and to prepare the way for the coming of *Olam Haba* [the world to come]."[66] According to Kinzer, Jesus' definitive self-sacrifice finally triumphs over the forces of chaos and destruction. Likewise, Christ bears God's refining judgment upon Israel and proleptically embodies Israel's eschatological restoration. Let us examine each of these concepts in turn.

### Jesus as the Ultimate Sacrifice

Kinzer expounds the Matthean account of Jesus' baptism, explaining that this event is an essential key to understanding Jesus' death. Just as Israel has been tasked with fighting against the forces of chaos (represented in the Psalms as raging waters), Jesus' baptism reveals his solidarity with

---

65. Ibid., 107–8.
66. Ibid., 123.

Israel's mission and his commitment to Israel's cause. In Kinzer's words, "Yeshua is immersed in the raging waters of Chaos on Israel's behalf, that those seas might be calmed through him."[67] The voice from heaven in Matthew 3:17 ("This is my son, whom I love ...") clearly alludes to Genesis 22:2 ("Take your son, your only son Isaac, whom you love ..."), further tightening the parallel between Jesus' story and Israel's story. While the Akedah provides the interpretive grid for Israel's sacrificial vocation, Matthew makes it clear that this vocation is finally and fully embodied in Jesus. In Kinzer's words, "Yeshua is God's beloved Son, whom God will give up for the sake of Israel and the world. But he is also the descendant of Abraham and Isaac whose self-offering on the cross completes Israel's sacrificial and atoning vocation implicit in the *Akedah* and rendered explicit in Isaiah 53."[68] In Mark 10:38 and Luke 12:49–50, Jesus refers to his impending death as a baptism, and his actual baptism is "a symbolic expression of his willingness to endure suffering and even death as Israel's representative."[69]

Jesus' struggle against the forces of chaos follows the pattern of Israel's sacrificial commission, and his death enacts the final and climactic defeat over these evil powers that hold creation in bondage: "Just as the Apostolic Writings [New Testament] portray the divine enfleshment in the priestly imagery of the *Mishkan*-Temple, so they portray the death of Yeshua in the priestly imagery of atoning sacrifice."[70] Revelation 5:5–6 describes Jesus as a slain lamb standing at the center of the throne, confirming that "the powers of chaos are defeated by the Messiah's act of whole-hearted worship, in the spirit of the *Akedah*. ... Yeshua is the great conqueror of the Dragon and the Beast, but his victory comes through his martyrdom, which is portrayed as a sacrifice presented before the heavenly throne."[71] Just as Israel fought against chaos by means of sacrifice, worship, and loving self-offering to God, Jesus' definitive victory takes the same shape: "If Yeshua is the perfect

---

67. Kinzer, "The Shape of Messianic Jewish Theology," Lecture 6, 4.

68. Mark Kinzer, "Israel's Eschatological Renewal in Water and Spirit: A Messianic Jewish Perspective on Baptism." A revised version of this paper was published in Kinzer, *Searching Her Own Mystery: Nostra Aetate, the Jewish People, and the Identity of the Church* (Eugene, OR: Cascade, 2015), ch. 5.

69. Kinzer, "The Shape of Messianic Jewish Theology," Lecture 6, 4.

70. Kinzer, "Beginning with the End," 108.

71. Kinzer, "The Shape of Messianic Jewish Theology," Lecture 6, 5.

one-man Israel, then his death as a martyr under the Romans sums up all of Israel's righteous suffering through the ages, provides the ultimate expression of the commitment to God and self-giving love shown first in the *Akedah*, and effects definitive atonement."[72]

According to John's eschatological vision of "a new heaven and a new earth," there is, fittingly, "no longer any sea";[73] the sea as the symbolic representation of the chaotic forces that oppose creation has finally been defeated. Israel's perpetual battle against chaos is definitively won in Christ. This linkage between Israel's vocation and Christ's victory demonstrates again that, for Kinzer, Christology is only intelligible against the backdrop of God's covenant with and purposes for Israel: "A Messianic Jewish version of the canonical narrative will see the death of Yeshua in continuity not only with Israel's temple system but also in continuity with Israel's ongoing life in this world. As with the incarnation, so with Yeshua's atoning death: the Messiah epitomizes and elevates Israel's story, rather than ending it and beginning something entirely new."[74]

### Jesus as the Bearer of Divine Judgment

While Jesus' baptism (both in its own right and in its foreshadowing of his sacrificial death) symbolizes his defeat over the forces of chaos, it also embodies Jesus' absorption of God's judgment upon Israel. In Matthew 3:11-12, John the Baptist declares, "I baptize you with water for repentance. But after me comes one who is more powerful than I, whose sandals I am not worthy to carry. He will baptize you with the Holy Spirit and fire. His winnowing fork is in his hand, and he will clear his threshing floor, gathering his wheat into the barn and burning up the chaff with unquenchable fire." Kinzer explains that the threefold baptism referred to by John (water, the Holy Spirit, and fire) is to be interpreted in light of Ezekiel 36-37 and Malachi 3-4.

Addressing Israel during the Babylonian exile, Ezekiel 36:24-28[75] speaks of God's promise to restore the people to their land, which necessarily

---

72. Kinzer, "Beginning with the End," 109.

73. Revelation 21:1.

74. Kinzer, "Beginning with the End," 108.

75. Ezekiel 36:24-28: "For I will take you out of the nations; I will gather you from all the countries and bring you back into your own land. I will sprinkle clean water on you, and you

includes cleansing them from the sins that drove them into exile. Kinzer explains the connection between Ezekiel's prophecy and John's proclamation: "As recent commentators have noted, many first-century Jews believed that the Babylonian exile had never really ended, and that the prophecies of restoration still awaited fulfillment. This was true even for many Jews living in the land of Israel. John appears to be among them, and he anticipates that the combined baptismal missions of the forerunner and his greater successor will achieve the full reality which Ezekiel prophesied."[76]

Thus, John administers water baptism, whose preparatory function focuses on repentance and the forgiveness of sins[77] and points forward toward the coming baptism with the Holy Spirit and with fire. According to Ezekiel 36:27, the placing of the divine Spirit within the people of Israel empowers them to live in covenant fidelity and obedience to the statutes and ordinances of the Torah. As for the baptism with fire, Malachi 3-4 describes the impending day of the Lord by employing imagery of a refining, purifying, and consuming fire.[78] Malachi speaks of a forerunner[79] who will prepare the way for this day of suffering and judgment, and Matthew identifies this forerunner as John.[80] As Kinzer explains, "Interpreted in the light of Malachi, the baptism of fire announced by John refers to the eschatological distress that will purify the righteous and destroy the wicked. It points not just to a post-mortem judgment that all human beings must endure, but specifically to the tribulation—centered in the holy city of Jerusalem—that accompanies the 'day of the Lord' and constitutes the 'birth-pangs of the Messiah.' Like the baptism with the Holy Spirit, this

---

will be clean; I will cleanse you from all your impurities and from all your idols. I will give you a new heart and put a new spirit in you; I will remove from you your heart of stone and give you a heart of flesh. And I will put my Spirit in you and move you to follow my decrees and be careful to keep my laws. Then you will live in the land I gave your ancestors; you will be my people, and I will be your God."

76. Kinzer, "A Messianic Jewish Perspective on Baptism," 4–5.

77. See Matthew 3:2, 6.

78. See Malachi 3:2–3; 4:1.

79. This forerunner is referred to as a "messenger" in Malachi 3:1 and as "the prophet Elijah" in Malachi 4:5.

80. See Matthew 3:4; 11:10, 14.

baptism of fire has as its object the restoration of Israel—in this case, the restoration of Israel's worship."[81]

This backdrop sets the context for John's resistance to baptizing Jesus in Matthew 3:13-14. As Kinzer explains, "John's words express more than the acknowledgement of a superior by a subordinate. John knows that he needs to be baptized by Yeshua because he knows that *all Israel needs to be baptized by Yeshua*—because Yeshua is the Coming One who baptizes with the Holy Spirit and with fire. He is the one who will bring Israel's purification, sanctification, and national restoration."[82] However, Jesus insists that he be baptized and thus reconfirms his tight identification with Israel; he is the one who will bear Israel's judgment. Once again, the crucifixion is already in view, as "Yeshua's submission to John's baptism anticipates the obedience that will lead him to the cross."[83] Jesus' connection to Israel is reinforced by the context of Jesus' baptism in Matthew 3. As Kinzer explains:

> Matthew 2 presents the story of Yeshua's infancy in terms of Israel's exodus from Egypt, and applies Hosea 11:1—"Out of Egypt have I called my Son"—to the return of Yeshua (with Joseph and Mary) from Egypt. Similarly, Matthew 4 recounts Yeshua's forty days of testing in the wilderness, in which he relives Israel's forty years of wandering before entering the land of promise. The Adversary challenges Yeshua to prove that he is "the Son of God." The biblical texts cited by Yeshua in response all derive from Deuteronomy, and speak of the covenantal requirements incumbent on the people of Israel. Thus, Yeshua demonstrates that he is the Son of God—the true representative of Israel—not by working signs and wonders, but by obeying the Torah as Israel was called to do.[84]

---

81. Kinzer, "A Messianic Jewish Perspective on Baptism," 6; see Matthew 24-25.

82. Kinzer, "A Messianic Jewish Perspective on Baptism," 6; see also Kinzer, *Postmissionary Messianic Judaism*, 218.

83. Kinzer, "A Messianic Jewish Perspective on Baptism," 7.

84. Ibid., 9.

Just as Jesus' bears Israel's judgment and embodies the obedience to which Israel is called, his resurrection guarantees the final restoration of Israel. Let us move on to address this aspect of Kinzer's Christology.

### THE RESURRECTION AND VICTORY OF CHRIST

Not surprisingly, Kinzer likewise points to Israel's history and theology as the key to understanding Jesus' resurrection. While Jesus' baptism at the hands of John connotes Israel's cleansing prophesied in Ezekiel 36, Jesus' resurrection by the Spirit points forward to Israel's national restoration prophesied in Ezekiel 37. According to Kinzer, the history of the Jewish belief in resurrection provides the interpretive grid for Jesus' resurrection: "Just as martyrdom first became a significant theme in Jewish life as a result of the persecutions during the Maccabean period, so resurrection likewise emerged as a major motif during the same period—and precisely in relation to the martyrs."[85] Here, Kinzer draws upon the thought of N. T. Wright, who claims that the belief in resurrection is "bound up with the struggle to maintain obedience to Israel's ancestral laws in the face of persecution. Resurrection is the divine reward for martyrs; it is what will happen after the great tribulation."[86] Wright is quick to mention that Israel's hope in resurrection was not an individual hope as much as it was a hope for national renewal and restoration. As Wright explains:

> The old metaphor of corpses coming to life had, ever since Ezekiel at least, been one of the most vivid ways of denoting the return from exile and connoting the renewal of the covenant and of all creation ... If Israel's god would "raise" his people (metaphorically) by bringing them back from their continuing exile, he would also, within that context, "raise" those people (literally) who had died in the hope of that national and covenantal vindication. "Resurrection," while focusing attention on the new embodiment of the individuals

---

85. Kinzer, "Beginning with the End," 109.

86. N. T. Wright, *The New Testament and the People of God* (Minneapolis: Fortress Press, 1992), 331–32.

involved, retained its original sense of the restoration of Israel by her covenant god.[87]

If Jesus is the one-man Israel who defeats the forces of evil and chaos as the ultimate Jewish martyr, Jesus' resurrection becomes the pledge of Israel's corporate renewal and restoration. Soulen makes this connection explicit: "Jesus, the firstborn from the dead, is also the first fruits of God's eschatological vindication of Israel's body. In light of Jesus' bodily resurrection, it is certain not only that God will intervene on behalf of the whole body of Israel at the close of covenant history but also that by this very act God will consummate the world."[88]

The connection Kinzer draws between Israel's vocation and hope for resurrection and Jesus' mission and actual resurrection can be seen through the New Testament reading cycle that Kinzer developed. In Judaism, the Torah is read publicly over the course of a year, with one major portion read each week in the Shabbat morning service. Likewise, a *Haftarah* portion from the Prophets[89] is also read each week, and these passages usually correspond thematically to the weekly Torah portion. Kinzer selected readings from the New Testament Gospels that would accompany the weekly Torah and Prophets readings in Messianic Jewish synagogue liturgies. As Kinzer explains, "The traditional annual cycle of Torah readings invites us to set our daily life in the context of Israel's founding events—the call of Abraham and Sarah, the exodus from Egypt, the giving of the Torah, and the journey to Cana'an. Similarly, this new annual cycle of readings from the *Besorah* [gospel] invites us to see both our own personal stories and the story of Israel in the light of Yeshua's redemptive journey, from his birth to his resurrection."[90]

The New Testament reading cycle begins with the birth of Jesus and his early work, just as the Torah cycle begins with the creation of the world

---

87. Wright, *People of God*, 332. See also Paul M. van Buren, *According to the Scriptures: The Origins of the Gospel and of the Church's Old Testament* (Grand Rapids: Eerdmans, 1998), 27–28.

88. R. Kendall Soulen, *The God of Israel and Christian Theology* (Minneapolis: Fortress, 1996), 166.

89. In Judaism, the Prophets (*Nevi'im*) includes the narrative books of Joshua through Kings as well as Isaiah, Jeremiah, Ezekiel and the twelve minor prophets.

90. Kinzer, "Chayyei Yeshua Shabbat Besorah Readings." Available at ourrabbis.org /main/resources/chayyei-yeshua-reading-cycle/.

and the call of the patriarchs and matriarchs. The three weeks between the 17th of Tammuz and the 9th of Av in the Jewish calendar are designated as a time of mourning the destruction of the temple, and the *Haftarah* readings for these three weeks are passages of admonition and judgment. For the New Testament readings for these three weeks, Kinzer selected passages that narrate Jesus' death, highlighting the direct connection between Jesus' atoning suffering and Israel's judgment and lament. The *Haftarah* passages for the seven weeks following the 9th of Av and leading up to Rosh Hashanah are readings of consolation and restoration, all drawn from Isaiah 40–66. To match these readings, Kinzer assigned New Testament texts about Jesus' resurrection. According to Kinzer, "the cycle thus points us to the truth that Yeshua, as the King of Israel and its representative, embodies in his person the meaning of the temple, the holy city, and Jewish history as a whole. His suffering sums up and purifies Israel's suffering, and his resurrection will bring about Israel's ultimate restoration."[91]

According to Kinzer, Jesus not only embodies Israel's history but also points forward to the final consummation of that history. While Jesus' life, death, and resurrection are intimately intertwined with Israel's ongoing story, Jesus inaugurates a future that Israel has not yet experienced: "Whereas the enfleshment of the *Memra* in Yeshua intensifies and elevates an eschatological reality already anticipated in Israel's life, and Yeshua in his death embodies and sums up all of Israel's martyrs through the ages and prepares the way for *Olam Haba*, in his resurrection he establishes a proleptic eschatological reality unprecedented in Israel's history."[92]

Overall, Kinzer's Christology aligns with Soulen's recasting of the canonical narrative, according to which "the gospel is the story of the God of Israel's victory in Jesus over powers that destroy. Just so, God's victory in Jesus is the center but not the totality of Christian faith. Faith in the gospel presupposes the God of Israel's antecedent purpose for creation, a purpose threatened by destructive powers but vindicated by God in the life, death, and resurrection of Jesus."[93]

---

91. Ibid.

92. Kinzer, "Beginning with the End," 111.

93. Soulen, *The God of Israel*, 156. It is important to note that Kinzer also critiques Soulen's Christology, which "seems to present Yeshua's death and resurrection primarily as a pledge

## THE SUFFERING OF CHRIST AND THE SUFFERING OF ISRAEL

We have seen in the previous chapters that both Barth and Rosenzweig draw a theological connection between the suffering of Israel and the suffering of Christ, and this connection gains additional traction in the work of Jewish and Christian post-Holocaust theologians. According to this trajectory of thought, Isaiah 53 is increasingly read with both the traditional Jewish interpretation and the traditional Christian interpretation in view, and new significance is ascribed to the idea that the Jewish people somehow participate in the atoning suffering of Christ.

Kinzer devotes ample attention to this topic, explicating what he perceives to be the bond between the suffering of Christ and the suffering of Israel. Kinzer exegetes Romans 9–11 with this connection in mind, noting that a traditional reading of this text "has seen the hardening of nonremnant Israel as exclusively punitive in nature." Kinzer, however, reaches a different conclusion. According to his reading, this text depicts "Israel's partial hardening as a form of suffering imposed by God so that God's redemptive purpose for the world might be realized."[94] Kinzer sees a tight parallel between the partial hardening of Israel in Romans 9–11 and the suffering of the ekklesia described in Romans 8, and questions whether Paul may be suggesting that "Israel's temporary unbelief in Yeshua is itself, paradoxically, a participation in Yeshua's vicarious, redemptive suffering."[95]

Kinzer notes the echoes of Genesis 22 in Romans 8:32 and 11:21, arguing that the Akedah sets the context for and provides a theological link between the suffering of Israel and the suffering of Christ. Kinzer follows Richard Hays' exegetical conclusion: "What Paul has done, in a word, is to interpret the fate of Israel christologically. ... Israel undergoes rejection for the sake of the world, bearing suffering vicariously."[96] According to this connection between Israel and Christ, Douglas Harink raises the following question: "Is it not possible to see Israel's present hardening as its

---

of God's final reign, rather than as a means of bringing it to pass" (Kinzer, "Beginning with the End," 118).

94. Kinzer, *Postmissionary Messianic Judaism*, 129 (for Kinzer's exegesis, see 122–40).

95. Ibid., 133.

96. Richard B. Hays, *Echoes of Scripture in the Letters of Paul* (New Haven: Yale University Press, 1993), 61, quoted in Kinzer, *Postmissionary Messianic Judaism*, 134.

unique (but unknowing) participation in the crucifixion of Jesus Christ, not as culpable 'failure,' but as its own share in suffering, waiting, and groaning with the church and the whole creation, as it too awaits the final redemption of all things?"[97]

We will recall that Kinzer interprets Israel's rejection of the gospel as it came to be preached in the second century (that is, as a rejection of Jewish corporate life) as an act of faithfulness to God. If Jesus as the Jewish Messiah embodies perfect covenant faithfulness, Kinzer proffers that Israel's refusal to accept a distorted gospel mirrors this faithfulness: "If the obedience of Yeshua that led him to death on the cross is rightly interpreted as the perfect embodiment and realization of Israel's covenant fidelity, then Jewish rejection of the church's message in the second century and afterward can rightly be seen as a hidden participation in the obedience of Israel's Messiah."[98] According to Kinzer, Israel's ongoing suffering and covenant fidelity to God mysteriously mirrors and participates in the atoning obedience of Christ.

Our exposition has made clear that Kinzer's Christology is thoroughgoingly informed by his doctrine of Israel, and every aspect of Christ's life reveals a deep resonance with the corporate life and vocation of the Jewish people. As Christ's flesh-and-blood community, the Jewish people indelibly and unwittingly participate in the redemptive work of their unrecognized Messiah. The connection that Kinzer draws between Jesus and the Jewish people informs his ecclesiology, which lies at the heart of his theological program. Kinzer's thought builds toward a unique ecclesiological proposal, and it is to this that we now turn.

## KINZER'S TWOFOLD ECCLESIOLOGY

Kinzer's ecclesiology focuses on both the distinction and the interrelatedness of three ecclesial groups within the one people of God. The people of Israel (the vast majority of whom do not believe in Jesus) and the body of Christ (the vast majority of whom are non-Jews) are linked together by the small but significant group of Jewish believers in Jesus (that is,

---

97.  Douglas Harink, *Paul among the Postliberals: Pauline Theology Beyond Christendom and Modernity* (Grand Rapids: Brazos, 2003), 180, quoted in Kinzer, *Postmissionary Messianic Judaism*, 134 n. 53.

98.  Kinzer, *Postmissionary Messianic Judaism*, 225.

Messianic Jews), who form an overlapping subsection of both Israel and the church. Kinzer's ecclesiological model builds on Barth's notion that Jesus Christ grounds the election of both Israel and the church and serves as the fundamental link between these two halves of the one people of God. Kinzer's Christology mirrors Barth's in this regard, and Kinzer takes one step further by assigning the Messianic Jewish community the task of serving as an ongoing visible representation of the ecclesiological bridge built by Christ.

While Kinzer's ecclesiology focuses most explicitly on his vision for the Messianic Jewish community, this community can only be understood in its connection to both the wider Christian church and the wider people of Israel. Because of the interrelatedness of these three subgroups of the people of God, Kinzer's ecclesiology has implications for both of these larger communities. As we seek to understand this aspect of Kinzer's thought, we must first rehearse the "postmissionary" posture of his Messianic Jewish theology, which undergirds his ecclesiology. We will then move on to an analysis of Kinzer's ecclesiological proposal, which he terms "bilateral ecclesiology in solidarity with Israel."

### POSTMISSIONARY MESSIANIC JUDAISM

The title of Kinzer's first book reveals the overall thrust of his theological paradigm and constructive ecclesiological agenda. As Kinzer explains, *Postmissionary Messianic Judaism* "is not mainly a book about Messianic Judaism. Instead, it is a book about the ekklesia—the community of those who believe in Yeshua the Messiah—and its relationship to the Jewish people."[99] Kinzer's usage of the term postmissionary is not meant as a critique of "the missionary endeavor in general and in every context."[100] Rather, it is a descriptor of the posture Messianic Judaism ought to assume toward Jewish life and the Jewish people. Kinzer offers three primary markers of a postmissionary stance:

> First, postmissionary Messianic Judaism summons Messianic Jews to live an observant Jewish life as an act of covenant fidelity rather than missionary expediency. ... Second, postmissionary Messianic

---

99.  Ibid., 12.
100.  Ibid., 13.

Judaism embraces the Jewish people and its religious tradition, and discovers God and Messiah in the midst of Israel. ... Third, postmissionary Messianic Judaism serves the (Gentile) Christian church by linking it to the physical descendants of Abraham, Isaac, and Jacob, thereby confirming its identity as a multinational extension of the people of Israel.[101]

Each of these three markers provides an important foundational element of Kinzer's theology. Kinzer's first claim is twofold, asserting unequivocally that Messianic Jews are indeed "to live an observant Jewish life." This core tenet of Kinzer's theology, stated firmly throughout his writings, is a significant statement in its own right. It necessarily assumes a close ongoing connection between Israel and Torah and challenges any Christian gospel that seeks to erode or eclipse this connection.[102] Kinzer's understanding of Jewish covenant fidelity is both theological and exegetical, and it is important to reiterate that Kinzer's reading of the New Testament undergirds his paradigm: "Contrary to what is usually assumed, I conclude that the New Testament— read canonically and theologically—teaches that all Jews (including Yeshua-believers) are not only permitted but are obligated to follow basic Jewish practice."[103]

The implications of this claim inform the rest of Kinzer's theological paradigm. Commenting on *Postmissionary Messianic Judaism*, Kinzer asserts that "while the message of *PMJ* goes far beyond the obligatory nature of Torah-based Jewish practice and identity for Jewish Yeshua-believers, one cannot underestimate the centrality of this proposition for the argument of the book as a whole. It is far more important as the basis for reaching other conclusions than as a conclusion in its own right."[104]

The second part of the first claim is equally important: Messianic Jewish covenant fidelity is not motivated by "missionary expediency." If Messianic

---

101. Ibid., 13–15.

102. Kinzer comments on the strange reversal perpetuated by the church with regard to Jews and Gentiles—"While the early Jewish Yeshua-movement decided that a Gentile did not need to become a Jew in order to be saved, the growing consensus among Christians was that in effect a Jew did need to become a Gentile to be saved!" (Ibid., 194).

103. Ibid., 23.

104. Kinzer, "Three Years Later," 184.

Jews understand themselves as part of the larger people of Israel, then their commitment to that people and their acceptance of Israel's covenant responsibilities are rooted in their identification with and participation in that covenant.[105] Here Kinzer agrees with Michael Wyschogrod, who claims that (as we saw in the last chapter) "to be a Jew means to labor under the yoke of the commandments." Wyschogrod goes on to explain the relevance of this claim for Jewish believers in Jesus. In his words, "The point is that once someone is a Jew, he always remains a Jew. Once someone has come under the yoke of the commandments, there is no escaping this yoke. So baptism, from the Jewish point of view, does not make eating pork into a neutral act. In fact, nothing that a Jew can do enables him to escape from the yoke of the commandments."[106]

The implication is clear—belief in Jesus as the Messiah does not cause a Jew to cease being a Jew, and thereby does not exempt them from Jewish covenant responsibilities. While Wyschogrod does not agree with Kinzer's theological convictions regarding Jesus, he does agree with Kinzer's position on how Messianic Jews ought to live. Wyschogrod explains that, "throughout the centuries, Jews who entered the Church very quickly lost their Jewish identity. Within several generations they intermarried and the Jewish traces disappeared. ... If all Jews in past ages had followed the advice of the Church to become Christians, there would be no more Jews in the world today." This historical observation leads Wyschogrod to pose a central set of questions:

> Does the Church really want a world without Jews? Does the Church believe that such a world is in accordance with the will of God? Or does the Church believe that it is God's will, even after the coming of Jesus, that there be a Jewish people in the world? ... If, from the Christian point of view, Israel's election remains a contemporary reality, then the disappearance of the Jewish people from the world

---

105. This, of course, raises questions about a Messianic Jewish stance toward oral Torah, the necessary bridge between biblical commandments and the execution thereof. Kinzer addresses this question in chapter 7 of *Postmissionary Messianic Judaism* as well as in "Messianic Judaism and Jewish Tradition in the Twenty-First Century: A Biblical Defense of Oral Torah," in *Israel's Messiah and the People of God*, 29-61.

106. Michael Wyschogrod, "A Letter to Cardinal Lustiger," in *Abraham's Promise*, 206.

cannot be an acceptable development. Closely related to the survival of the Jewish people is the question of the Mosaic Law.[107]

For Wyschogrod as well as Kinzer, the connection between Israel and Torah is a key factor for the continued existence of the Jewish people.[108] Just as Wyschogrod offers the above challenge to the church, Kinzer sees his theology as a clarion call for the church to reconsider its stance toward Torah observance for the Jewish people: "Christians who now affirm the irrevocable nature of the covenant between God and Israel must rethink their approach to Jewish practice as rooted in the Torah—for all Jews, including Jewish Yeshua-believers."[109]

Drawing on the thought of Wyschogrod, Soulen explains that the church's stance toward a Torah-observant Messianic Judaism reveals to what extent it has actually renounced the anti-Judaism and supersessionism that have persistently clung to Christian history:

> For Wyschogrod, the acid test of the church's theological posture toward Israel's election is the church's conduct toward Jews in its own midst, that is, toward Jews who have been baptized. For it is here that the church demonstrates in an ultimate way whether it understands itself in light of God's eternal covenant with the seed of Abraham. If the church acknowledges the abiding reality of Israel's corporeal election, it will naturally expect baptized Jews to maintain faithfully their Jewish identity. But if the church truly believes that it has superseded God's covenant with Israel, it will prohibit or discourage Jews from preserving their identity as Jews and members of the Jewish people. In short, the problem of supersessionism turns on the church's capacity to acknowledge

---

107. Ibid., 207–8.

108. On this topic, Kinzer writes the following: "In the absence of entrenched and widespread anti-Semitism, or some other form of enforced ghettoization, I would agree with Elliott Abrams, who argues that only distinctive religious observance can secure Jewish communal survival" (Kinzer, "Response to Mishkan Reviewers of My Book," *Mishkan* 48 [2006]: 58; see Elliott Abrams, *Faith or Fear* [New York: The Free Press, 1997]).

109. Kinzer, *Postmissionary Messianic Judaism*, 210. This aspect of Kinzer's theology directly addresses Marshall's concern that the link between Israel and Torah remain intact, and we will see in our assessment the way in which Kinzer's paradigm tightly coheres with Marshall's criteria.

the abiding religious significance of Israel's corporeal election and hence the abiding religious significance of the distinction between Gentile and Jew.[110]

The connection between Israel (including Jesus-believing Israel) and Torah paves the way for Kinzer's second marker of postmissionary Messianic Judaism, which highlights the solidarity between Messianic Jews and the larger Jewish world. That postmissionary Messianic Judaism "embraces the Jewish people and its religious tradition, and discovers God and Messiah in the midst of Israel" points toward a Christology that is firmly rooted in God's covenant with Israel and posits significant continuity between the Old and New Testaments. As we saw above, Kinzer argues that Messianic Judaism is to be a branch of Judaism, not a denomination of the Christian church. If God continues to dwell and work amid the Jewish people, Jewish followers of Christ need not sever their connections to their people or its unique way of life. In fact, to do so would be to act unfaithfully toward their divinely appointed covenantal calling. According to Kinzer, upholding this covenantal vocation and following Jesus as the Messiah are not competitive, but are rather mutually reinforcing. As Kinzer explains, "Messianic Jews with this orientation discern the hidden sanctifying reality of Yeshua already residing at the center of Jewish life and religious tradition. They understand their inner mission as the call to be a visible sign of this hidden messianic presence."[111]

Here Kinzer intentionally departs from the overarching trend of Messianic Jewish theology and practice. Kinzer explains that Messianic Judaism has traditionally treated "postbiblical Jewish history, customs, and institutions with wariness or even disdain," viewing "even devout Jews who do not believe in Yeshua as lacking a life-giving relationship with God."[112] According to this traditional Messianic Jewish paradigm, Jewish believers in Jesus could never truly feel at home in the Jewish world, which is

---

110. Soulen, *The God of Israel*, 11, quoted in Kinzer, *Postmissionary Messianic Judaism*, 182.

111. Kinzer, *Postmissionary Messianic Judaism*, 14. For more on the idea of the "hidden Messiah," see Richard Harvey, "The 'Hidden Messiah' in Judaism" (paper presented at the LCJE International Conference, Keszthely, Hungary, August 2007). Available through the Lausanne Consortium on Jewish Evangelism at www.lcje.net/papers/2007/intl/Harvey.doc.

112. Kinzer, *Postmissionary Messianic Judaism*, 15.

perceived to be "a domain bereft of Yeshua's sanctifying presence."[113] Kinzer
challenges this viewpoint, arguing instead that Messianic Judaism's witness to the wider Jewish community points to a reality internal to that
community's covenantal life. If Jesus sums up and epitomizes Jewish covenant faithfulness to God, then pointing the Jewish people toward their
Messiah does not entail directing them away from their communal context
and extant covenantal relationship with God. In essence, to bear witness to
Jesus is to point the Jewish people inward into their corporate life and vocation. This, according to Kinzer, is where their Messiah is to be discovered.

The third marker of Kinzer's postmissionary paradigm lays the
groundwork for understanding Messianic Judaism as an essential link
between Israel and the church. Like Rosenzweig, Kinzer propounds a
model whereby the Jewish people and the ekklesia are oriented toward
the same *telos* while retaining their unique, complementary distinctions.[114]
Kinzer's ecclesiological model is buttressed by his Christology, which portrays Christ as a bridge rather than a wedge between these two covenant
communities. Construing Christology and ecclesiology as such combats
supersessionism, as the church becomes an extension—rather than a
replacement—of Israel. Messianic Judaism thus serves as a witness to
Israel of the abiding presence of its Messiah in its midst, and as a witness to the larger Christian church of God's unfailing love for and election of the Jewish people. Kinzer describes these two facets of Messianic
Judaism's witness as its "inner" and "outer" vocation.[115] Kinzer fleshes out
the implications of this third marker in his ecclesiological proposal, and
it is to this that we now turn.

## BILATERAL ECCLESIOLOGY IN SOLIDARITY WITH ISRAEL

Having explored Kinzer's Christology and theology of Israel, as well as his
postmissionary Messianic Jewish paradigm, we are now prepared to turn
to the distinct ecclesiological implications of his position. As we have noted,

---

113. Ibid.

114. Following Paul in Galatians 3:28, Kinzer treats the union between Jew and Gentile
as analogous to the union between man and woman in marriage. Kinzer claims that "the
unity of Jew and Gentile does not imply the elimination of all distinction between the two,
any more than the unity of husband and wife eliminates all gender differentiation" (Kinzer,
*Postmissionary Messianic Judaism*, 170).

115. Ibid., 16.

Kinzer's ecclesiology—which is prescriptive as well as descriptive—is the capstone of his entire theological system.[116]

As the practical outworking of Kinzer's theological system, bilateral ecclesiology builds upon the theological pillars we have explored thus far. First, Kinzer states that, "according to New Testament teaching, the ekklesia does not replace Israel. The Jewish people as a whole retains its position as a community chosen and loved by God." That Israel has experienced a "partial hardening" (to use Paul's language) does not nullify its status as a "holy people, set apart for God and God's purposes."[117] As we have seen, Kinzer (like Wyschogrod) contends that God dwells amid the Jewish people and calls them to live a life of corporate fidelity to the commands and statutes of the Torah. Second, "the ekklesia contains at its core a portion of Israel," which Paul refers to as "the remnant." According to Kinzer, this remnant of Israel within the ekklesia is called to be "a representative and priestly component of Israel that sanctifies Israel as a whole."[118] If the remnant is to fulfill its God-given role, "this portion of Israel must truly live as Israel—that is, it must be exemplary in observing those traditional Jewish practices that identify the Jewish people as a distinct community chosen and loved by God."[119]

However, Kinzer acknowledges that the New Testament is also the story of God's salvific and redemptive purposes flowing outward from Israel via the person and ministry of Jesus and his early followers. As the gospel message begins to be preached to and received by non-Jews, it becomes clear that the body of Christ is to include gentiles who are not required to live as Jews.[120] The interwoven story lines of Israel's continued role as a holy nation (and enduring call to covenant fidelity) and the inclusion of gentiles in the transnational and increasingly diverse body of Christ raises an important ecclesiological question: How is the ekklesia to accommodate both the calling of the remnant to live as Israel and the acknowledgment that gentile believers need not adopt Jewish practice?

---

116. See Kinzer, *Postmissionary Messianic Judaism*, ch. 4.

117. Ibid., 151.

118. Ibid.

119. Ibid.

120. See, for example, the story of Peter and Cornelius in Acts 10 and the ruling of the Jerusalem Council in Acts 15.

According to Kinzer, "only one structural arrangement would allow for distinctive Jewish communal life within the context of a transnational community of Jews and Gentiles: the one ekklesia must consist of two corporate subcommunities, each with its own formal or informal governmental and communal structures."[121] Within such an arrangement, the Jewish branch of the ekklesia remains distinct from the gentile branch and serves as a link between the wider ekklesia and wider Israel. As Kinzer explains:

> In contrast to the Jewish people, whose identity is essentially particular and circumscribed, the community of the Messiah encompasses those from among all the nations of the world. ... The Jewish people remain at the center of this new catholic reality as a distinct national entity, a sanctified community of kinship and common ethnicity. But the circle of oneness and holiness has now been widened to include all those from the nations who are reconciled with the God of Israel and the Israel of God. Within this widened circle, all are holy—with distinctions in role but no distinctions in access or proximity to God differentiating Jew from Greek, male from female.[122]

Kinzer explains the way in which bilateral ecclesiology "provides the Gentile branch of the ekklesia with a way of sharing in Israel's life and blessings without succumbing to supersessionism."[123] As we saw in chapter 3, theologians across the spectrum are increasingly acknowledging the deep and destructive supersessionism woven throughout the church's history. Kinzer's proposed ecclesiological shift offers a promising step

---

121. Kinzer, *Postmissionary Messianic Judaism*, 152. Kinzer summarizes his ecclesiological proposal in the following five basic principles: (1) the perpetual validity of God's covenant with the Jewish people; (2) the perpetual validity of the Jewish way of life rooted in the Torah as the enduring sign and instrument of that covenant; (3) the validity of Jewish religious tradition as the historical embodiment of the Jewish way of life rooted in the Torah; (4) the bilateral constitution of the ekklesia, consisting of distinct but united Jewish and Gentile expressions of Yeshua-faith; and (5) the ecumenical imperative of the ekklesia, which entails bringing the redeemed nations of the world into solidarity with the people of Israel in anticipation of Israel's—and the world's—final redemption (see ibid., 264).

122. Kinzer, "Messianic Jewish Community: Standing and Serving as a Priestly Remnant," 12.

123. Ibid.

toward repairing and renouncing this corrosive shadow-side of church history. In Kinzer's assessment, "The rise of Christian supersessionism is correlated with schism between the Jewish and Gentile branches of the ekklesia, schism between the Jewish branch and the wider Jewish people, and the demise of Jewish Yeshua-faith as a viable corporate reality."[124] If these are the factors that led to supersessionism's triumph, each must be addressed in order to repair the church's derailment with regard to the Jewish people.

Kinzer believes that restoring the Jewish branch of the ekklesia is a key factor in righting history's wrongs and healing the schism between Jews and Christians. Thus, as Kinzer states, "While I am arguing for the legitimacy and importance of Messianic Judaism, my thesis is that the church's own identity—and not just the identity of Messianic Jews—is at stake in the discussion."[125] While church history has perpetuated supersessionism, according to Kinzer, the church nonetheless remains fundamental in God's plan for reconciliation and redemption:

> Supersessionism and the crumbling of the ecclesiological bridge, i.e., the Jewish ekklesia, damaged the church in a profound way. But we must avoid the temptation to see church history in purely negative terms. The Gentile ekklesia preserved the essential message entrusted to it. It continued to proclaim Israel's risen Messiah. It rejected Marcionism and accepted the Jewish Bible as inspired, authoritative, and canonical. It collected the books of the New Testament and arranged them in a manner that further countered Marcionite anti-Judaism. The most virulent forms of anti-Jewish teaching in the second century did not carry the day but were moderated by Irenaeus and later by Augustine. *The church faithfully preserved and carried within it the truths that would allow it eventually to reexamine its history and recognize supersessionism as an error demanding correction.* At the same time, the triumph of supersessionism and the crumbling of the ecclesiological bridge produced a schism in the heart of the people of God.[126]

---

124. Kinzer, *Postmissionary Messianic Judaism*, 152.

125. Ibid., 13.

126. Ibid., 211. Italics added.

In other words, buried within the church's tradition and heritage lies the resources to repair the schism. However, these resources alone are not sufficient. Because the Jewish people remain a people elected by God and shaped according to his purposes, their role in salvation history is equally significant and necessary for the reunification of God's people. As we have already seen, Kinzer nuances the traditional interpretation of the Jewish people's rejection of Christ and asserts that in its insistence upon upholding Jewish tradition and practices, Israel was demonstrating a profound faithfulness to God. According to Kinzer, God has continued to work amidst the Jewish people as a whole, safeguarding within rabbinic Judaism[127] a key element of Jesus' own mission and message.

Kinzer argues that in order for God's consummative purposes to prevail, the church must acknowledge and embrace the contribution Jewish tradition has to make. Here Kinzer's theology closely resembles Rosenzweig's, for Kinzer claims that the message of God in Christ is structurally flawed when it unhitches itself from Judaism, its source and counterpart. To the extent that Christians embrace a de-Judaized Jesus and proclaim a gospel that disregards God's covenant with Israel, their understanding and embodiment of God's purposes is distorted and truncated. Similarly, Judaism is ultimately incomplete without the reminder—issued by Christians and Messianic Jews—that the whole world is God's beloved creation, destined for redemption. God's covenant with Israel was always intended to expand outward to include all nations, and Judaism must remember that the God of Israel is also the God of the gentiles. To the extent that Jews seek to follow and honor God while remaining indifferent or hostile to their Messiah and his mission, their understanding of and ability to fulfill their own redemptive vocation will always be limited.

According to Kinzer's thought, Messianic Judaism plays a mediating role between the church and wider Israel, and its calling is to represent

---

127. According to Peter Ochs, "there is, in one sense, no other Judaism for Jews than that which comes by way of Rabbinic Judaism, or the Judaism of the *Mishnah*, Talmud, synagogue, prayer book, and Torah study that emerged after, in spite of, and in response to the loss of the Second Temple. All of the new Judaisms that have appeared since have appeared from out of and in terms of this Rabbinic Judaism" (Peter Ochs, "Yoder's Witness to the People of Israel," in *Jewish-Christian Schism Revisited*, by John Howard Yoder, ed. Michael G. Cartwright and Peter Ochs [Grand Rapids: Eerdmans, 2003], 3).

and recommend each to the other. Messianic Jews are to live under the messiahship of Jesus while fully identifying with the corporate existence and life of the Jewish people: "Bilateral ecclesiology in solidarity with Israel summons the Messianic Jewish congregational movement to take a step towards the Jewish world and a step away from its evangelical matrix. Only by being distinct from evangelicalism, and connected to Judaism, can such a Messianic Judaism fulfill its vocation as an ecclesiological bridge enabling the church to discover its identity in relationship to Israel and enabling the Jewish people to encounter its Messiah as it has never done before."[128]

Bilateral ecclesiology presumes an ongoing distinction between Jews and gentiles, even and perhaps especially within the body of Christ. Here Kinzer agrees with Soulen, who asserts that "the distinction between Jew and Gentile, being intrinsic to God's work as the Consummator of creation, is not erased but realized in a new way in the sphere of the church."[129] This implies that while there is only one gospel of Jesus Christ, the acceptance and appropriation of that gospel looks different for Jews than it does for gentiles. In the words of Thomas Torrance, acceptance of the validity of God's ongoing covenant with Israel "means that we cannot expect Jews to become Christians in the same sense that we are, for they could only become followers of Christ as Lord and Saviour within the obedience laid upon them by God in the covenant bond which God has not revoked." Torrance rightly concludes that this matter "needs much more attention than Christians have yet given to it."[130]

Kinzer's bilateral ecclesiology posits that Jewish followers of Christ are to live as covenantally faithful Jews, thus linking the wider ekklesia to the wider people of Israel. Likewise, Kinzer's theology (in consonance with the New Testament) maintains that gentiles are not called to become Jews or to live as Jews. While gentiles may gain insight into the Israel onto which they have been grafted by having an awareness of Jewish life and ritual, their covenantal calling is to live fully within their own non-Jewish identity.

---

128. Kinzer, "Three Years Later," 191.

129. Soulen, *The God of Israel*, 169.

130. Thomas F. Torrance, "Christian/Jewish Dialogue," Appendix A(2), in *The Witness of the Jews to God*, ed. David W. Torrance (Edinburgh: Handsel Press, 1982), 143–44.

## CONCLUSION

Having reviewed the contours of Kinzer's theology as well as his ecclesiological proposal, we may now assess Kinzer's thought through the lens of Marshall's question. To what extent does Kinzer uphold the universal, ecclesially mediated saving mission of Christ? How does he connect Christology to the irrevocable election of Israel, necessarily expressed through faithful Jewish practice? And in what ways does Kinzer's thought open theological avenues that remained obstructed in the thoughts of Barth, Rosenzweig, and the post-Holocaust thinkers we surveyed?

It is important to state at the beginning of our assessment that any conclusions we draw about Kinzer's theology must be provisional. While the works that Kinzer has produced allow us to glimpse the novelty of his thought, it is likely the case that the bulk of Kinzer's theology has yet to be written. While we are able to evaluate the contribution that Kinzer's theology makes to an affirmation of Marshall's criteria as well as point toward areas of potential concern, much of this will ultimately serve to suggest work that still must be done. Our assessment of Kinzer will thus point the way forward toward potential future directions in the new Jewish-Christian encounter. With this proviso in place, let us assess Kinzer's theology from the two foci of Marshall's question.

Kinzer's Christology positions Christ's mission and work within the context of Israel's vocation to be both an agent of sanctification in creation's movement toward consummation and an agent of redemption against the destructive forces of chaos and disorder. The holiness that dwells uniquely in the people of Israel was always intended to expand outward to all nations and to all of creation, and it is through Christ that this movement takes place. Indeed, Kinzer's Christology maintains both the universal scope of Christ's mission as well as its particular relevance for Israel. For Kinzer, Christ embodies the definitive sacrifice that finally defeats the forces of chaos and absorbs the judgment associated with Israel's disobedience.

Certain aspects of Kinzer's Christology bear a deep resemblance to the thought of both Barth and Rosenzweig. Kinzer's Christology resonates with Barth's Christology in that Israel's no to Christ is couched within and ultimately overcome by Christ's yes to Israel, which sums up Israel's vocation to usher in humanity's intended *telos*. Christ's sacrificial service to God guarantees both God's definitive acceptance of Israel as well as the ultimate defeat of the forces that oppose God's good creation. However, while Barth declares that the "Synagogue" is blind and its alleged obedience to God is bankrupt, Kinzer's thought moves in a different direction. For Kinzer, rabbinic Judaism represents a truly faithful movement before God whose rejection of the Christian gospel stems primarily from fidelity to its covenant with God. Furthermore, Judaism's ongoing existence serves as a corrective to Christianity's anti-Judaic and supersessionist tendencies.

Here Kinzer's thought mirrors Rosenzweig's, as Kinzer sees both the people of Israel and the ekklesia as holding complementary redemptive vocations that prevent one another from falling into error. Yet, unlike Rosenzweig, Kinzer unequivocally affirms Christ's relevance for the Jewish people. Whereas Rosenzweig merely gestures toward a Christology in light of Israel, Kinzer offers a robust and nuanced understanding of Christ that derives entirely from Israel's election and vocation. According to Kinzer, all Jews are called to embrace Jesus as their Messiah—and to embrace him as Jews.

This is perhaps the most novel aspect of Kinzer's thought, and it has direct relevance to providing a workable answer to Marshall's question. A Torah-observant Messianic Judaism allows us to simultaneously affirm the universal applicability of Christ's mission and call to discipleship without undermining or eclipsing Israel's unique covenantal vocation. Kinzer's bilateral ecclesiology provides a tangible model of what it means for the ekklesia—composed of both Jews and gentiles—to be an extension of the people of Israel by virtue of Christ and the ongoing presence of the remnant (that is, the Messianic Jewish community).

As a Messianic Jewish theologian, Kinzer is able to bypass the key dangers we observed in chapter 3. There, we saw the way in which an affirmation of Israel's ongoing election (which includes the ongoing practice of Judaism) is often competitive with orthodox Christology. Because Kinzer challenges a mutually exclusive construal of Judaism and Christianity and construes Christ as the indelible link between these two communities, this tension virtually disappears. Kinzer's Messianic Jewish perspective allows him to uphold both a high Christology and a high doctrine of Israel (and Torah), which none of the theologians in chapter 3 were fully able to do.

However, if we are to approach the issue of Christology from Marshall's perspective, we must ask what exactly the "saving mission of Christ" is according to Kinzer. In his review essay of *Postmissionary Messianic Judaism*, Rich Robinson critiques Kinzer for "focusing greatly on issues of community ... to the exclusion of salvation issues."[131] Robinson likewise questions whether Kinzer has "sufficiently appreciated the reality of sin in the shaping of religious systems, Jewish or otherwise."[132]

While Kinzer's response to Robinson's review raises serious concerns about whether Robinson adequately grasped Kinzer's argument throughout the book,[133] these two critiques in particular do indeed carry some weight. Christian conceptions of soteriology generally hinge upon a robust doctrine of human sinfulness, and Robinson is correct to point out that this doctrine receives relatively little attention in Kinzer's thought. While Kinzer draws a direct connection between human disobedience and the forces of chaos, one wonders whether complete human obedience and submission to God (beginning with Israel) is hypothetically possible. If so, might human obedience alone suffice to overthrow these destructive forces? If this is the case, why was Christ's sacrifice necessary? If human obedience is not actually a possibility, then why not? A more thorough account of sin and its consequences would help to fill in some of the christological and soteriological gaps that remain in Kinzer's theology.

Closely related to the issue of human sinfulness is the doctrine of atonement. While Kinzer's treatment of both the tabernacle/temple and the death of Christ make reference to atonement, the precise meaning and dynamic of this concept in Kinzer's thought are difficult to discern. With regard to the temple/tabernacle, Kinzer's emphasis falls on the way in which these institutions perpetuate Israel's vocation to remain holy, with the sacrificial system modeling Israel's faithfulness according to the pattern of the Akedah. If obedience to God is carried out through sacrifice and submission, what role does the atoning dimension of the sacrifices

---

131. Robinson, "*Postmissionary Messianic Judaism:* A Review Essay," 11.

132. Ibid., 16.

133. See Kinzer, "Response to Mishkan Reviewers of My Book," 55–60.

play? Sacrifice and obedience are indeed key themes of both the temple/
tabernacle as well as Christ's death, but can these events be adequately
understood without recourse to atonement for sins? At the very least, this
aspect of Kinzer's work requires further clarity.

As we claimed above, Kinzer's theology clearly asserts that the universal scope of Christ's work includes its relevance for Israel. In fact, for
Kinzer, Christ's work is carried out with special reference to Israel and its
ongoing vocation. However, the question remains as to how Kinzer envisions this connection playing out in actuality. As we have already noted,
Kinzer's bilateral ecclesiology mirrors Barth's notion of the twofold people
of God as well as Rosenzweig's construal of the complementary vocations
of Judaism and Christianity. Like Barth, Kinzer's ecclesiology stems from
his Christology. Christ's mission as Israel's Messiah and the emissary of
God's presence to the nations informs Kinzer's doctrine of both Israel and
the church. However, like Rosenzweig, Kinzer posits that Israel's vocation
remains intact despite Israel's rejection of Christ. In fact, Israel's rejection
of Christ serves to reveal the errancy of the gospel that has been preached
to the Jewish people and directs the church back to the fact that Christ did
not come to abolish Judaism. Kinzer's bilateral ecclesiology enables him to
assert that both the church and Israel faithfully carry out aspects of Christ's
mission and message. While the church witnesses to Christ's universality,
Israel witnesses to his particularity.

Like Rosenzweig and Soulen, Kinzer maintains that the coming of
Christ does not erase the distinction between Jew and gentile. Even within
the ekklesia, faithfulness for Jews and faithfulness for gentiles looks different. As we have seen, this core tenet lies at the heart of Kinzer's bilateral
ecclesiology. While this claim contributes to answering Marshall's question by providing a way for Jews to follow Jesus without ceasing to live as
Jews, it also raises a few key questions from the perspective of Marshall's
framework.

We will recall from the introduction that Marshall suggests Kinzer's theology as one potential means of answering his central question, claiming
that this option "surely deserves more attention than it has yet received."[134]
According to Marshall, Kinzer's theology "recognizes both the necessity of

---

134. Marshall, "Elder Brothers," 125.

distinctively Jewish practice and identity for Jewish election, and the universality of Christ's saving mission."[135] Nonetheless, Marshall does raise a number of potential concerns. First, he asks whether Kinzer's theology is actually "the best of both worlds,"[136] or whether it might represent a form of syncretism that finally compromises its ability to uphold either aspect of Marshall's question. Second, Marshall wonders whether Kinzer's bilateral ecclesiology adequately accounts for the unity between Jew and gentile created by the cross of Christ (see Ephesians 2:11–22). Let us address each of these concerns in turn.

Marshall's first worry is clearly manifest in the thought of David Novak, who claims that the truth claims of Judaism and Christianity are fundamentally incompatible and thus there is no way that someone who holds to orthodox Christian theology (particularly the doctrines of the Trinity and the incarnation) could legitimately be accepted as a rabbinic Jew. In his words, "The ultimate truth claims of Judaism and Christianity are not only different but mutually exclusive. ... One cannot live as a Jew and a Christian simultaneously."[137] Within the framework of Novak's mutually exclusive construal of Judaism and Christianity, "the highest form of worship of the Lord God of Israel is either by the Torah and the tradition of the Jewish people or by Christ and the tradition of the Church."[138] Novak claims that while adherents of these two religions can seek to understand one another, such understanding is grounded in the distinction between the two religions. It is this boundary that, according to Novak, Messianic Judaism transgresses.[139]

---

135. Ibid.

136. Ibid.

137. David Novak, "What to Seek and What to Avoid in Jewish-Christian Dialogue," in *Christianity in Jewish Terms*, ed. Tikva Frymer-Kensky et al. (Boulder, CO: Westview, 2000), 5.

138. Ibid.

139. In his 2010 book *Jewish-Christian Dialogue and the Life of Wisdom: Engagements with the Theology of David Novak*, Matthew Levering dedicates a full chapter to putting Kinzer's thought in dialogue with Novak's. As well as questioning Kinzer's New Testament theology and portrayal of church history, Levering echoes Novak's objection to Messianic Judaism claiming to be a branch of Judaism when the rest of the Jewish world does not accept it as such. Following Novak, Levering asserts that "Rabbinic Judaism ... has rejected the view that Rabbinic Jews can practice Judaism faithfully and affirm Jesus as Messiah at the same time" (Matthew Levering, *Jewish-Christian Dialogue and the Life of Wisdom: Engagements with the Theology of David Novak* [London: Continuum, 2010], 43).

Novak's critique of Messianic Judaism highlights the way in which Kinzer's theology presumes a radically different understanding of the relationship between Judaism and Christianity than the traditional model that Novak upholds. When Kinzer claims that his ecclesiology has implications for the larger Jewish world and the larger Christian world, this is no doubt among the issues that he has in mind. Kinzer posits a deep underlying resonance between these two religious communities that undergirds their apparent irreconcilable differences. However, the precise nature of the relationship between Israel and the church—and the definition of the "solidarity" Kinzer prescribes—is not entirely clear. In Richard Harvey's review of *Postmissionary Messianic Judaism*, he writes that "the phrase 'in solidarity with' can be variously interpreted to allow for the inclusion of Israel within the Church, the inclusion of the Church within Israel, and parallel co-existences of the two in partnership, complementarity, or even antagonism."[140] While it is clear that Kinzer's theological starting point differs fundamentally from Novak's, this is yet another area of Kinzer's thought that requires additional explanation.

With regard to the second concern, that of the christological unity between Jew and gentile, Marshall remarks that, according to a Messianic Jewish approach, "it sometimes seems as though Christ has two bodies—two churches—neither of which has a universal saving mission. With that, the sense in which Christ himself has a single saving purpose for all ceases to be apparent."[141] If the Jewish people and the ekklesia each have separate vocations, and Jews and gentiles within the ekklesia have different expressions of covenant faithfulness, how does Kinzer maintain an abiding, christologically grounded sense of unity between Jews and gentiles? Richard Harvey echoes this concern, claiming "Kinzer's bilateral ecclesiology runs the risk of producing a 'bilateral Christology' and a 'bilateral soteriology' in its wake."[142] Rich Robinson raises a similar concern from an exegetical perspective, and wonders whether Jewish believers can maintain central Jewish practices (that is, Shabbat, dietary practices, circumcision) in the

---

140. Richard Harvey, "Shaping the Aims and Aspirations of Jewish Believers," *Mishkan* 48 (2006): 24 n. 5.

141. Marshall, "Elder Brothers," 125.

142. Harvey, "Shaping the Aims," 24.

midst of the gentile ekklesia. He asks: "Is it necessary to conclude that there had to be distinct corporate structures in order for this to take place?"[143]

With regard to Robinson's question, Kinzer's model is untenable along the lines Robinson proposes. According to Kinzer, "Jewish practice is inherently corporate in nature. Circumcision is a social rite, performed by a trained official within the community. Sabbath observance requires social support and communal expression. The dietary laws require kosher meat processing and a network of relating families following similar food customs. The practical need for communal support reinforces the underlying meaning of all Jewish practice, which is to be an effective sign marking Israel as a people set apart for God."[144] That Kinzer resolutely defends the corporate nature of Jewish life leaves him open to the concerns expressed by Marshall and Harvey. This is yet another area of Kinzer's thought that requires additional clarification.

Related to Kinzer's maintenance of a firm distinction between Jew and gentile, another question arises. If, according to Kinzer, neither Christ nor Israel's rejection of Christ nullifies Israel's ongoing mission as God's agent of consummation and redemption, what is ultimately at stake in Israel's acceptance or rejection of its Messiah? By positing that Israel demonstrates a certain fidelity to God by rejecting a distorted gospel, Kinzer follows Marshall in affirming a "divinely willed disharmony between the order of knowing and the order of being."[145] In other words, the ontic nature of Israel's enduring election (in Christ) and Israel's noetic rejection of Christ (who grounds its election) remain at odds. The ensuing question becomes, if Christ is inseparable from the Jewish people and exists as Israel's "hidden Messiah," then what finally does Israel's noetic understanding of Christ's identity add?

Along these lines, Harvey re-raises the issue of soteriology. Harvey's assessment of Kinzer directly addresses Kinzer's appropriation of Barth and Rosenzweig, and Harvey is ultimately concerned that Kinzer's theology (like Barth's) leans toward universalism. According to Harvey, "Barth's Christological election (with its suggestive overtones of universalism)

---

143. Robinson, "*Postmissionary Messianic Judaism: A Review Essay*," 19.
144. Kinzer, *Postmissionary Messianic Judaism*, 151–152.
145. Marshall, "Christ and the Cultures," 90.

leaves room for the inclusion of unbelieving Israel 'in solidarity with the Church' though they may deny what the Church affirms. If this is a correct reading of Barth, Kinzer appears to have adopted the same logic, and a 'bilateral Christology and soteriology' emerges, following Rosenzweig."[146] From a Christian perspective, it seems inevitable that the question of Israel's acceptance of its Messiah will remain tied to soteriological concerns. According to Harvey, "whilst Christians recognise a continuing election of Israel (the Jewish people) and thus a continuing commitment of Jesus to His people, they will be reluctant to admit that this commitment in itself is salvific, or that the hidden presence of the Messiah with His people is the means by which he is revealed to them."[147] In order to adequately address this issue, Kinzer would need to explain more thoroughly his understanding of salvation.[148]

Kinzer is not unaware of these (and other) critiques of his thought. He recognizes that "*PMJ* raises as many questions as it answers," and he plans to "elaborate and defend my views on Christology, soteriology, missiology and Torah ... in the coming years."[149] That Kinzer's thought necessitates additional clarification on certain key points does not nullify the significant contribution it makes to elucidating the interrelationship between Israel and the church, not least from the perspective of Marshall's question. Marshall's own acknowledgement of the value of Kinzer's thought makes its significance clear, and one can only hope that Kinzer's thought continues to receive the attention Marshall believes it deserves.

Having assessed the theology of Barth, Rosenzweig, Kinzer, and the post-Holocaust theological architects of the new Jewish-Christian encounter, all with regard to Marshall's theological criteria, we will now move on to draw some general conclusions about what has emerged

---

146. Harvey, "Shaping the Aims," 25–26.

147. Richard Harvey, "Implicit Universalism in Some Christian Zionism and Messianic Judaism," in *Jesus, Salvation and the Jewish People: The Uniqueness of Jesus and Jewish Evangelism,* ed. David Parker (Carlisle: Paternoster, 2011), 232–33.

148. It is important to note that Kinzer's soteriology is expressed in his essay "Final Destinies: Qualifications for Receiving an Eschatological Inheritance." However, it seems clear that Kinzer's theology as expounded in this essay would not satisfy the concerns of Harvey and Robinson. Neither Kinzer's definition of salvation nor his purported means of attaining salvation appease the concerns of his critics. See "Final Destinies: Qualifications for Receiving an Eschatological Inheritance," in *Israel's Messiah and the People of God,* 126–55.

149. Kinzer, "Response to Mishkan Reviewers of My Book," 54.

throughout our study as well as point toward potential future directions in this developing tradition of thought.

# CONCLUSION

—

# WHERE DO WE GO FROM HERE?

As we noted in the introduction to this study, the context in which Jewish-Christian relations are currently being carried out is in large part a product of four key twentieth-century events: the demise of Christendom, the Holocaust, the creation of the modern state of Israel, and the emergence of Messianic Judaism. The irreducible complexity and historical significance of these events provide the backdrop for the theologians we have addressed in this study and the doctrinal developments we have highlighted. These key events, whose magnitude cannot be overestimated, set the frame for our particular reflections as well as a new chapter in Jewish-Christian relations more broadly.

As we have seen, the theologians engaged in this study are deeply committed to their respective traditions while at the same time pressing to redefine those traditions in light of interaction with the religious other. Because each thinker views Judaism and Christianity as being somehow intertwined and inseparable, the new Jewish-Christian encounter is beginning to erode the static and historically entrenched construal whereby Judaism and Christianity are conceived in mutually exclusive terms.[1] While Karl Barth and Franz Rosenzweig served as pioneers of this new dialogical engagement, the post-Holocaust thinkers we engaged in chapters 3 and 4 continue to extend the scope and trajectory of this burgeoning intellectual tradition. The Christian emphasis on affirming the irrevocable election of Israel and renouncing supersessionism, and the Jewish willingness to reconsider Christianity's central doctrinal claims in Jewish terms, marks a watershed moment in the history of Jewish-Christian relations. As we conclude this study, let us reflect upon a few key issues that sum up the

---

1. See Introduction, New Jewish-Christian Encounter, for an explanation of the four distinct characteristics of the new Jewish-Christian encounter.

theological journey we have embarked upon and point forward to the future of the new Jewish-Christian encounter.

## CONTINUED RECASTING OF CHRISTIAN THEOLOGY IN LIGHT OF ISRAEL

If, as Pope John Paul II contends, Judaism is somehow "intrinsic" to Christianity, then the full implications of the new Jewish-Christian encounter on Christian theology are only beginning to become clear. Ultimately, if the enduring and thoroughgoing connection between Jews and Christians is real, it must work its way through every doctrine of Christian theology. It cannot be isolated merely to Christian views on evangelism or ecclesiology; it must inform each and every Christian doctrine. In other words, its effect on Christian self-understanding must be total. The following is a list of only a few examples of the theological work that still must be done in this regard:

- Christian sacramental theology can no longer be conducted in isolation from the Jewish practices that lie in the background of these distinct Christian rituals;

- The universal scope of Christianity's outward-focused mission must include the Jewish people, though not in such a way as to draw Jews away from Judaism;

- Christ's atonement must increasingly be rethought in categories that cohere with a Jewish narrative framework;

- The sin-redemption paradigm (particularly in Protestant and Reformed theology) must be conceived in such a way as to fit within the larger, overarching, creation-consummation paradigm;

- The election of Israel must increasingly serve to inform our understanding of both the election of Christ and the election of the church;

- The resonance between God's incarnation in the Jewish people and God's incarnation in Jesus Christ must be brought to the fore in Christian incarnational theology;

- The connection between the suffering of Israel and the suffering of Christ must be more fully exposed and expounded;

- The overarching narrative of salvation history must be reconceived such that the ongoing existence and faithful practice of the Jewish people plays a positive and significant role in God's ongoing redemptive plans for the world;

- Christian reflection on the ongoing role of God's covenant with the people of Israel must also include adequate attention to the *land* of Israel, which stands at the heart of that covenant.[2]

In sum, if Judaism is intrinsic to Christianity, then *no doctrine of Christian theology can be understood without reference to Judaism and the Jewish people*. It seems as though this realization is just beginning to sink in, and the future of Christian theology will undoubtedly include both a greater awareness of this reality and a heightened effort to address it. Christian theology in the twenty-first century must increasingly be done in conversation with Judaism, Jewish tradition, and the input of Jewish scholars. Additional reflection on the particular doctrinal issues listed above (as well as many others) will hopefully mark the future of the new Jewish-Christian encounter and Christian theology more broadly.

## REVISITING MARSHALL'S FOUR OPTIONS

With regard to Marshall's framing question, this study has—if nothing else—shed additional light on why an adequate answer continues to prove elusive. We will recall that Marshall proposes four possible answers to this riddling question. First, one can assert that "the Jews, or at least some of them, are not really called to life in the Church, or at least not in the same way, or to the same life, that the gentiles are."[3] As Marshall points out, this option upholds the irrevocable election of Israel and the

---

2. See Mark Kinzer's *Jerusalem Crucified, Jerusalem Risen: The Resurrected Messiah, the Jewish People, and the Land of Promise* (Eugene, OR: Cascade, 2018), Edjan Westerman's *Learning Messiah:* (Eugene, OR: Wipf & Stock, 2018), and *The New Christian Zionism: Fresh Perspectives on Israel and the Land*, ed. Gerald McDermott (Downers Grove, IL: IVP Academic, 2016). For my review of the first two books, see *Pro Ecclesia* 30 no. 1 (2021): 114-23.

3. Marshall, "Elder Brothers," 123.

ongoing practice of Torah, but it fails to affirm the universality of Christ's saving mission. According to the second option, God's saving purposes are offered "figuratively" through the "old law" and then enacted "with temporally unsurpassable clarity by the incarnation of the Word" whose life, death, and resurrection inaugurates a new law.[4] While this option safeguards Christology's universal scope, it precludes construing Israel's ongoing Torah observance in positive (and divinely willed) terms. Third, Marshall points to the Messianic Jewish option (particularly as embodied in Kinzer's thought), though he questions whether this option represents an undesirable form of syncretism and whether it is able to maintain an abiding sense of unity in the body of Christ. Finally, Marshall proposes that perhaps the church's faith in Christ and Israel's observance of Torah point to one and the same eschatological *telos* and await one and the same coming Messiah. However, this option too seems problematic because it erects and relies upon a certain barrier between Israel and the church.

As we have seen throughout this study, these various stances (especially the first two) have been well treaded in twentieth-century Jewish and Christian theology. While Barth's theology fails to maintain a positive construal of Israel's ongoing Torah observance, Rosenzweig's Christology places a gap between Christ and the Jewish people. Likewise, the post-Holocaust theologians we assessed in chapter 3 tend to either downplay Christology for the sake of Israel or present an attenuated view of Israel's ongoing positive vocation. Kinzer's theology presents a unique ecclesiological proposal whereby Christ's universality and Israel's ongoing covenantal vocation are both affirmed, though his theology too leaves a number of key questions unanswered.

While we have not succeeded in providing a definitive answer to Marshall's question, we have achieved a more thorough understanding of both the options Marshall lists and the enduring complexity of the question itself. Perhaps at this point we can be encouraged by the words of Rabbi Tarfon: "It is not incumbent upon you to complete the work, but neither are you at liberty to desist from it."[5]

---

4. Marshall, "Elder Brothers," 124.
5. Pirkei Avot 2:21.

This study has also provided a more thorough exegesis of Kinzer's thought, which Marshall himself flags as meriting further attention.[6] The areas of potential or actual inadequacy notwithstanding, it seems clear that Kinzer's thought indeed deserves more careful consideration, and Torrance and Wyschogrod concur with Marshall on this point. This leads us back to the question of syncretism and the way in which Judaism and Christianity are understood vis-à-vis one another. Because the new Jewish-Christian encounter begs the question of boundary redefinition, the trajectory of this study led us into a deeper consideration of Messianic Jewish theology and its potential contribution to this unique dialogical endeavor. Let us briefly reflect on the contribution of Messianic Jewish theology and the possibility of Messianic Judaism's increased role in the future of the new Jewish-Christian encounter.

## THE CONTRIBUTION AND SIGNIFICANCE
## OF MESSIANIC JUDAISM

The emergence of the Messianic Jewish movement in the latter half of the twentieth century coincides with the widespread constructive reengagement between Christians and Jews embodied in the new Jewish-Christian encounter. Messianic Judaism thoroughly deconstructs a mutually exclusive understanding of Judaism and Christianity, and Kinzer's theology does so in a way that upholds the distinctive ethos of the new Jewish-Christian encounter. In an atmosphere in which the relationship between Judaism and Christianity is being reconsidered and reconceived, it seems that the question of Messianic Judaism cannot be disregarded. In the words of Douglas Harink, "Christians and Jews can no longer 'dialogue' as if Messianic Judaism did not exist."[7] As we look toward the future of the new Jewish-Christian encounter, it increasingly appears as though Messianic Judaism is at the very least a movement to be seriously evaluated, and perhaps represents a newcomer whose voice contributes to the continued development of this emerging intellectual tradition.

Many scholars (particularly from the Jewish side) are troubled by Messianic Judaism's existence and attempt at theological self-justification,

---

6. Marshall, "Elder Brothers," 125.
7. Kinzer, *Postmissionary Messianic Judaism*, back cover.

and this cautionary stance embodies an understandable reception to any new theological position whose contours are unfamiliar and whose impact is unpredictable. It is for this reason that, just as our assessment of Kinzer's thought must remain tentative, so too must our conclusions with regard to Messianic Judaism. Only time will tell whether the established players in the new Jewish-Christian encounter will receive this newcomer at the table.

While Messianic Judaism has not yet made significant inroads into the key epicenters of the new Jewish-Christian encounter, several indications point to its increased recognition within these dialogical circles. That Marshall offers Messianic Judaism as one potential answer to his framing question indicates that what Messianic Judaism has to offer may be relevant indeed. Without endorsing Messianic Judaism's doctrinal convictions, Michael Wyschogrod has coined the term "Wyschogrod-Kinzer hypothesis,"[8] making explicit the resonance between Kinzer's paradigm and his own.

Similarly, Soulen affirms that a thorough renunciation of supersessionism requires that the church encourage the Jews in its midst to uphold their unique covenantal obligations (i.e., Torah observance).[9] All of these signs point to the necessity of affording (postmissionary) Messianic Judaism further consideration.

Furthermore, what is unique about Kinzer's proposal is that it is not merely theological and theoretical. Rather, it is a concrete ecclesial model that Kinzer (and others) are working to bring into existence. The assessment of Kinzer's paradigm therefore cannot merely be ideological; it must take into account these unique communities that embody the vision Kinzer has pioneered. Marshall's concern that, according to Kinzer's model, "it sometimes seems as though Christ has two bodies—two churches,"[10] reflects this concrete dimension of Messianic Judaism's existence. Thus, it has yet to be seen not only how the larger arena of Jewish-Christian dialogue responds to Messianic Judaism's presence, but also how this presence itself becomes tangibly manifest. If the kinds of communities that Kinzer is

---

8. Michael Wyschogrod in discussion with the author, October 31, 2010.

9. See R. Kendall Soulen, *The God of Israel and Christian Theology* (Minneapolis: Fortress, 1996), 11.

10. Marshall, "Elder Brothers," 125.

advocating prove somehow unsustainable, this will be a direct reflection upon the theological paradigm undergirding those communities. However, if such communities continue to grow and thrive, perhaps this in itself will be an additional sign that Messianic Judaism does indeed have a unique and significant contribution to make.

While we cannot predict what the future will bring—with regard to the next chapter of the new Jewish-Christian encounter, Messianic Judaism, or Christian theology more generally—this study has sought to trace the key influences in the emergence of a developing strand of Jewish-Christian dialogue and to outline the dominant features of its present incarnation. At the very least, what this study has made clear is that the twentieth century saw the dawn of a new era in Jewish-Christian relations, the full impact and implications of which are only just beginning to be revealed. We can only hope that the type of theologically honest engagement embodied in the new Jewish-Christian encounter will indeed bring healing to the deep schism that exists in the one people of God. And together we can give thanks to the God of Israel, who has sustained us and enabled us to reach this occasion.

—

# THE JEWISH PEOPLE'S RELATIONSHIP TO LAND, LANGUAGE, AND LAW IN ROSENZWEIG'S THOUGHT

## LAND

Rosenzweig explains that the other peoples of the world are dependent on land for their permanence. Their confidence is anchored in "the solid ground of the earth," and their "will to eternity clings to the soil and to the soil's dominion, the territory."[1] The problem with this arrangement is that the land is indeed stronger than blood. The land endures even if conquered, but the people become dominated by the conquerors in a way that compromises their identity: "In this way the earth betrays the people that entrusts to the permanence of the earth its own permanence; the earth itself persists, but the people on it perish."[2] Here Rosenzweig reviews the history of the Jewish people's formation, noting that, whereas Adam (the "father of humanity") was "sprouted from the earth," Abraham (the father of the Jewish people) was not indigenous to the land that would become Israel but instead was *called into* the land.[3]

Even after Abraham's family becomes landed, the Jewish people are repeatedly formed during times of exile, first in Egypt and later in Babylon. This removal from the land does not, however, cause the Jewish people to forget its land and become disconnected from it, but rather serves to

---

1. Franz Rosenzweig, *The Star of Redemption*, trans. Barbara E. Galli (Madison: University of Wisconsin Press, 2005), 318.
2. Ibid., 318–19.
3. Ibid., 319.

strengthen both its connection to the land and its fundamental rootedness in itself rather than in the land. The Jewish people are like "a knight truer to his land when he lingers in his travels and adventures and longs for the homeland it has left than in the times when he is at home."[4]

The Jewish people yearn for the land even as they exist—and resolve to exist—independent of it. Their will to be a people "can be realized only by means of the people itself; the people is a people only through the people."[5] The people's relation to the land is most notably forward-pointing, echoing again this people's fundamental orientation vis-à-vis time: "The land is in the deepest sense its own only as land of longing, as—holy land."[6] The holiness of the land reminds the Jewish people that it is not theirs but God's, and has the effect of infinitely increasing the people's longing for the land and precluding them from ever feeling truly at home anywhere else. The Jewish people are thus fundamentally a people in exile, where "exile is less a political reality than an ontological category,"[7] for even when they do inhabit their homeland, it is not theirs to possess. Exile here indicates this people's essential *separation* from world history with all its component parts.

## LANGUAGE

Rosenzweig contends that language is bound to the life of a people rather than any external reality, and thus can die with the death of a people. Language is thus firmly entrenched in time, as it mirrors the life and development of historical peoples. Just as with the land, the Jewish people are in exile regarding language as well. Long ago Hebrew fell out of common usage, yet it did not die. It remained for the Jewish people the language of prayer and study, and its status as the "holy language" endures. For the Jewish people, "the holiness of its own language has the same effect as the holiness of its own land: it deflects the ultimate of feeling from the

---

4. Ibid.

5. Ibid.

6. Ibid.

7. Stéphane Mosès, *System and Revelation: The Philosophy of Franz Rosenzweig*, trans. Catherine Tihanyi (Detroit: Wayne State University Press, 1982), 179.

everyday; it prevents the eternal people from ever living entirely at one with the times."[8]

As the Jewish people in geographical exile live under host lands, they also adopt the languages of these lands for their vernacular. However, in the same way that they perpetually long for their own land and never consider these host lands to be home, the host languages never become their natural tongue. Whereas the identity of other peoples is tied to their language, the Jewish people employ hybrid dialects that both reflect their current geographical locale as well as their ultimate allegiance to their sacred tongue. This situation again reinforces the Jewish people's fundamental disconnectedness from the life of the times: "The holiness of the holy language, in which alone he can only pray, does not allow his life to take root in the soil of a language of his own; evidence for the fact that his linguistic life always senses itself faraway and knows its real linguistic homeland is elsewhere, in the domain of the holy language that is inaccessible to everyday speech."[9]

## LAW

Similar to land and language, the customs of the peoples of the world ground their existence in time. Customs and laws change and flux, following and tracking the historical progression of societies. "And again the eternal people purchases its eternity at the price of temporal life."[10] For the Jewish people, "custom and law, having become non-augmentable and unchangeable, flow into the one basin of that which is valid now and forever; a unique form of life that unites custom and law fills the moment and makes it eternal."[11] Torah serves both to separate the Jewish people from the flow of historical time and to make their customs and law distinct from the other peoples of the world. It represents that which is equally binding on all Jews for all time, for "every individual is supposed to regard the Exodus out of Egypt as if he himself had also gone out,"[12] as if he was physically present at the forming event of his people.

---

8. Rosenzweig, *The Star of Redemption*, 321.
9. Ibid.
10. Ibid., 322.
11. Ibid.
12. Ibid., 323.

The history of the Jewish people is unchanging, as is the way in which that history bears upon the present life of the people. "Whereas the myth of peoples is continuously changing, parts of the past are continuously forgotten, and others are memorialized into myth, here the myth becomes eternal and does not change any longer; and whereas the peoples live in revolutions in which the law continuously sheds its skin, here reigns the law that no revolution could repeal, and that can probably be evaded but not changed."[13] The living out of *this* law, specific to *this* people, continuously from one generation to the next, further evidences the Jewish people's existence as the eternal people.

---

13. Ibid.

# APPENDIX 2(A)
—
# MARC CHAGALL'S *WHITE CRUCIFIXION*

# APPENDIX 2(B)

—

# MARC CHAGALL'S *EXODUS*

# BIBLIOGRAPHY

—

Abrams, Elliott. *Faith or Fear*. New York: The Free Press, 1997.

Adam, Adolf. *The Liturgical Year*. New York: Pueblo Publishing Company, 1981.

Alexander, Philip S. "'The Parting of the Ways' from the Perspective of Rabbinic Judaism." In *Jews and Christians: The Parting of the Ways A.D. 70 to 135*, edited by James D. G. Dunn, 1–25. Grand Rapids: Wm. B. Eerdmans Publishing, 1999.

Ausmus, Harry J. *Will Herberg: From Right to Right*. Chapel Hill: University of North Carolina Press, 2009.

Bader-Saye, Scott. *Church and Israel after Christendom: The Politics of Election*. Eugene, OR: Wipf & Stock Publishers, 2005.

Barth, Karl. *Church Dogmatics*. Edited by T. F. Torrance and G. W. Bromiley. Translated by G. W. Bromiley. 14 vols. London: T&T Clark, 2004.

———. *The Christian Life: Church Dogmatics IV/4 Lecture Fragments*. Translated by Geoffrey W. Bromiley. Grand Rapids: Wm. B. Eerdmans Publishing, 1981.

———. *The Church and the Political Problem of Our Day*. New York: Charles Scribner's Sons, 1939.

Barth, Markus. *Jesus the Jew*. Translated by Frederick Prussner. Atlanta: John Knox Press, 1978.

Batnitzky, Leora. *Idolatry and Representation: The Philosophy of Franz Rosenzweig Reconsidered*. Princeton: Princeton University Press, 2000.

———. *How Judaism Became a Religion: An Introduction to Modern Jewish Thought*. Princeton: Princeton University Press, 2011.

Berkovits, Eliezer. *Not in Heaven: The Nature and Function of Jewish Law*. Jerusalem: Shalem Press, 2010.

Biggar, Nigel. *The Hastening That Waits: Karl Barth's Ethics*. Oxford: Oxford University Press, 1993.

Bosch, David J. *Transforming Mission: Paradigm Shifts in Theology of Mission*. Maryknoll, NY: Orbis Books, 1991.

Bowler, Maurice G. "Rosenzweig on Judaism and Christianity: The Two Covenant Theory." *Judaism* 22, no. 4 (1973): 475–81.

Braaten, Carl E. and Robert W. Jenson. "Introduction." In *Jews and Christians: People of God*, edited by Carl E. Braaten and Robert W. Jenson, i–xi. Grand Rapids: Wm. B. Eerdmans Publishing, 2003.

Bromiley, Geoffrey W. *Introduction to the Theology of Karl Barth*. Grand Rapids: Wm. B. Eerdmans, 1979.

———, ed. and trans. *Karl Barth Letters, 1961–1968*. Grand Rapids: Wm. B. Eerdmans, 1981.

Brown, Colin. *Karl Barth and the Christian Message*. London: Tyndale Press, 1967.

Buber, Martin. *Two Types of Faith*. Translated by Norman P. Goldhawk. Syracuse: Syracuse University Press, 2003.

Burge, Gary. *Whose Land? Whose Promise? What Christians Are Not Being Told About Israel and the Palestinians*. Cleveland: Pilgrim Press, 2004.

Busch, Eberhard. *Karl Barth: His Life from Letters and Autobiographical Texts*. Grand Rapids: Wm. B. Eerdmans Publishing, 1994.

Cohen, Jeremy. *Living Letters of the Law: Ideas of the Jew in Medieval Christianity*. Berkeley: University of California Press, 1999.

Colyer, Elmer M. *How to Read T. F. Torrance: Understanding His Trinitarian and Scientific Theology*. Downers Grove: InterVarsity, 2001.

Cowie, L. W. and John Selwyn Gummer. *The Christian Calendar*. Springfield: G. & C. Merriam, 1974.

de Lange, Nicholas. *Ignaz Maybaum: A Reader*. New York: Berghahn Books, 2001.

Donin, Hayim Halevy. *To Be a Jew: A Guide to Jewish Observance in Contemporary Life*. New York: Basic Books, 1972.

———. *To Pray as a Jew: A Guide to the Prayer Book and the Synagogue Service*. New York: Basic Books, 1980.

Eisenbaum, Pamela. *Paul Was Not a Christian*. New York: HarperCollins, 2010.

Fackenheim, Emil. *To Mend the World: Foundations of Post-Holocaust Jewish Thought.* Bloomington: Indiana University Press, 1994.

Fishbane, Michael. *Judaism: Revelation and Traditions.* New York: HarperOne, 1987.

Flett, John G. *The Witness of God: The Trinity, Missio Dei, Karl Barth, and the Nature of Christian Community.* Grand Rapids: Wm. B. Eerdmans Publishing, 2010.

Fredriksen, Paula. *Jesus of Nazareth, King of the Jews.* New York: Vintage, 2000.

Frymer-Kensky, Tikva et al., eds., *Christianity in Jewish Terms.* Boulder, CO: Westview Press, 2000.

Glatzer, Nahum. *Franz Rosenzweig: His Life and Thought.* Indianapolis: Hackett Publishing, 1998.

Gorringe, Timothy. *Karl Barth: Against Hegemony.* New York: Oxford University Press, 1999.

Greenberg, Irving. *For the Sake of Heaven and Earth: The New Encounter between Judaism and Christianity.* Philadelphia: Jewish Publication Society, 2004.

Guder, Darrell L. *Missional Church: A Vision for the Sending of the Church in North America.* Grand Rapids: Wm. B. Eerdmans Publishing, 1998.

Guretzki, David. "Karl Barth on Mark Kinzer's 'Non-supersessionist and Post-Missionary Ecclesiology': Yes! and No!" Paper presented at conference of the Canadian Evangelical Theological Association, Carleton University, Ottawa, May 23, 2009.

Gustafson, James. *Ethics from a Theocentric Perspective.* Vol. 2 of *Ethics and Theology.* Chicago: University of Chicago Press, 1984.

Halevi, Judah. *Book of Kuzari.* Translated by Hartwig Hirschfeld. Whitefish, MT: Kessinger Publishing, 2003.

Harink, Douglas. *Paul among the Postliberals: Pauline Theology Beyond Christendom and Modernity.* Grand Rapids: Brazos Press, 2003.

———. "Barth's Apocalyptic Exegesis and the Question of Israel in Römerbrief, Chapters 9–11." *Toronto Journal of Theology* 25, no. 1 (2009): 5–18.

Hart, David B. "Israel and the Nations." *First Things* 105 (August/September 2000): 51–54.

Hartman, David. *A Heart of Many Rooms: Celebrating the Many Voices within Judaism*. Woodstock, VT: Jewish Lights Publishing, 2002.

Harvey, Richard. "The 'Hidden Messiah' in Judaism." Paper presented at LCJE International Conference, Keszthely, Hungary, August 2007. Available at http://www.lcje.net/papers/2007/intl/Harvey.doc.

———. "Shaping the Aims and Aspirations of Jewish Believers." *Mishkan* 48 (2006): 18–21.

———. "Implicit Universalism in Some Christian Zionism and Messianic Judaism." In *Jesus, Salvation and the Jewish People: The Uniqueness of Jesus and Jewish Evangelism*, edited by David Parker, 209–234. Carlisle: Paternoster Press, 2011.

Haynes, Stephen. *Prospects for Post-Holocaust Theology*. Atlanta: Scholars Press, 1991.

Hays, Richard B. *Echoes of Scripture in the Letters of Paul*. New Haven: Yale University Press, 1993.

Held, Shai. "The Promise and Peril of Jewish Barthianism: The Theology of Michael Wyschogrod." *Modern Judaism* 25, no. 3 (2005): 316–26.

Herberg, Will. "Judaism and Christianity: Their Unity and Difference." In *Jewish Perspectives on Christianity*, edited by Fritz A. Rothschild, 240–55. New York: Crossroad, 1990.

Heschel, Abraham Joshua. *God in Search of Man: A Philosophy of Judaism*. New York: Farrar, Straus & Giroux, 1976.

———. *The Sabbath*. New York: Farrar, Straus & Giroux, 1951.

Hoffman, Matthew. *From Rebel to Rabbi: Reclaiming Jesus and the Making of Modern Jewish Culture*. Stanford: Stanford University Press, 2007.

Hunsinger, George. "Election and the Trinity: Twenty-Five Theses on the Theology of Karl Barth." *Modern Theology* 24, no. 2 (2008): 179–98.

Jenson, Robert W. "Toward a Christian Theology of Israel." *Pro Ecclesia* 9, no. 1 (1999): 43–56.

John Paul II. *Spiritual Pilgramage: Texts on Jews and Judaism, 1979–1995*. New York: Crossroad, 1996.

———. "Toward a Christian Theology of Judaism." In *Jews and Christians: People of God*, edited by Carl E. Braaten and Robert W. Jenson, 1–13. Grand Rapids: Wm. B. Eerdmans Publishing, 2003.

Juster, Daniel C. *Jewish Roots: A Foundation of Biblical Theology.* Shippensburg, PA: Destiny Image Publishers, 1995.

Kaplan, Gregory. "In the End Shall Christians Become Jews and Jews, Christians? On Franz Rosenzweig's Apocalyptic Eschatology." *Cross Currents* 54, no. 4 (2004): 511–29.

Kessler, Edward and Neil Wenborn, eds. *A Dictionary of Jewish-Christian Relations.* Cambridge: Cambridge University Press, 2008.

Kinzer, Mark. "Final Destinies: Qualifications for Receiving an Eschatological Inheritance." In *Israel's Messiah and the People of God: A Vision for Messianic Jewish Covenant Fidelity*, edited by Jennifer M. Rosner, 126–55. Eugene, OR: Cascade, 2011.

———. "Finding Our Way Through Nicaea: The Deity of Yeshua, Bilateral Exxlesiology, and Redemptive Encounter with the Living God." In *Searching Her Own Mystery: Nostra Aetate, the Jewish People, and the Identity of the Church*, 218. Eugene, OR: Cascade, 2015.

———. "Israel's Eschatological Renewal in Water and Spirit: A Messianic Jewish Perspective on Baptism." Paper presented at the Messianic Jewish-Roman Catholic Dialogue Group in Jerusalem, September 2009.

———. *Jerusalem Crucified, Jerusalem Risen: The Resurrected Messiah, the Jewish People, and the Land of Promise.* Eugene, OR: Cascade, 2018.

———. "Lumen Gentium, through Messianic Jewish Eyes." In *Israel's Messiah and the People of God: A Vision for Messianic Jewish Covenant Fidelity*, edited by Jennifer M. Rosner, 156–74. Eugene, OR: Cascade, 2011.

———. "Messianic Jewish Community: Standing and Serving as a Priestly Remnant." Kesher 28 (2014), 79–101.

———. "Modern Judaism," Lectures 1–8. Lectures presented at Messianic Jewish Theological Institute, online course, 2011.

———. *Postmissionary Messianic Judaism.* Grand Rapids: Brazos Press, 2005.

———. "Postmissionary Messianic Judaism, Three Years Later: Reflections on a Conversation Just Begun." In *Israel's Messiah and the People of God: A Vision for Messianic Jewish Covenant Fidelity*, edited by Jennifer M. Rosner, 175–96. Eugene, OR: Cascade, 2011.

———. "Response to Mishkan Reviewers of My Book." *Mishkan* 48 (2006): 54–65.

———. "The Shape of Messianic Jewish Theology," Lectures 1–8. Lectures presented at Messianic Jewish Theological Institute, online course, 2011.

———. "Toward a Theology of 'Messianic Judaism.'" In *Israel's Messiah and the People of God: A Vision for Messianic Jewish Covenant Fidelity*, edited by Jennifer M. Rosner, 14–28. Eugene, OR: Cascade, 2011.

*The Koren Sacks Siddur: A Hebrew/English Prayerbook*, translated by Jonathan Sacks. Jerusalem: Koren, 2009.

Krell, Marc A. *Intersecting Pathways: Modern Jewish Theologians in Conversation with Christianity*. Oxford: Oxford University Press, 2003.

Kren, George M. and Leon Rappoport. *The Holocaust and the Crisis of Human Behavior*. Teaneck, NJ: Holmes & Meier, 1994.

Küng, Hans. *On Being a Christian*. New York: Image Books, 1984.

Küng, Hans et al. *Christianity and the World Religions: Paths of Dialogue with Islam, Hinduism and Buddhism*. New York: Doubleday, 1986.

Leighton, Christopher M. "Christian Theology After the Shoah." In *Christianity in Jewish Terms*, edited by Tikva Frymer-Kensky, 36–48. Boulder, CO: Westview Press, 2000.

Levenson, Alan T. *An Introduction to Modern Jewish Thinkers: From Spinoza to Soloveitchik*, 2nd ed. Lanham, MD: Rowman & Littlefield Publishers, 2006.

Levenson, Jon D. *Sinai and Zion: An Entry into the Jewish Bible*. New York: HarperOne, 1985.

Levering, Matthew. *Jewish-Christian Dialogue and the Life of Wisdom: Engagements with the Theology of David Novak*. London: Continuum, 2010.

Levine, Amy-Jill. *The Misunderstood Jew: The Church and the Scandal of the Jewish Jesus*. New York: HarperOne, 2007.

Lilla, Mark. *The Stillborn God: Religion, Politics and the Modern West*. New York: Random House, 2007.

Lindsay, Mark. *Barth, Israel and Jesus: Karl Barth's Theology of Israel*. Burlington, VT: Ashgate Publishing, 2007.

Marquardt, Friedrich-Wilhelm. *Die Entdeckung des Judentums für die christliche Theologie: Israel im Denken Karl Barths*. Munich: Kaiser, 1967.

———. *Theologie und Sozialismus: Das Beispiel Karl Barths,* 3rd ed. Munich: Kaiser, 1985.

Milgrom, Jacob. *Leviticus 1–16.* Anchor Bible 3A. New York: Doubleday, 1991.

Marshall, Bruce D. "Christ and Israel: An Unsolved Problem in Catholic Theology." The 20th Annual Aquinas Lecture presented at the Dominican School of Philosophy & Theology. Berkeley, CA, March 3, 2010.

———. "Christ and the Cultures: The Jewish People and Christian Theology." In *The Cambridge Companion to Christian Doctrine,* edited by Colin E. Gunton, 81–100. Cambridge: Cambridge University Press, 1997.

———. "Elder Brothers: John Paul II's Teaching on the Jewish People as a Question to the Church." In *John Paul II and the Jewish People: A Jewish-Christian Dialogue,* edited by David G. Dalin and Matthew Levering, 113–29. Lanham, MD: Rowman & Littlefield, 2008.

———. "Quasi in Figura: A Brief Reflection on Jewish Election, after Thomas Aquinas." *Nova et Vetera* (English Edition) 7, no. 2 (2009): 439–76.

———. *Trinity and Truth.* Cambridge: Cambridge University Press, 2000.

———. "Truth Claims and the Possibility of Jewish-Christian Dialogue." *Modern Theology* 8, no. 3 (1992): 221–40.

Maybaum, Ignaz. *The Face of God after Auschwitz.* Amsterdam: Polak & Van Gennep, 1965.

———. *Trialogue Between Jew, Christian and Muslim.* London: Routledge & Kegan Paul, 1973.

McCormack, Bruce. "Election and the Trinity: Theses in Response to George Hunsinger." *Scottish Journal of Theology* 63, no. 2 (2010): 203–24.

———. "Grace and Being: The Role of God's Gracious Election in Karl Barth's Theological Ontology." In *The Cambridge Companion to Karl Barth,* edited by John Webster, 92–110. Cambridge: Cambridge University Press, 2000.

McCready, Wayne O. and Adele Reinhartz, eds. *Common Judaism: Explorations in Second-Temple Judaism.* Minneapolis: Fortress Press, 2008.

McDermott, ed. *The New Christian Zionism: Fresh Perspectives on Israel and the Land.* Downers Grove, IL: IVP Academic, 2016.

McGarry, Michael B. *Christology After Auschwitz.* Mahwah, NJ: Paulist Press, 1977.

Migliore, Daniel. "Reforming the Theology and Practice of Baptism: The Challenge of Karl Barth." In *Toward the Future of Reformed Theology: Tasks, Topics, Traditions,* edited by David Willis and Michael Welker, 494–511. Grand Rapids: Wm. B. Eerdmans Publishing, 1999.

Moloney, Francis. *The Gospel of John.* Collegeville, MN: Liturgical Press, 1998.

Mosès, Stéphane. *System and Revelation: The Philosophy of Franz Rosenzweig.* Translated by Catherine Tihanyi. Detroit: Wayne State University Press, 1982.

Neuhaus, Richard John. "Salvation Is From the Jews." *First Things* 117 (2001): 17–22. Previously published in *Jews and Christians: People of God,* edited by Carl E. Braaten and Robert W. Jenson, 65–77. Grand Rapids: Wm. B. Eerdmans Publishing, 2003.

Neusner, Jacob. *A Short History of Judaism: Three Meals, Three Epochs.* Minneapolis: Fortress Press, 1992.

———. *Judaism in Modern Times: An Introduction and Reader.* Cambridge: Blackwell Publishing, 1995.

———. *Judaism in the New Testament: Practices and Beliefs.* London: Routledge, 1995.

———. *The Way of Torah: An Introduction to Judaism.* Belmont, CA: Wadsworth, 1993.

Newbigin, Lesslie. *The Open Secret: An Introduction to the Theology of Mission.* Grand Rapids: Wm. B. Eerdmans Publishing, 1995.

Novak, David. "'And after the fire a soft murmuring sound ...' The Abiding Significance of Judaism for Christian Identity." *Studies in Jewish-Christian Relations* 2, no. 2 (2007): 140–54.

———. "Beyond Supersessionism." Review of The God of Israel and Christian Theology, by R. Kendall Soulen. *First Things* 81 (March 1998): 57–58.

———. *The Election of Israel: The Idea of a Chosen People.* Cambridge: Cambridge University Press, 1995.

——. "From Supersessionism to Parallelism in Jewish-Christian Dialogue." In *Jews and Christians: People of God*, edited by Carl E. Braaten and Robert W. Jenson, 95–113. Grand Rapids: Wm. B. Eerdmans Publishing, 2003.

——. *Halakhah in a Theological Dimension*. Chico, CA: Scholars Press, 1985.

——. *Jewish-Christian Dialogue: A Jewish Justification*. New York: Oxford University Press, 1989.

——. "Karl Barth and Divine Command: A Jewish Response." In *Talking with Christians: Musings of a Jewish Theologian*, 127–45. Grand Rapids: Wm. B. Eerdmans Publishing, 2005.

——. *Talking with Christians: Musings of a Jewish Theologian*. Grand Rapids: Eerdmans, 2005.

——. "When Jews Are Christians." In *Talking with Christians: Musings of a Jewish Theologian*, 218–28. Grand Rapids: Wm. B. Eerdmans Publishing, 2005.

Ochs, Peter. *Another Reformation: Postliberal Christianity and the Jews*. Grand Rapids: Baker Academic, 2011.

——. "A Rabbinic Pragmatism." In *Theology and Dialogue: Essays in Conversation with George Lindbeck*, edited by Bruce D. Marshall, 213–48. Notre Dame: University of Notre Dame Press, 1990.

——. "Yoder's Witness to the People of Israel." In *Jewish-Christian Schism Revisited* by John Howard Yoder, edited by Michael G. Cartwright and Peter Ochs, 2–6. Grand Rapids: Wm. B. Eerdmans Publishing, 2003.

Parkes, James. *The Conflict of the Church and the Synagogue: A Study in the Origins of Antisemitism*. London: Macmillan, 1969.

Pawlikowski, John. "Christology and the Jewish-Christian Dialogue: A Personal Theological Journey." *Irish Theological Quarterly* 72, no. 2 (2007): 147–67.

Putnam, Hilary. "Jewish Ethics?" In *The Blackwell Companion to Religious Ethics*, edited by William Schweiker, 159–165. Oxford: Blackwell, 2005.

Ramsey, Paul. "Elements of a Biblical Political Theory." *Journal of Religion* 29, no. 4 (1949): 258–83.

Rashkover, Randi. "Jewish Responses to Jewish-Christian Dialogue: A Look Ahead to the Twenty-First Century." *Cross Currents* 50, no. 1-2 (2000): 211–20.

———. *Revelation and Theopolitics: Barth, Rosenzweig and the Politics of Praise*. London: T&T Clark, 2005.

Reno, R. R. "The Carnal Reality of Revelation." *First Things* (August 26, 2010). firstthings.com/web-exclusives/2010/04/the-carnal-reality-of-revelation.

Robinson, Rich. "*Postmissionary Messianic Judaism:* A Review Essay." *Mishkan* 48 (2006): 8–21.

Rosenstock-Huessy, Eugen, ed. *Judaism Despite Christianity*. New York: Schocken, 1969.

Rosenzweig, Franz. *Briefe*. Berlin: Schocken Verlag, 1935.

———. *On Jewish Learning*. Edited by Nahum Glatzer. Madison: University of Wisconsin Press, 1955.

———. *Philosophical and Theological Writings*. Translated and edited by Paul W. Franks and Michael L. Morgan. Indianapolis: Hackett Publishing, 2000.

———. *The Star of Redemption*. Translated by Barbara E. Galli. Madison: University of Wisconsin Press, 2005.

———. *The Star of Redemption*. Translated by William W. Hallo. Boston: Beacon Press, 1972.

———. "'Urzelle' to the Star of Redemption (1917)." In *Philosophical and Theological Writings*, translated and edited by Paul W. Franks and Michael L. Morgan, 48–72. Indianapolis: Hackett Publishing, 2000.

Rosner, Jennifer M., ed. *Israel's Messiah and the People of God: A Vision for Messianic Jewish Covenant Fidelity*. Eugene, OR: Cascade, 2011.

Rothschild, Fritz A., ed. *Jewish Perspectives on Christianity*. New York: Crossroad, 1990.

Rubenstein, Jeffrey L. *Talmudic Stories: Narrative Art, Composition, and Culture*. Baltimore: Johns Hopkins University Press, 1999.

Sacks, Jonathan. *A Letter in the Scroll: Understanding Our Jewish Identity and Exploring the Legacy of the World's Oldest Religion*. New York: Free Press, 2000.

———. *To Heal a Fractured World: The Ethics of Responsibility*. New York: Schocken Books, 2005.

Samuelson, Norbert. *An Introduction to Modern Jewish Philosophy*. Albany: State University of New York Press, 1989.

Sanders, E. P. *Judaism: Practice and Belief, 66 BCE–66 CE*. London: SCM Press, 1992.

Sandmel, Samuel. *We Jews and Jesus*. New York: Oxford University Press, 1973.

Soloveichik, Meir Y. "No Friend in Jesus." *First Things* 179 (January 2008): 29–32.

Soloveitchik, Joseph B. "Confrontation." *Tradition* 6, no. 2 (1964): 5–29.

Sonderegger, Katherine. "Barth's Christology and the Law of Israel." Paper presented at the Center for Barth Studies Conference, Princeton, NJ, June 21–24, 2009.

———. "Response to Indissoluble Unity." In *For the Sake of the World: Karl Barth and the Future of Ecclesial Theology*, edited by George Hunsinger, 80–94. Grand Rapids: Wm B. Eerdmans Publishing, 2004.

———. *That Jesus Christ Was Born a Jew: Karl Barth's "Doctrine of Israel."* University Park: The Pennsylvania State University Press, 1992.

Soulen, R. Kendall. *The God of Israel and Christian Theology*. Minneapolis: Fortress Press, 1996.

Thoma, Clemens. *A Christian Theology of Judaism*. Translated by Helga B. Croner. New York: Paulist Press, 1980.

Torrance, Thomas. *The Mediation of Christ*. Colorado Springs: Helmers and Howard, 1992.

———. "Christian/Jewish Dialogue: Report of the Overseas Council of the Church of Scotland." Appendix A(2) in *The Witness of the Jews to God*, edited by David W. Torrance, 139–50. Edinburgh: Handsel Press, 1982.

———. "The Divine Vocation and Destiny of Israel in World History." In *The Witness of the Jews to God*, edited by David W. Torrance, 85–104. Edinburgh: Handsel Press, 1982.

Twersky, Isadore, ed. *A Maimonides Reader*. Springfield, NJ: Behrman House, 1972.

Van Buren, Paul M. *According to the Scriptures: The Origins of the Gospel and of the Church's Old Testament*. Grand Rapids: Wm. B. Eerdmans Publishing, 1998.

———. *A Theology of the Jewish-Christian Reality, Part Two: A Christian Theology of the People Israel*. Lanham: University Press of America, 1995.

Ward, Graham. *Cultural Transformation and Religious Practice*.
     Cambridge: Cambridge University Press, 2005.

Webster, John. *Barth's Ethics of Reconciliation*. Cambridge: Cambridge
     University Press, 1995.

Westerman, Edjan. *Learning Messiah: Israel and the Nations: Learning to
     Read God's Way Anew*. Eugene, OR: Wipf & Stock, 2018.

Wiesel, Elie. "Art and Culture after the Holocaust." In *Auschwitz:
     Beginning of a New Era? Reflections on the Holocaust*, edited by Eva
     Fleischner, 403–415. New York: KTAV, 1977.

Wigoder, Geoffrey. *Jewish-Christian Relations Since the Second World War*.
     Manchester: Manchester University Press, 1988.

Willis, Robert E. *The Ethics of Karl Barth*. Leiden: Brill, 1971.

Wright, Christopher J. H. *The Mission of God: Unlocking the Bible's Grand
     Narrative*. Downers Grove: InterVarsity Press, 2006.

Wright, N. T. *The New Testament and the People of God*. Minneapolis:
     Fortress Press, 1992.

Wolfson, Elliot R. "Facing the Effaced: Mystical Eschatology and the
     Idealistic Orientation in the Thought of Franz Rosenzweig."
     *Zeitschrift für Neure Theologiegeschichte* 4 (1997): 39–81.

———. "Judaism and Incarnation: The Imaginal Body of God." In
     *Christianity in Jewish Terms*, edited by Tikva Frymer-Kensky et al.,
     239–53. Boulder, CO: Westview, 2000.

———. "Light Does Not Talk But Shines: Apophasis and Vision in
     Rosenzweig's Theopoetic Temporality." In *New Directions in Jewish
     Philosophy*, edited by Aaron W. Hughes and Elliot R. Wolfson,
     87–148. Bloomington: Indiana University Press, 2009.

Wyschogrod, Michael. *Abraham's Promise: Judaism and Jewish-Christian
     Relations*. Edited by R. Kendall Soulen. Grand Rapids: Wm. B.
     Eerdmans Publishing, 2004.

———. *The Body of Faith: God and the People Israel*. Northvale, NJ: Jason
     Aronson, 1996.

———. "Franz Rosenzweig's *The Star of Redemption*," In *Abraham's Promise:
     Judaism and Jewish-Christian Relations*, edited by R. Kendall Soulen,
     121–30. Grand Rapids: Wm. B. Eerdmans Publishing, 2004.

———. "Israel, the Church, and Election." In *Abraham's Promise: Judaism
     and Jewish-Christian Relations*, edited by R. Kendall Soulen, 179–87.

Grand Rapids: Wm. B. Eerdmans Publishing, 2004.

———. "A Jewish Perspective on Incarnation." *Modern Theology* 12, no. 2 (1996): 195–209.

———. "A Jewish Perspective on Karl Barth." In *How Karl Barth Changed My Mind*, edited by Donald McKim, 156–61. Grand Rapids: Wm. B. Eerdmans Publishing, 1986.

———. "Judaism and the Land." In *Abraham's Promise: Judaism and Jewish-Christian Relations*, edited by R. Kendall Soulen, 91–103. Grand Rapids: Wm. B. Eerdmans Publishing, 2004.

———. "A Letter to Cardinal Lustiger." In *Abraham's Promise: Judaism and Jewish-Christian Relations*, edited by R. Kendall Soulen, 202–10. Grand Rapids: Wm. B. Eerdmans Publishing, 2004.

———. "Paul, Jews, and Gentiles." In *Abraham's Promise: Judaism and Jewish-Christian Relations*, edited by R. Kendall Soulen, 188–201. Grand Rapids: Wm. B. Eerdmans Publishing, 2004.

———. "Why Was and Is the Theology of Karl Barth of Interest to a Jewish Theologian?" In *Abraham's Promise: Judaism and Jewish-Christian Relations*, edited by R. Kendall Soulen, 211–24. Grand Rapids: Wm. B. Eerdmans Publishing, 2004.

Yoder, John Howard. *The Jewish Christian Schism Revisited*. Edited by Michael G. Cartwright and Peter Ochs. Grand Rapids: Wm. B. Eerdmans Publishing, 2003.

Zetterholm, Magnus. *Approaches to Paul: A Student's Guide to Recent Scholarship*. Minneapolis: Fortress Press, 2009.

# SCRIPTURE INDEX

—

## Old Testament

## New Testament

# SUBJECT INDEX

—

Abel (biblical figure), 207

Abraham, 4, 5–18, 11, 16, 33, 48, 136n148, 146n2, 177, 188, 189, 190, 205, 208, 215, 217, 222, 227

Abrams, Elliott, 229n108

Absolutism, 25n84, 91n223

Actualism, 57, 59, 69, 94

Adam and Eve, 207, 207n35

Ahavah Rabbah, 18n61

Akedah (binding of Isaac), 160, 208–9, 216–18, 224, 239

"Akhnai, Oven of," 89

Albo, Joseph, 132

Altmann, Alexander, 135n142

Anthropomorphism, 154–55, 192

Antinomianism, 176

Anti-Judaism, 2–3, 182, 185, 210–11

Anti-Semitism, 73–74, 82, 183, 229n108

Atonement, 71, 141, 151–52, 158, 165, 179, 191, 193, 209n39, 218, 239, 247. *See also* Yom Kippur (Day of Atonement)

Augsburg College, 26–27

Augustine, 178, 234

Auschwitz, 159, 161–63, 166, 183

Averah, 207n35

Babylon, 253

Bader-Saye, Scott, 1–2, 81, 172, 180–83, 188, 195

Baeck, Leo, 83, 163

Baptism, 22, 66, 66n139, 107, 109, 120, 167n70, 176, 177n110, 178, 195, 216–217, 218–221, 228

Bar Kochba, 168

Barth, Karl, 211n46, 237

on Christianity and Christology, 44, 143–44

on Christianity and supersessionism, 169

on Christology and ecclesiology, 95–97, 114–16, 121, 145–53, 155n28, 177, 178, 181n124, 183, 187, 190–93, 194–95, 196–97, 226

on command of God, 56–67

on election of God, 46–56

on election of Israel, 80–94, 180, 213

on faithfulness/unfaithfulness, 212

on his own theological method, 43n4

on Israel and church, 42–94, 166, 243–44

on Israel's negative witness, 138

on Jewish-Christian encounter, 31–33, 40–41, 246–47

on Jewishness of Jesus, 70–75

on Jewish people (Israel), 80–85

on Judaism (Torah), 85–94, 124, 250

on Judaism and Christianity, 97n6, 167–68

on mission of Christ, 67–70

on suffering, 158, 224

on synagogues, 50n39, 84

timeline, 42n2

Barth, Markus, 178

Batnitzky, Leora, 162–63

Bava Metzia, 89

Besorah (gospel), 222

Bet Mikdash [temple], 205, 215

Bible, 27–28, 43, 63, 64, 71, 76, 84, 135, 154–55, 168, 169n78, 234

Biggar, Nigel, 86, 92

Blood community, 136, 157, 166, 225

LEXHAM PRESS

# STUDIES IN HISTORICAL & SYSTEMATIC THEOLOGY

Studies in Historical and Systematic Theology is a peer-reviewed series of contemporary monographs exploring key figures, themes, and issues in historical and systematic theology from an evangelical perspective.

—

**Learn more at LexhamPress.com/SHST**